**Corte and
the Interior**
Pages 134–155

**Bonifacio and
the South**
Pages 110–133

AJACCIO AND
THE WEST COAST

Tiuccia

Porticcio

Bocognano

Bastelica

Cozzano

Propriano

Sartène

Zonza

BONIFACIO AND
THE SOUTH

Solenzara

Aléria

Porto-Vecchio

Figari

Île Cavallo

Îles Lavezzi

Îles Sanguinaires

D1638118

0 kilometres   5   15

0 miles   15

CORSICA

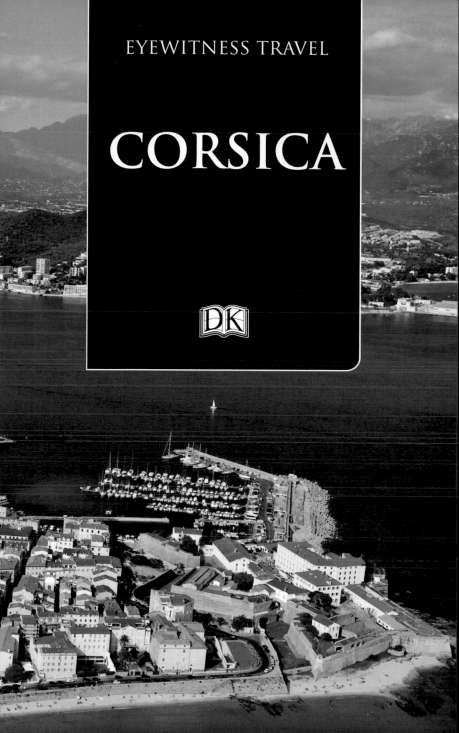

EYEWITNESS TRAVEL

CORSICA

DK | Penguin Random House

Produced by Fabrizio Ratti Editoria Srl, Milan, Italy
Project Editor Donatella Ceriani
Art Editor Oriana Bianchetti
Editors Marina Beretta, Angela Magrì
Designer Elisabetta Mancini

Contributors Fabrizio Ardito, Cristina Gambaro, Angela Magrì

Photographers Fabrizio Ardito, Adriano Bacchella,
Cristina Gambaro, Lucio Rossi, Marco Stoppato

Cartographers Grafema Cartografia Srl, Novara

Illustrators Modi Artistici, Anna Mucciarelli, Tiziano Perotto

English Translation Richard Pierce

Editors Sylvia and David Tombesi-Walton
(Sands Publishing Solutions); Lauren Robertson
Consultant David Abram
Senior DTP Designer Jason Little
Production Melanie Dowland

Printed and bound in China

First published in Great Britain in 2003
by Dorling Kindersley Limited,
80 Strand, London WC2R 0RL

17 18 19 10 9 8 7 6 5 4 3 2

Reprinted with revisions 2006, 2008, 2010, 2012, 2014, 2016

Copyright © 2003, 2016 Dorling Kindersley Limited, London
A Penguin Random House company

ISBN: 978 0 24120 847 2

MIX
Paper from
responsible sources
FSC
www.fsc.org   FSC™ C018179

**The information in this
DK Eyewitness Travel Guide is checked regularly/annually.**
Every effort has been made to ensure that this book is as up-to-date as possible
at the time of going to press. Some details, however, such as telephone numbers,
opening hours, prices, gallery hanging arrangements and travel information are
liable to change. The publishers cannot accept responsibility for any consequences
arising from the use of this book, nor for any material on third party websites, and
cannot guarantee that any website address in this book will be a suitable source of
travel information. We value the views and suggestions of our readers very highly.
Please write to: Publisher, DK Eyewitness Travel Guides, Dorling Kindersley,
80 Strand, London, WC2R 0RL, UK, or email: travelguides@dk.com.

Front cover main image: The idyllic Plage d'Arone at Piana, Corsica

◀ Aerial view of Ajaccio

Contents

The Romanesque church of
San Michele de Murato

Introducing Corsica

Laricio pines in the beautiful
Forêt d'Aïtone

A crystal-clear sea and white rocks in a cove in front of Îles Lavezzi

Cheese and charcuterie – two of the many specialities of Corsica

Corsica Area by Area

Travellers' Needs

Survival Guide

Snow-capped mountains near Monte Cinto

A typical maquis plant, *Euphorbia dendroides*, in bloom

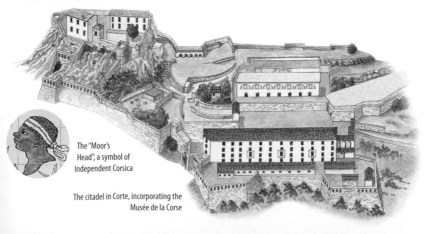

The "Moor's Head", a symbol of Independent Corsica

The citadel in Corte, incorporating the Musée de la Corse

HOW TO USE THIS GUIDE

This guide helps visitors to get the most out of their stay in Corsica by providing detailed descriptions, practical information and expert advice. *Introducing Corsica* sets the island in its geographical, historical and cultural context. *Corsica Area by Area* describes the main sights in detail, with maps, photographs and illustrations. *Travellers' Needs* offers recommendations on hotels, restaurants, local food, bars, shopping, sports and entertainment, while the *Survival Guide* provides useful information on safety, health, transport and local currency.

Corsica Area by Area

Corsica has been divided into four main areas, each coded with a coloured thumb tab *(see the front flap and inside front cover)*. The sights described in the regions are plotted and numbered on a *Regional Map*. The key to symbols and a *Road Map* can be found on the back flap and inside back cover.

1 Introduction
The history, landscape and character of each area are described here, showing how the region has developed over time and what it has to offer visitors.

A locator map shows the colour of each area in relation to the island of Corsica for quick reference.

The area colour code is in the top margin of each page.

2 Regional Map
This gives an illustrated overview of the area. All the sights covered in the chapter are numbered, and there is useful information on getting around by car and public transport.

3 Major Towns
All major towns are described on two or more pages, with the most interesting sights described individually.

The Town Map shows the main streets. The key sights are plotted, along with the parking areas, churches and tourist information offices.

Corsica at a Glance

This presents the island divided into four areas, whose colours correspond to those on the colour-coded tabs.

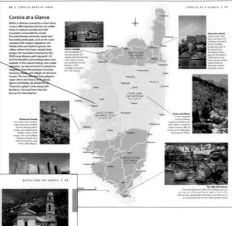

Practical Information
includes the location of the towns and villages on the Road Map.

4 Detailed Information
All important places to visit are described individually, and also have detailed practical information. The entries are listed in order, following the numbering on the Regional Map.

Boxes highlight special or unique aspects of an area or sight.

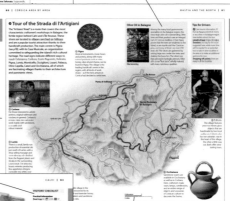

5 Tours
These features provide useful tips on interesting artistic or nature tours. The stages of each tour are numbered, and information is given on refuges and where to buy provisions.

A Visitors' Checklist provides a summary of the practical information necessary for planning a visit.

The scale gives an idea of the distances and a wind rose indicates north.

6 Corsica's Top Sights
In two or more pages, historic buildings or fortifications are dissected to reveal their interiors, while photographs highlight the most interesting features.

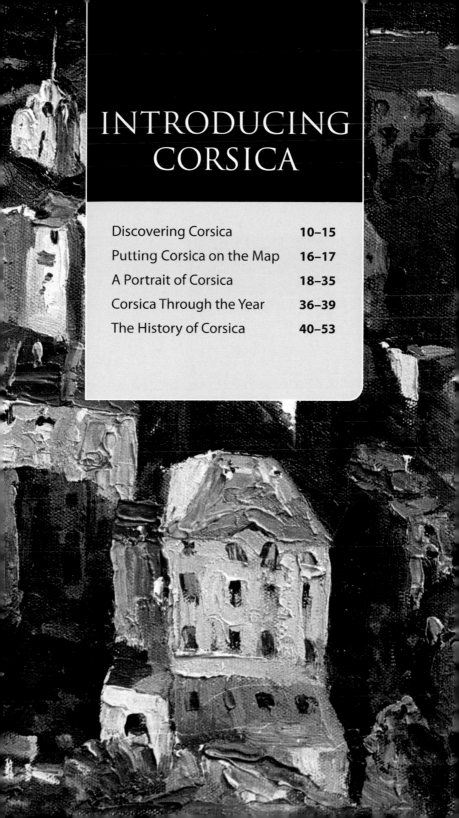

INTRODUCING
CORSICA

DISCOVERING CORSICA

The following tours have been designed to cover as many of Corsica's highlights as possible, while keeping long-distance travel manageable. First come a pair of two-day routes around the island's principal cities, Ajaccio and Bastia. Next is a five-day itinerary taking in some of Corsica's most beautiful beaches, with some suggestions on how to extend the trip to a week, if desired. Finally, for those with a little more time,

two seven-day tours of the north and south of Corsica cover the must-see sights of these contrasting regions, stopping off at cities, towns, villages and areas of great natural beauty. These last two routes can be combined to create the ultimate fortnight-long trip around the whole of the *Île de Beauté*. Choose your tour based on the time you have to explore and be inspired by what Corsica has to offer.

Alta Rocca
Located in the south of Corsica, this region is characterized by a mountainous landscape with oak forests.

A Week in Southern Corsica

- Mingle with the beau monde at **Ajaccio**'s stylish marina.
- Visit idyllic **Campomoro**, an isolated fishing village on the southwest coast.
- Head into the unspoilt **Alta Rocca** region for a taste of authentic mountain cuisine.
- Cross the Corsican watershed at the **Col de Bavella**.
- Relax on **Porto-Vecchio**'s famous beaches.
- Wonder at the location of **Bonifacio**'s *haute ville*.
- Explore the medieval streets of **Sartène**.
- Marvel at the carved faces of **Filitosa**'s 3,500-year-old standing stones.

Key
— A Week in Northern Corsica
— A Week in Southern Corsica

L'Île-Rousse

Pigna

Calvi · Sant' Antonin

Calenzana

Asco Stagnu

Monte Cinto

Girolata

Col de Verghio

Gorges de Spelunca

Fôret d'Aïtone

Porto

Piana

Plage d'Arone

Golfe de Sagone

Gravón

CORSE-DU-SUD

Ajaccio

Prunelli

Golfe d'Ajaccio

Filitosa

Porto Pollo

Golfe de Valinco

Campomoro

Sartène

Megaliths of Cauria

Roccapina

Bonifacio
The Old Town of Bonifacio is situated right on the rim of a sheer chalk cliff and enjoys spectacularly dramatic views.

◀ A Corsican village depicted by Xiaoyang Galas in her oil painting *Sea, Sun and Village*

Cap Corse
The small village of Pino, on the west coast of the Cap Corse peninsula, is surrounded by lush vegetation and maquis-covered hills.

A Week in Northern Corsica

- Gaze over **Bastia**'s Vieux Port from the ramparts of a Genoese citadel.
- Drive the corniche road around **Cap Corse**.
- Bathe in the dazzling turquoise waters off the **Désert des Agriates** coast.
- Explore the pretty villages of inland **Balagne**.
- Admire sweeping views of sea and mountains from **Calvi**'s fortress.
- Experience the epic grandeur of **Porto**'s gulf and its forested hinterland.
- Delve into Corsica's rugged heart at **Corte**, the starting point for some unforgettable trips into the mountains.

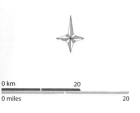

A Tour of Corsica's Best Beaches

- Enjoy the pure white sands of **Plage de Loto**, jewel in the crown of the Désert des Agriates.
- Recline on a sunbed and enjoy an astounding view of **Calvi**'s Genoese Citadelle.
- Experience Corsican-style wild swimming at **Arone**, a gorgeous bay of pale-blue water framed by bare mountains and maquis.
- Snorkel in the transparent waters at **Roccapina** beach, overlooked by a headland of giant boulders.
- Avoid the peak-season crowds by heading to **Rondinara**, a hidden gem of the far southeast.
- Take in the vivid white and turquoise colours of **Palombaggia** and **Santa Giulia** beaches.

Two Days in Ajaccio

The birthplace of Napoleon Bonaparte, Corsica's capital has a sleek French Riviera feel that contrasts with the island's rugged hinterland.

- **Arriving** Ajaccio's Napoleon Bonaparte Airport, served by shuttle buses and taxis, is 6 km (3 miles) to the east.

- **Moving on** The terminus for the Ajaccio–Bastia train line is off the north end of Cours Napoleon.

See pp90–95 for information on sights in Ajaccio.

Day 1
Morning The cafés overlooking Ajaccio's boat-jammed **marina** provide the perfect springboard for a stroll around nearby **Place Foch**, a palm-lined square where the **Salon Napoléonien** holds an exhibition devoted to the city's most illustrious son. Cross the square to reach Rue Fesch and the **Palais Fesch – Musée des Beaux-Arts**, where the world-class collection of Renaissance art includes works by Botticelli, Titian and Michelangelo.

Afternoon Napoleon's birthplace, the **Maison Bonaparte**, is the highlight of the old town – an area where colour-washed, terracotta-tiled houses and narrow backstreets have changed little in centuries. Be sure to visit the weathered

Genoese **Citadelle**, overlooking the town beach, Plage St-François; and the Venetian-Renaissance-style **cathedral**, where Napoleon and his siblings were baptized. Ajaccio's best shops and Second Empire-style cafés dot the city's main thoroughfare, **Cours Napoleon**, which is only a short stroll away.

Day 2
Morning Jump on a bus or ferry from the marina to **Porticcio** *(see p97)*, on the far east shore of the gulf. Here, you can swim in turquoise water while gazing across the bay to the city. Buses also run further around the coast, to the less frequented coves of Agosta and Ruppione. Head back to Ajaccio in time for lunch.

Afternoon After lunch, take a cruise out to the **Îles Sanguinaires** *(see p96)*. Situated off the **Pointe de la Parata** *(see p96)*, at the southernmost tip of the Golfe d'Ajaccio, these scattering of islets are crowned by lighthouses and watchtowers. Return either by boat or by bus via the coast road, the Route des Sanguinaires, which skirts a string of attractive **beaches** *(see p96)*.

To extend your trip...
Follow the D55 for 29 km (18 miles) southeast to **Côti-Chiavari** *(see p97)*, an orange-granite village boasting stupendous views of the gulf.

Two Days in Bastia

A vibrant, modern port city, Bastia also has a warren-like old harbour overlooked by a citadel and a number of Baroque churches.

- **Arriving** Poretta Airport, 16 km (9 miles) south, is served by shuttle buses.

- **Moving on** The train journey across the mountains to Ajaccio on the Micheline line takes just under four hours.

The imposing façade of the church of St-Jean-Baptiste, Bastia

See pp62–7 for information on sights in Bastia.

Day 1
Morning Start the day with breakfast under the palms at one of the terrace cafés lining **Place St-Nicholas**. From there, stroll south via the fresh-produce market at Place du Marché to the **Vieux Port**, overshadowed by the twin campaniles of the church of **St-Jean-Baptiste**, Bastia's most iconic building. Don't miss two equally extravagant Baroque churches nearby, the **Chapelle St-Roch** and the **Oratoire de l'Immaculée Conception**.

Afternoon Savour the cobbled squares, pastel hues and sea views of the Terra Nova quarter, in the Genoese Citadelle above the Vieux Port. In the Palais des Gouverneurs, the **Musée de Bastia** charts the city's history

Fishermen's boats moored in Ajaccio's marina

The idyllic surroundings of Roccapina beach, in the south of Corsica

and affords fine vistas over the old and new harbours below. The famous statue of *Christ des Miracles* is housed in the Rococo **Oratoire Ste-Croix**.

Day 2
Morning Hire a car to explore Bastia's scenic fringes, starting with a 16-km (9-mile) drive south down the slither of land that divides La Marana beach from the **Étang de Biguglia** lagoon, an important stopover for migratory birds, including pink flamingos. It's worth making the trip just to see **La Canonica** *(see p152)*, a splendidly preserved 12th-century Pisan cathedral. Spend the rest of the morning browsing the chic boutiques along **Boulevard Paoli**, Bastia's stylish main street.

Afternoon Far reaching views across the Ligurian Sea to Elba and the Tuscan coast can be had from the **Route de la Corniche Supérieure**, which contours north from Bastia around the folds of **Cap Corse** *(see p71)*. Admire the schist-roofed hamlet of San Martino di Lota before dropping down to the shoreline again at **Erbalunga** *(see p70)*, a picturesque harbour.

To extend your trip…
Continue north to **Macinaggio** *(see pp70–71)*. From here, take a boat trip along the wild shore of the Cape's northern tip.

A Tour of Corsica's Best Beaches

- **Duration** Five days, but can be extended to seven with the extra suggestions.
- **Airports** Arrive and depart from Bastia's airport.
- **Transport** This tour is most easily done by car, though all of the beaches, with the exception of Arone, are accessible by bus in summer.

Day 1: Loto
The remote coastline of the **Désert des Agriates** *(see p76)*, to the west of Bastia, is spangled with beaches of breathtaking beauty, and Loto is the loveliest. A cove of brilliant white sand and translucent water, it can be reached only by boat from **St-Florent** *(see p74)*, on the opposite side of the gulf.

Day 2: Calvi
The sweep of pale-orange sand in **Calvi** *(see p85)* is famous for its superb setting: the sun-bleached walls of the Genoese Citadelle rise above it to the north, while the snow-capped peaks of Monte Cinto soar through clouds to the south. It is an impossibly scenic backdrop for a swim.

Day 3: Arone
Wild, pristine and expansive enough to soak up even the large summer crowds, **Plage d'Arone** *(see p102)* is enclosed on all sides by rocky, maquis-covered hills.

Day 4: Roccapina
The idyllic white-sand beach of **Roccapina** *(see p130)*, in the far southwest, is overlooked by a pile of eroded boulders that look eerily like a recumbent lion, but it's the clarity of the water that really astonishes here.

Day 5: Rondinara
Consistently voted France's most beautiful bay, **Rondinara** *(see p25)* is a secluded, shell-shaped beach with fine white sand and turquoise water. Sheltered and shallow, it's perfect for families with small children. A shaded café at its southern end provides a welcome pit stop.

To extend your trip…
Palombaggia and **Santa Giulia** *(see p124)*, just up the coast from Rondinara, offer ample incentive to prolong your stay in the far south.

One of the many sandy beaches around the town of Calvi

A Genoese tower on a cliff just outside the village of Pino

A Week in Northern Corsica

- **Airports** Arrive and depart from Bastia's Poretta Airport.

- **Transport** In summer, buses cover all of this route, but departures are usually limited to one per day. A car is essential to complete the itinerary in a week.

- **Book ahead** Musée de Bastia, Musée de la Corse (Corte), boat trip to Girolata (Porto).

Day 1: Bastia
Follow the first day of the city itinerary on pp12–13.

Day 2: St-Florent, via Cap Corse
The corniche road around Cap Corse makes for a perfect day's sightseeing. Stop at **Macinaggio** *(see p70)* for a boat ride, or walk the **Sentier des Douaniers** *(see pp72–3)*. Descending the western cape in the afternoon, admire the Latinate villas and mausolea at **Pino** *(see p73)* and the sea views from medieval **Nonza** *(see p74)*. Be sure to arrive at **St-Florent** *(see p74)* in time to watch *boules* on the plane-shaded village square.

Day 3: L'Île Rousse, via the Nebbio
Catch a boat from St-Florent to Plage de Loto, one of the many gorgeous beaches along the rocky shoreline of the **Désert des Agriates** *(see p76)*. In the afternoon, head inland, through the hill villages of the **Nebbio** region *(see p76)*, to the 13th-century Pisan chapel of **San Michele de Murato** *(see p75)*. Call at a vineyard or two in **Patrimonio** *(see p74)* before the drive up the Balagne coast to **L'Île Rousse** *(see p78)*.

Day 4: Calvi, via the Balagne
The villages inland from L'Île Rousse survey the coast from a giant amphitheatre of crags and hilltops. Visit **Pigna** *(see p78)*, famous for its music and handicraft workshops, then pause at **Sant'Antonino** *(see p79)* for a view of the peaks to the south. When you reach Calvi, see the Citadelle and stroll along the marina.

> **To extend your trip…**
> Take the D151 inland from Calvi, looping through the pretty mountain village of **Calenzana** *(see p79)*.

The entrance to a ceramics exhibition in Pigna, a hamlet famous for art and music

Day 5: Porto
The journey down Corsica's rugged northwest coast crosses landscapes of surreal beauty, with red porphyry headlands emerging from bays of cobalt blue. From **Porto** *(see p106)*, boats cross the gulf to **Girolata** *(see p107)*, a tiny fishing village at the foot of maquis-covered hills. At sunset time, follow one of the marked trails winding through the unusual **Calanque** rock formations *(see pp104–5)*, south of Porto. End the day with an aperitif at the Hôtel Roches Rouges in **Piana** *(see p102)*.

> **To extend your trip…**
> Follow the D824 west from Piana to reach one of the island's hidden gems, **Plage d'Arone** beach *(see p102)*.

Day 6: Porto to Corte
There are many opportunities to swim in mountain streams on the drive up to the grandiose **Gorges de Spelunca** *(see p106)*. At its head, the **Fôret d'Aïtone** *(see p107)* is filled with fragrant Laricio pine trees and crashing waterfalls. Continue on the D84 over the **Col de Verghio** *(see p155)* and through the **Scala di Santa Regina** canyon *(see p154)* to reach **Corte** *(see pp138–41)*. Visit the Musée de la Corse and the adjacent Citadelle, then stroll around the cobbled streets and squares of the *haute ville*, especially Place Gaffori.

> **To extend your trip…**
> Make a detour to the ski station Asco Stagnu and experience **Monte Cinto** *(see p27)*, Corsica's highest massif.

Day 7: Corte to Bastia
Corte is a quintessentially Corsican town, with a towering Genoese citadel and a somewhat forbidding atmosphere. Some astounding mountain scenery awaits nearby. Head up the **Gorges de la Restonica** *(see p143)* to the sparkling glacial lakes of Mélo and Capitellu, set in a vast bowl of vertical grey granite. Bastia lies only a couple of hours' drive away.

A Week in Southern Corsica

- **Airports** Arrive and depart from Ajaccio's airport.
- **Transport** In summer, buses cover the entire route, except for the final stage (via Filitosa). A car is recommended.
- **Booking ahead** Cucuruzzu, Levie, Musée de la Préhistoire (Sartène), boat from Bonifacio.

Day 1: Ajaccio
Follow the first day of the city itinerary on p12.

Day 2: Campomoro and the Sartenais
On the south side of the Golfe de Propriano is **Campomoro** *(see p132)*, one of Corsica's loveliest seaside villages, with a cluster of stone houses strung around a gently curving white sandy beach that is overlooked by a Genoese watchtower. When the heat subsides, visit the nearby **Megaliths of Cauria** *(see p131)*, an important scattering of enigmatic prehistoric monuments.

Day 3: The Alta Rocca
Deep valleys cloaked in oak and chestnut trees dominate the gloriously unspoilt Alta Rocca region, inland from Campomoro. Here, winding mountain roads lead through a succession of red-tiled villages swathed in greenery. Don't miss **Levie** *(see pp128–9)* and the Musée Départemental d'Alta Rocca, the nearby prehistoric site of **Cucuruzzu** *(see p129)* or pretty **Zonza** *(see p128)*, where ancient houses nestle in the shadow of the Aiguilles de Bavella, a cluster of vast granite needles rising from the Corsican watershed. Follow one of the delightful walks from the **Col de Bavella** *(see pp126–7)*, at the foot of the peaks, to visit nearby rock formations and viewpoints.

Day 4: Porto-Vecchio, via the Route de Bavella
Some of the most breathtaking scenery in the entire Mediterranean flanks the Route de Bavella, the road leading from the island's craggy spine

to **Solenzara** *(see p125)*, on the east coast. Pull over for a refreshing dip in the river en route to the harbour town of **Porto-Vecchio** *(see p124)*, a former Genoese stronghold with a medieval citadel that now hosts a wide range of smart restaurants and boutiques.

> **To extend your trip…**
> Between Solenzara and Porto-Vecchio is the turning to **Araggio** *(see p125)*, a superb prehistoric fortress.

Day 5: Bonifacio, via the beaches
Nearly everyone comes to Porto-Vecchio for the amazing beaches scalloping the coast to the south. With water that wouldn't look out of place in the Caribbean, **Palombaggia** and **Santa Giulia** *(see p124)* tend to attract the largest crowds in the summer, though **Rondinara** *(see p25)*, further south, is a less well-known alternative with equally spectacular colours. In the afternoon, explore the extraordinary *haute ville* of **Bonifacio** *(see pp114–21)*, where ancient houses cluster on a narrow chalk promontory facing the straits across to Sardinia.

> **To extend your trip…**
> Follow the footpath along the clifftops running east from Bonifacio to reach the dramatically situated lighthouse at **Capo Pertusato** *(see p119)*.

Day 6: Sartène
Catch an excursion boat out of Bonifacio for an unrivalled view of this clifftop town. After lunch, head north up the coast and have a swim at **Roccapina** beach *(see p130)*. Finish the day with a meal on the square in the medieval fortress town of **Sartène** *(see p130)*, where the Musée de la Préhistoire Corse displays fascinating archaeological finds from the region.

Day 7: Ajaccio, via Filitosa
Bring the trip back to Ajaccio and, on the way, visit Corsica's most illustrious prehistoric site, **Filitosa** *(see p133)*. The carved menhirs here date from the second millennium BC.

> **To extend your trip…**
> Visit great beaches without the crowds at the village of **Porto-Pollo** *(see p132)*, on the Golfe de Propriano.

An aerial view of Sainte-Lucie-de-Tallano, in the Alta Rocca region

The Stantari menhirs of Cauria, a fascinating collection of megalithic monuments

Putting Corsica on the Map

Corsica is a region of France, but geographically it lies closer to Italy, between the Ligurian and Tyrrhenian seas, separated from Sardinia by the windswept Straits of Bonifacio, and only a few nautical miles from the coast of Tuscany. The island has an area of 8,680 sq km (3,350 sq miles) and a population of around 316,000, which increases considerably in the summer, when tourists arrive. The administrative capital is Ajaccio, while Corte is referred to as the historical capital and Bastia as the economic capital.

0 kilometres 50
0 miles 50

Barcelona,
Tangier, Tunis

Mediterranean Sea

Europe

Barcelona

A PORTRAIT OF CORSICA

The light-reflecting granite rocks, the dense, dark forests, the sandy coves, the expansive panoramas of Cap Corse or the compressed Bozio valley – Corsica is an enigmatic island with many and varied facets. Despite its large number of visitors, the island remains a wild and fascinating place.

A long, slow continental drift moved Corsica from the coast of Provence to its present position, in the northernmost waters of the Tyrrhenian Sea, with the Côte d'Azur and the Tuscan archipelago only a stone's throw away. A central chain of tall mountains culminating in Monte Cinto (2,706 m/8,878 ft) descends from Calvi, in the northwest, towards Porto-Vecchio, in the southeast corner of the island, separating it into two distinct regions. Pisan and Genoan rulers called the northeastern part *Diqua dei monti* ("Hither the mountains") while the inaccessible, untamed southwestern part was known as *Dila dei monti* ("Beyond the mountains").

Geologically, the divide separates the schist regions to the east from the predominantly granite areas descending towards the west coast. The exceptions to this rule are the extraordinary landscapes along the coasts of the Scandola Nature Reserve, the result of ancient volcanic eruptions, and the bright limestone rich in fossils on the cliffs of the south coast, especially around Bonifacio. Inland, mountains, gorges and torrents make Corsica a hiker's paradise. "Imagine a world still in the midst of chaos, a tempest of mountains separating narrow gorges in which torrents flow," wrote the French author Guy de Maupassant.

The pretty coloured buildings of Bastia, with the jetty and lighthouse in the foreground

◄ Picturesque village in Corsica's mountainous interior

Traditional Corsican products

He continues "No plains, but rather immense waves of granite and colossal undulations of earth covered with maquis or tall chestnut and pine forests." Much of Corsica's fascination is due to this lush interior cut through by wild torrents, a sign that it receives a heavier rainfall than the other Mediterranean islands. Corsica also has a splendid sea that is much admired by travellers from all over the world. This means, of course, that the coastline is often crowded, but it is still possible to find secluded coves, only accessible by foot or boat.

A local handmade marionette

An Age-Old Culture

Archaeologists say that the first humans arrived in Corsica around 9,000 years ago, probably after dangerous, but short, sea journeys from the Tuscan coast. The first Corsicans owed their survival to the breeding of livestock and hunting,

Sheep on their way to pasture – an age-old Corsican scene

which later gave rise to their own unique megalithic culture. The best examples of this can be found in the southwest region of the island: the menhirs of Filitosa, the dolmens at Sartène and the *castelli* at Cucuruzzu and Capula. Agricultural products were introduced by Greek colonists and then spread when the Romans conquered the island and made the principal city, Aléria, their capital. With the grim and chaotic Middle Ages came invaders, pirates, preachers and, above all, merchants. A bone of contention between the agile ships of Pisa and Genoa, Corsica became a Genoese colony in the 13th century and was to remain so, amid revolts and battles, up to the 18th century.

The "Corsican Nation"

The Corsicans were fierce opponents already of the Roman legions and have always felt they were a separate people with their own language (still a hallmark of the "Corsican nation") and ancient traditions. The downfall of Genoese power paved the way for the French and, at the same time, for the brief but crucial period of independence, linked to the figure of Pascal Paoli, the "Father of the Nation" *(see pp50–51)*. Renowned as the birthplace of Napoleon Bonaparte – who was born in Ajaccio on 15 August 1769 – Corsica has been part of France for over two centuries.

The Corsicans' continued demands for independence from France are a sign of their national pride, which is rooted in the distant past. Although there is still an ardent yearning for the "Corsican nation", support for the violent paramilitary groups so active in the 1970s is no longer very strong. Since the Matignon Agreement, finally reached in 2001, France has been investing

Starting a sailing trip from a Corsican beach

heavily in both economy and infrastructure on the island, a fact that perhaps has made total autonomy less tempting. The wish for cultural independence and identity, however, is still deeply felt, with manifestations centred at the University of Corte, and through an abundance of websites relating to the island's language, history and traditions *(see also pp34–5)*.

The People and the Land

There are only about 316,000 Corsicans on the island; three times as many work in mainland France. During the winter, as fewer jobs are available in the tourism sector, many leave for temporary work on the continent. The majority of the population live along the coast, mostly near the main towns such as Ajaccio and Bastia. Apart from Corte, the interior is sparsely inhabited – a fact that makes it appealing to the many visitors who come here to experience wilderness, leaving behind the hustle and bustle of modern life. Paradoxically, what leads to a diminishing population and lack of conventional work opportunities, is in some way still beneficial since it attracts tourists.

Luckily tourism, despite being a major source of income, has not been allowed to take over the island, not even along the coasts. So far, the natural environment and local traditions have been respected, thanks to projects such as the Parc Régional de la Corse *(see p103)*, and there are no sprawling highrise resorts on the island.

Corsicans are generally quite traditional, and family comes first – a reflection of the old clan values *(see p35)*. Women might no longer be the cause of vendettas, but the attitude towards them is very conservative and, compared to northern Europe, equality is a very remote goal. On the other hand, no one receives more respect than a Corsican mother.

The locals' reputation of aloofness or suspiciousness towards strangers is not altogether an exaggeration, but visitors who show respect and admiration for this captivating island will be welcome and treated with Mediterranean warmth

One of Corsica's many beaches

Corsica's Landscape and Fauna

Corsica is essentially a tall, craggy peak descending to the sea, with valleys furrowed by mountain torrents and small plains around the river estuaries. As well as the coastline and the sea, the mountains also offer spectacular natural scenery, with summits over 2,500 m (8,200 ft) high and the large Corsican pine forests that cover the central zone of the island. Many rivers, mostly along the east coast, create coastal lakes called *étangs* near their outlets. There is an abundance of flora, with almost 3,000 species of plants, 80 of which are endemic, providing a marvellous carpet of Mediterranean maquis *(see p77)*.

A river along the route to the Col de Bavella

The Coastline
The maquis undergrowth dominates the coastline up to the first hill ranges. In the eastern plain around Porto-Vecchio and in the peninsula of Cap Corse, there are cork oaks and holm oaks. In the inhabited coastal areas, the century plants (Mexican agave), palm trees, prickly pears and aloes create an exotic atmosphere. The large umbrella pine woods are particularly thick around Porto-Vecchio and Calvi.

The Hills
Maquis shrubs cover the first hill ranges and are present up to 1,000 m (3,300 ft). Olive trees grow to an altitude of 600 m (2,000 ft). At a lower level, vineyards cover the seaward slopes of Cap Corse, the Nebbio area, and the eastern and southern coastal plains. The numerous citrus-fruit orchards boast fine oranges, lemons, mandarins, limes and clementines. There are also many eucalyptus trees, introduced in 1868 to drain the swampy coasts and eradicate malaria.

The aloe is a succulent plant with spinous leaves that, from January to April, has lovely red or yellow tubular flowers that bloom in thick clusters.

Woodpeckers live in the woods of Corsica. Visitors may hear their characteristic pecking and glimpse their bright plumage among the pine and cork oak trees.

Myrtle is a fragrant evergreen shrub that thrives in sunny areas. Its lovely white flowers bloom in spring, while the berries mature in the autumn.

Olive trees are among the trees that live longest, becoming gnarled with time. Olives are harvested by hanging large nets under each tree.

Wildlife

As well as the wild boar and the rarely seen mouflon, which is the symbol of the island, the Corsican deer has also returned to the area, thanks to a reintroduction project. The rocky coasts are the habitat of such marine birds as seagulls, ospreys and cormorants.

Tyrrhenian wall lizard

In the maquis, the Hermann's tortoise can be found, which is closely related to a species now extinct on the European continent. There are no vipers in Corsica, but there are two endemic species of lizard, the Tyrrhenian wall lizard and the Bedriaga's wall lizard, as well as the harmless Aesculapian snake. The sea is rich in fish, including groupers and breams, and also provides tasty molluscs and crustaceans.

A family of boars, common in Corsica

The Forests

The central zone of the island is an immense forest, except for the valley floors and the areas destroyed by fire. At an altitude of 500–800 m (1,600–2,600 ft), there are chestnut trees, planted by the Genoese. Chestnuts were a staple in the diet of the mountain population. Further up, at 700–1,500 m (2,300–5,000 ft), are the conifers, with the marvellous Valdu-Niellu, Aïtone and Vizzavona forests, dominated by giant Laricio pines.

The Mountains

Covered by snow from autumn to late spring, the mountains in Corsica are tall and solitary, inhabited only by a few shepherds. At 1,500 m (5,000 ft), the woods give way to alders, junipers and barberries. Higher up, just before the rocky peaks, are the grassy mountain pastures. The tallest peaks are Monte Cinto (2,706 m/8,878 ft), Monte Rotondo (2,622 m/8,602 ft), Monte Padro (2,393 m/ 7,851 ft) and Monte d'Oro (2,389 m/7,838 ft).

Mushrooms thrive in the damp underbrush of the forests, at the foot of conifers and beech trees. They are gathered from late summer onwards.

The golden eagle is a formidable raptor that lives on the tallest peaks. It can catch large prey, such as lambs, in its powerful talons.

Chestnuts mature in early autumn. As the prickly burs fall to the ground, they break, showing the nuts inside. September and October are the ideal times for hikes among the chestnut orchards.

The juniper is one of the characteristic and most fragrant plants of the high mountain zones. It can be recognized by its silver-green needles and almost black berries.

The Corsican Coastline

From the small isolated bays among granite rocks on the west coast, to the long sandy beaches between Bastia and Bonifacio that are ideal for family holidays, Corsica is a paradise for sunbathers. The island's 1,000 km (620 miles) of coastline offer visitors the chance to lie in the sun from May to October, and it is possible to find secluded spots even in July and August. Except for the major beaches near towns such as Calvi, Porto-Vecchio and Ajaccio, most have no lifeguards, so it is advisable to be cautious when bathing, especially when the wind is strong and the sea is rough.

From St-Florent to L'Île Rousse, small bays with fine sand alternate with cliffs covered in maquis.

From Calvi to Ajaccio, steep cliffs line the coast and many beaches can be reached only by sea. Landing is not possible along the red cliffs of the Scandola Nature Reserve.

Golfe d'Ajaccio has many beaches and rocky areas. The Pointe de la Parata peninsula extends into the sea towards the Îles Sanguinaires, where the sea is crystal clear.

The white cliffs along the southern coast around Bonifacio are among the best known in Corsica. Some of the large rocks even have a name, such as the famous Grain de Sable ("grain of sand"), seen here in the background.

Map labels:
L'Île Rousse
N197
② Calvi
D81
Galéria
Fango
Golo
D84
Golfe de Porto
③ Porto
D84
Tavign
D81
D70
Sagone
Liamone
Cruzini
Gravo
Golfe de Sagone
D81
Bocognano
N193
Ajaccio
D27
Golfe d'Ajaccio
④ Porticcio
D83
N196
Taravo
D157
Zo
Golfe de Valinco
Propriano
Sartène
N196
Tonnara ⑤
Boni

Along the Cap Corse, high cliffs frame many bays with picturesque little harbours, such as this one at Centuri.

The coast south of Bastia is known for its coastal lakes, which are called *étangs*. These form interesting marshy zones at the river mouths, such as the Étang de Biguglia, seen above.

0 kilometres 25

0 miles 15

South of Porto-Vecchio, the coastline becomes less steep and has magnificent coves with incredibly crystal-clear water and fine sand. Rondinara bay, seen here from above, is one of the best examples of these.

Ten of Corsica's Most Varied Beaches

① **The most inaccessible**
Saleccia beach *(see p76)*, one of Corsica's most arresting white-sand bays, is accessible only by boat or via an 11-km (7-mile) rutted track. At weekends, the bay is dotted with yachts.

② **The most fashionable**
Shallow, crystal-clear water and a charming harbour: Calvi beach, with fine bathing facilities, is one of the liveliest in Corsica.

③ **The best for diving**
Surrounded by a eucalyptus grove, the beach at Porto is the best starting point for those who want to explore the west coast's sea floor.

④ **The most urban**
The beaches at Porticcio, opposite Ajaccio, have white sand and good facilities and are frequented by the locals. The best known is La Viva.

⑤ **The best for kite-surfing and windsurfing**
Tonnara beach, at the end of the deep Golfe de Figari, is a favourite with kite- and windsurfers because there is always a stiff breeze.

⑥ **The most sheltered**
The small coves of the Îles Lavezzi, bordered by rocks sculpted by the sand and wind, can be reached by boat from Bonifacio.

⑦ **The most tropical**
A shell-shaped cove with brilliant turquoise water and white sand, the beach at Rondinara also has a camp site and a restaurant.

⑧ **The best for watersports**
The beach at Santa Giulia, a tranquil sandy bay bordered by dunes and pine trees, is equipped for all aquatic sports, such as windsurfing, canoeing and sailing.

⑨ **The most photogenic**
With its white sand, pink cliffs, dunes, pines and a lovely blue sea, the beach at Palombaggia, south of Porto-Vecchio, is perhaps the most spectacular.

⑩ **The most family-friendly**
Of the long, sandy beaches fit for families, the best is at Aléria, on the east coast.

GR20: Stages 1–5

Crossing Corsica from northwest to southeast, the GR20 (Grande Randonnée 20) is 200 km (124 miles) long. The path runs at an average altitude of 1,000–2,000 m (3,300–6,600 ft), linking Calenzana, in the Balagne region, with Conca, in the Porto-Vecchio hinterland. Every year, several thousand hikers try this tour, which is only for those in very good condition. The GR20 is divided into 15 stages, and the hikes last from 8am–5pm on terrain with altitude differences as much as 800 m (2,600 ft). Stages 1 to 5 have spectacular but difficult stretches, the most notorious being Cirque de la Solitude, a route fitted with fixed ladders, chains and cables.

The Sentier de Spasimata is a path that skirts the slopes of the Cirque de Bonifatu. It is famous for the restored footbridge suspended over a torrent.

The refuges along the route are small stone constructions built in the local mountain architectural style, so that they blend in well with the natural setting. The Carozzu refuge is immersed in the surrounding vegetation; other refuges are in open meadows.

Warning

The GR20 route takes about 14 days to complete, hiking an average of seven hours a day. As such, it is recommended only for persons in good physical condition, with some experience in hiking and climbing. Hikers must be equipped with mountain boots, waterproof jackets, fleece wear, sun hats and first-aid kits. In the summer, food is available at some refuges, but it is safest to bring your own provisions. You can restock (on food and drink) at points where the trail descends to road level.

Calvi

D751

Calenzana, a tiny village in the Balagne region, is where the GR20 begins. The first stage has a steep ascent and is quite challenging.

Capo a u Den

2,032 m (6,667

Ortu di u Piobbu

Stage 1
Start: Calenzana (275 m/902 ft)
Finish: Ortu di u Piobbu refuge (1,570 m/5,151 ft)
Length: 10 km (6 miles)
Degree of difficulty: hard
Average duration: 7 hours
Maximum altitude: 1,570 m (5,151 ft)
Stopover: Ortu di u Piobbu refuge (bed space for 30)

Cirque de Bonifatu

Carozzu

Cirque de la Solitude

The alpine asphodel is a species of plant that blooms between late May and June.

Stage 5
Start: Bergeries de Ballone (1,440 m/4,724 ft)
Finish: Castel de Verghio (1,404 m/4,606 ft)
Length: 13 km (8 miles)
Degree of difficulty: average
Average duration: 7 hours
Maximum altitude: 2,000 m (6,562 ft)
Stopover: Castel de Verghio hotel (29 rooms and restaurant)

Col de Verghio

Castel de Verg

D84

Evisa

Capo Stranciacone is a large rock face that borders the valley descending towards Asco. It can be seen from the GR20 near Haut-Asco, in the vicinity of Stage 3 of the path.

Calenzana

Castel de Verghio

Bergeries de
Capannelle

Conca

Stage 2
Start: Ortu di u Piobbu refuge (1,570 m/5,151 ft)
Finish: Carozzu refuge (1,270 m/4,167 ft)
Length: 8 km (5 miles)
Degree of difficulty: hard
Average duration: 6 1/2 hours
Maximum altitude: 1,950 m (6,400 ft)
Stopover: Carozzu refuge (bed space for 24)

Key

━━━ *GR20: Stages 1–5*

▢ *Parc Naturel Régional*

Stage 3
Start: Carozzu refuge (1,270 m/4,167 ft)
Finish: Asco Stagnu refuge (1,422 m/4,665 ft)
Length: 6 km (4 miles)
Degree of difficulty: average
Average duration: 6 hours
Maximum altitude: 2,010 m (6,594 ft)
Stopover: Asco Stagnu refuge (bed space for 32)

nte Corona
▲
4 m (7,034 ft)

ASCO

L'ASCO

D147

🏠 ⛰ **Asco Stagnu**

Monte Cinto
▲
2,706 m (8,878 ft)

Large flocks of mountain goats live on these peaks and can be spotted by hikers during their climb.

Monte Cinto is the tallest peak in Corsica and dominates the third and fourth stages of the Grande Randonnée long-distance path.

Stage 4
Start: Asco Stagnu refuge (1,422 m/4,665 ft)
Finish: Bergeries de Ballone (1,440 m/4,724 ft)
Length: 8 km (5 miles)
Degree of difficulty: hard, with rock climbs in the Cirque de la Solitude
Average duration: 6 hours
Maximum altitude: 2,218 m (7,277 ft)
Stopover: Tighjiettu refuge (1,683 m/5,520 ft; bed space for 39), or tents at the Bergeries de Ballone

**Bergeries
de Ballone**

Corte

🏠 **Albertacce**

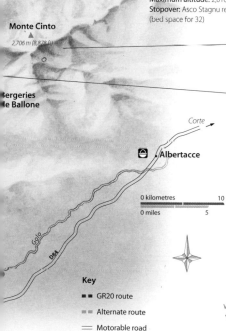

0 kilometres   10
0 miles   5

Golo

D84

Key

▪▪ GR20 route

▪▪ Alternate route

══ Motorable road

Snow-capped peaks appear near Haut-Asco, which during the winter months is a popular ski resort *(see p154).*

GR20: Stages 6–10

Stage 7 of the GR20 offers the best views but is one of the toughest stretches. It does not climb any peaks, but it crosses the GR20's highest pass, the Brêche de Castillo, at 2,225 m (7,300 ft). The easiest part is the eighth stage, a shaded route without steep slopes.

Col de Verghio

Albertacce

Golo

D84

D84

Castel de Verghio

Forêt de Valdu-Niellu

Evisa

Lac de Nino

Tavignan

At the Col de Verghio, the view opens on to a pass crossed by a motorable road. This is the edge of the Valdu-Niellu woods. A little further up are the alpine meadows and rocky zones.

Soccia

Orto

Vico

Guagno

Stage 6
Start: Castel de Verghio (1,404 m/4,606 ft)
Finish: Manganu refuge (1,601 m/5,253 ft)
Length: 14 km (9 miles)
Degree of difficulty: average
Average duration: 5 1/2 hours
Maximum altitude: 1,760 m (5,774 ft)
Stopover: Manganu refuge (bed space for 31)

0 kilometres 10
0 miles 10

Lac de Nino (Lake Nino) is a glacial lake that feeds the Tavignano river. It forms a marshy area called Pozzine ("the wells") that from above looks like lacework.

Key

■ ■ GR20 route
■ ■ Alternate route
— Motorable road
■ ■ Other paths

Lac de Capitello is surrounded by rocky scenery. The Punta dei Sette Laghi (Seven Lakes Peak) is so named because it affords an excellent view of a series of glacial lakes.

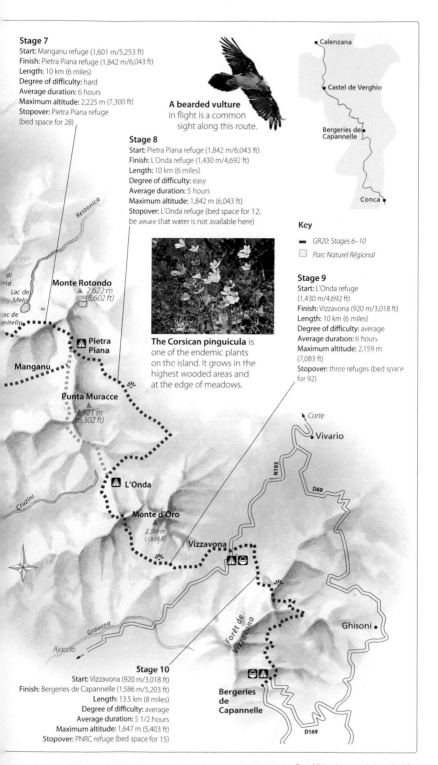

Stage 7
Start: Manganu refuge (1,601 m/5,253 ft)
Finish: Pietra Piana refuge (1,842 m/6,043 ft)
Length: 10 km (6 miles)
Degree of difficulty: hard
Average duration: 6 hours
Maximum altitude: 2,225 m (7,300 ft)
Stopover: Pietra Piana refuge (bed space for 28)

A bearded vulture in flight is a common sight along this route.

Stage 8
Start: Pietra Piana refuge (1,842 m/6,043 ft)
Finish: L'Onda refuge (1,430 m/4,692 ft)
Length: 10 km (6 miles)
Degree of difficulty: easy
Average duration: 5 hours
Maximum altitude: 1,842 m (6,043 ft)
Stopover: L'Onda refuge (bed space for 12; be aware that water is not available here)

The Corsican pinguicula is one of the endemic plants on the island. It grows in the highest wooded areas and at the edge of meadows.

Key
— GR20: Stages 6–10
▢ Parc Naturel Régional

Stage 9
Start: L'Onda refuge (1,430 m/4,692 ft)
Finish: Vizzavona (920 m/3,018 ft)
Length: 10 km (6 miles)
Degree of difficulty: average
Average duration: 6 hours
Maximum altitude: 2,159 m (7,083 ft)
Stopover: three refuges (bed space for 92)

Stage 10
Start: Vizzavona (920 m/3,018 ft)
Finish: Bergeries de Capannelle (1,586 m/5,203 ft)
Length: 13.5 km (8 miles)
Degree of difficulty: average
Average duration: 5 1/2 hours
Maximum altitude: 1,647 m (5,403 ft)
Stopover: PNRC refuge (bed space for 15)

Calenzana

Castel de Verghio

Bergeries de Capannelle

Conca

Restonica

Monte Rotondo ▲ 2,622 m (8,602 ft)

di ria
Lac de Melo
Lac de nitello

Pietra Piana

Manganu

Punta Muracce ▲ 1,921 m (6,302 ft)

Cruzini

L'Onda

Monte d'Oro 2,389 m (7,838 ft)

Corte

Vivario

N193

D69

Vizzavona

Gravona

Ajaccio

Ghisoni

Forêt de Vizzavona

Bergeries de Capannelle

D169

GR20: Stages 11–15

The last stages of the GR20 path offer no respite to those who have come this far without descending to the valley. Almost all stages have difficult stretches but make up for this with spectacular views, especially in the Aiguilles de Bavella area. Two weeks should be enough to walk the entire GR20, finishing at Conca.

The mouflon (*muvra* in Corsican) was once near extinction but has been a protected species since 1956. There are still only around 600 mouflons on the island.

Stage 11
Start: Bergeries de Capannelle (1,586 m/5,203 ft)
Finish: Prati (1,820 m/5,970 ft)
Length: 16.5 km (10 miles)
Degree of difficulty: average
Average duration: 6 1/2 hours
Maximum altitude: 1,840 m (6,040 ft)
Stopover: San Pedru di Verde refuge (bed space for 26)

Stage 12
Start: Prati (1,820 m/5,970 ft)
Finish: Usciolu refuge (1,750m/5,741 ft)
Length: 9 km (6 miles)
Degree of difficulty: hard
Average duration: 5 1/2 hours
Maximum altitude: 2,041 m (6,700 ft)
Stopover: Usciolu refuge (bed space for 29)

The Coscione Plateau lies west of Monte Incudine and is skirted by the GR20, which offers beautiful panoramic views towards the Golfe d'Ajaccio.

Stage 13
Start: Usciolu refuge (1,750 m/5,741 ft)
Finish: Asinao refuge (1,530 m/5,020 ft)
Length: 14.5 km (9 miles)
Degree of difficulty: average
Average duration: 8 hours
Maximum altitude: 2,134 m (7,001 ft)
Stopover: Asinao refuge (bed space for 29)

Bergeries de Capannelle

Monte Renoso
2,352 m (7,716 ft)

Monte Tortu
2,262 m (7,421 ft)

Col de Verde

Taravo

Prati

Palneca

Ciamannacce

Cozzano

Uscio

Zicavo

Aullene

Coscione Plateau

Monte Incudine
2,134 m (7,00 ft)

Asinao

Aiguilles de Ba

Quenza

Col de Bavella
(see pp126–7)

Zonza

Levie

D69

Key
■■ GR20 route
■■ Alternate route
══ Motorable road
■■ Other paths

0 kilometres ———— 10
0 miles ———— 10

Ghisonaccia
Fium'Orbo

Calenzana

Castel de Verghio

Bergeries de Capannelle

Conca

The kite is commonly seen in the Parc Naturel Régional (Regional Park). Kites can be recognized by their distinctive forked tail.

The martagon lily is one of the most spectacular alpine bulbous plants, with stems standing over a metre (4 ft) tall, and pulled-back petals in colours ranging from white to maroon.

Key

GR20: Stages 11–15

Parc Naturel Régional

Asinao

Stage 14
Start: Asinao refuge (1,530 m/5,020ft)
Finish: Paliri refuge (1,055 m/3,461 ft)
Length: 13 km (8 miles)
Degree of difficulty: hard
Average duration: 7 hours
Maximum altitude: 1,530 m (5,020 ft)
Stopover: Paliri refuge (bed space for 20)

Punta Paliri dominates the Bavella forest and rises up behind the Bavella refuge, which is the last high-altitude stage in the GR20 route before it descends back to "civilization".

The "Sea and Mountains" and "Sea to Sea" Paths

Solenzara
Solenzara

Paliri

The GR20 is not the only long hiking route in Corsica. There are two *Mare e Monti* (between sea and mountains) paths: the first links Calenzana to Cargèse in ten easy stages and the second goes from Porticcio to Propriano in five stages overlooking the sea. There are also three *Mare a Mare* (from sea to sea) paths: the northern one stretches from Moriani to Cargèse in 12 stages, the central one from Ghisonaccia to Porticcio in seven stages, and the southern path goes from Porto-Vecchio to Propriano in five stages. These paths are relatively easy to walk, although in the central zone they intersect with the GR20. *Gîtes d'étape* (hikers' hostels) along these routes offer half-board stopovers. See also page 188.

A hiker halfway between the mountains and the sea

Punta d'Ortu
695 m (2,280 ft)

Conca

Porto-Vecchio

Stage 15
Start: Paliri refuge (1,055 m/3,461 ft)
Finish: Conca (252 m/827 ft)
Length: 12 km (7 miles)
Degree of difficulty: average
Average duration: 5 hours
Maximum altitude: 1,055 m (3,461 ft)
Stopover: Gîte La Tonnelle (bed space for 30)

Architecture in Corsica

The various peoples that have ruled Corsica have left their imprint in the cities and around the island. The Pisans built the Romanesque churches, while the Genoese built almost all the splendid Baroque ones as well as the defensive structures indispensable for an island: the watchtowers along the coastline and the citadels. In the field of domestic architecture, the mortuary chapels, which were often constructed along the sides of roads, are particularly interesting. They were a mark of distinction of the rich families, especially those that had made their fortunes abroad.

Polychrome marble on the façade of a Romanesque church

Romanesque

Corsica has some splendid examples of Romanesque church architecture, mostly dating from the late 11th century onwards, during Pisan rule. These churches often have an aisle-less nave with a semicircular apse, while the façade is decorated with blind arches and panels that continue along the sides. Polychrome marble is also a characteristic feature.

Greek cross

Gilded grey marble reflects the sunlight.

The striation is orange, light green and light blue.

Bas-relief with the Lamb of God above the portal.

Half-pilasters with simple lines

Single portal

La Canonica Church (see p152) has extremely simple lines and an interior with two aisles. The only other church with this feature is Santa Maria Assunta at St-Florent (see p74).

Baroque

In the 17th and 18th centuries, the Genoese imported a northern Italian Baroque style to Corsica. In the rich areas, such as Castagniccia, Balagne and Bastia, large churches were built, the linear façades of which were animated by cornices, pilasters, pediments and volutes. The interiors feature spectacular stucco work, multicoloured marble and trompe l'oeil.

Wrought-iron railing

Lantern

Belfry, usually with four bells.

The bell tower of a Baroque church, such as St-Jean-Baptiste in Porta, is next to the church but not adjacent to its main body.

Base

St-Jean-Baptiste in Porta (see p151) is the best-known example of Baroque architecture in Corsica. Like many other churches, it has an aisle-less nave and central plan.

Curved pediment

Overhanging courses consisting of the frieze and cornice.

Rinceau

Volute

Cartouche

Pilaster

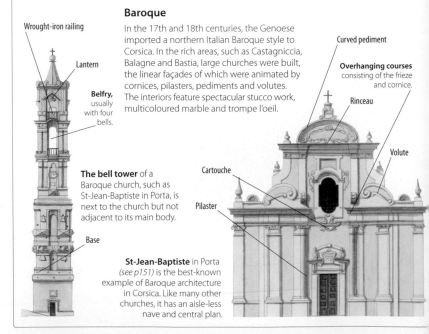

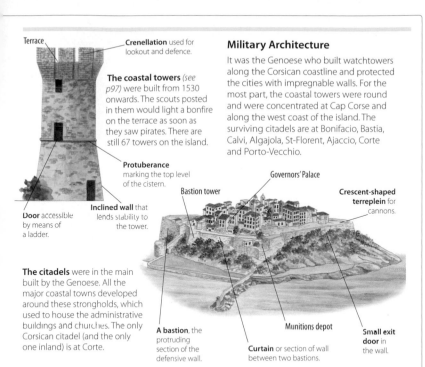

Terrace

Crenellation used for lookout and defence.

The coastal towers *(see p97)* were built from 1530 onwards. The scouts posted in them would light a bonfire on the terrace as soon as they saw pirates. There are still 67 towers on the island.

Protuberance marking the top level of the cistern.

Inclined wall that lends stability to the tower.

Door accessible by means of a ladder.

Military Architecture

It was the Genoese who built watchtowers along the Corsican coastline and protected the cities with impregnable walls. For the most part, the coastal towers were round and were concentrated at Cap Corse and along the west coast of the island. The surviving citadels are at Bonifacio, Bastia, Calvi, Algajola, St-Florent, Ajaccio, Corte and Porto-Vecchio.

Governors' Palace

Bastion tower

Crescent-shaped terreplein for cannons.

The citadels were in the main built by the Genoese. All the major coastal towns developed around these strongholds, which used to house the administrative buildings and churches. The only Corsican citadel (and the only one inland) is at Corte.

A bastion, the protruding section of the defensive wall.

Munitions depot

Curtain or section of wall between two bastions.

Small exit door in the wall.

Cemetery Architecture

A hallmark of the rich families in the north of the island are the mortuary chapels, which are true mausoleums built on private land, often at the side of minor roads. They reflect different styles, from the small Classical Roman temple to Baroque and Neo-Classical styles, and Byzantine architecture.

The Neo-Classical catafalque displays this 18th-century style's simple lines. The pilasters and tympanum are inspired by ancient temples, while the dome, often crowned by the statue of a saint or the Virgin Mary, is in the Christian tradition.

Statue of the Virgin

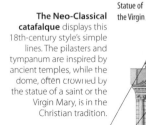

Decorative element in the shape of a vase adorned with a flame, typical of Classical architecture.

Main chapel

The double staircase is a distinctive feature.

Ornament resembling a piece of leather with rolled edges.

Lunette consisting of a fixed glass panel.

Byzantine-style dome

Tile roof

Side chapel

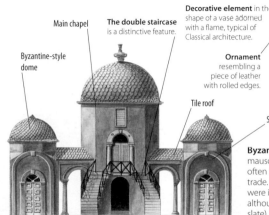

Byzantine taste is often visible in the mausoleums of merchant families, who often travelled widely to carry out their trade. The superimposed tile domes were inspired by those on mosques, although the material (schist, a local slate) is less precious.

Language, Literature, Music and Traditions

Corsica is a bilingual region, and all road signs are written in both Corsican and French. The Corsican language is similar to Italian and is still spoken and written everywhere, though less by young people. The island's literary tradition is mostly oral, based on legends that were handed down during cold winter months around the hearth, or in the songs describing the salient events in the lives of the locals. The ancient melodies are now being performed by music groups that sing in the local language and are also famous outside of Corsica.

An allegory of Corsica in an 18th-century print

Page from an old encyclopedia with the entry "Corsica"

The Corsican Language

In the northeast, the Corsican language (Corsu) is soft and musical, with an inflection and many words that are similar to Tuscan dialects. It is harsher and more crisp in the southwest, bearing influences of neighbouring Sardinia. The "double d" is used a lot in the southwest. For example, the word for "beautiful" in Bastia is bellu, while in Ajaccio it becomes beddu.

The Corsican language derived from Latin and, over the centuries, has been influenced by the various populations that ruled the island, mainly Tuscan – and not only because of Pisan dominion. In fact, Genoa, which ruled Corsica for five centuries, used Tuscan as the official and written language. The few Genoese words that have remained exist mostly in maritime and technical terminology. Influences also came from southern Italy, especially Calabria and Sardinia, and from French, which determined the spread of generic terms such as cammi di ferru, or railway, (chemin de fer in French).

The French language was first used in Corsica in 1769, when the island was annexed by France. It began to spread in the late 19th century, with the introduction of compulsory education.

Two ancient "foreign" dialects have remained on the island, but are disappearing due to the predominance of French. In Bonifacio, the Ligurian dialect of the 13th-century Genoese colonists can still be heard, while at Cargèse, Greek, imported by refugees from the Peloponnese in the 17th and 18th centuries, is virtually extinct. As for books, all the texts printed before the 18th century are in Italian. After that time, French became widespread, even though Italian was still used.

Recognized as a regional language in 1974, Corsican is now enjoying a revival thanks to the courses at the University of Corsica (see p141), where a vast data bank on the language has been created. Although most children on the island learn Corsican at home, the language is also taught at school, and many schools offer bilingual education.

Many associations and periodicals have also promoted Corsican, and there are several radio stations broadcasting in Corsican. The first newspaper in Corsican, A Tramuntana, was published in 1896, followed by others, especially in the period between the two World Wars.

The phrasebook on page 221 gives some examples of Corsican words.

Corsican Literature

Corsican has always been a spoken language and the local literary production was passed on orally, expressed as stories (stabato-ghji) and legends (fole) that were handed down from generation to generation. Then there were poems and songs that narrated life experiences: the lamentu for a death or a departure,

Honoré de Balzac (1799–1850)

and the *voceri*, the cries of black-clad women for a violent death.

Written literature made its appearance around the 17th century, with the establishment of the first literary circles, most of which were linked to liberation movements. The literature of this period dealt mainly with history and politics. Only at the end of the 19th century were the first poems, short stories and novels published in the Corsican language.

Between the World Wars, *A Muvra* became the newspaper of the Partitu Corsu d'Azione (Corsican Action Party), the main independence-movement party.

In the 19th century, many prominent French authors wrote works inspired by the island: Honoré de Balzac's *The Vendetta*; Guy de Maupassant's *The Corsican Bandit*, *A Vendetta* and *Histoire Corse*; and Alexandre Dumas' *Corsican Brothers*. Among contemporary authors, Angelo Rinaldi paints a ruthless portrait of his home town, Bastia, in the novels *La Dernière Fête de l'Empire* and *Les Roses de Pline*, and Marie Susini deals with the Corsican family and provinciality in novels such as *L'Île sans Rivage* and *La Renfermée*. Sisters Hélène and Jeanne Bresciani, both authors in their own right, together wrote *2, rue de la Marine*, a poetic account of coming to terms with the death of their father, reflected through Corsican culture.

Cetera, a 16-string cittern

Music

Songs are undoubtedly the best expression of Corsican musicality. An excellent example of this discipline is the *paghjella*, a traditional polyphonic song for three male voices that may have been imported from the Balearic Islands and is still sung during mass and other religious ceremonies in some towns and villages. Each voice has a specific function: the first, a tenor, provides the melodic and tonal base; the second, which is lower, provides the background; and the third, the highest, adds improvised embellishments.

According to tradition, the singers must all be dressed in black. All Corsican songs express an emotion, a state of mind, or retell a joyful or painful event. In the past, they were used to hand down traditions orally.

A particularly sorrowful song, the *voceru*, is sung by women dressed in black on the occasion of a wake: they weep and sing while rocking their bodies back and forth to mourn the deceased. A more playful genre is the *chjama e rispondi*, a form of choral competition in which two contestants improvise insults in verse.

Instruments in Corsica are traditionally wind-based, and typical of a pastoral society: flutes and fifes made of wood or animal horns (*a ciallamella, u liscarolu, a caramusa, u fischju*). Jew's harps (*ghjerbula*) and castanets (*chjoche*) are also used, as well as violins and guitars. Some instruments have been revived – for example, the 16-string *cetera*, a sort of cittern; the *pifane*, a goat horn used in the past by local shepherds; and the *pirula*, a wind instrument made from a hollow reed.

Some local groups – such as I Muvrini, A Filetta, Canta U Populu Corsu and Donasulana – have specialized in polyphonic music and have become famous on and off the island.

Local Traditions

Almost all Corsicans are Catholic and the local traditions that have been preserved are mostly of a religious nature. The most fascinating are the processions held during Easter Week, for example in Bonifacio, Calvi, Sartène and Erbalunga. Local saints' days are well celebrated in the cities and villages, as are ceremonies for the dead, accompanied by solemn processions to the cemeteries or to the unusual and impressive mortuary chapels (*see p33*) along the roads of Cap Corse and the west coast. However, the best-known "custom" in Corsica is the vendetta, which was common practice up to the mid-19th century. The physical distance and perceived indifference of Genoese justice led Corsican families to take the law into their own hands and seek revenge for offences. Rivalry for love, the division of a plot of land or any other dispute, even the most futile, could trigger a chain of murders – or even wars – that would carry on for generations. The feud would end only if the parish priest managed to broker an agreement between the families. Avengers going into hiding in the maquis were known as *bandits d'honneur* ("bandits of honour") to differentiate them from common highway robbers.

Scene of a vendetta between Corsican clans in a period print

CORSICA THROUGH THE YEAR

The best months to visit Corsica are May, June and September: the climate is mild, the prices are lower, and the beaches are not crowded. In addition, the risk of fires is low. In the summer, the island is filled with tourists and it is more difficult to find convenient and comfortable accommodation. Hikers and cyclists especially should avoid July and August because of the heat. From November to April, Corsica comes to a halt, and only a few hotels are open in the cities and main tourist locations along the coast. In these colder months, transport connections with the island are reduced to a minimum, and the sea can be quite rough.

Rockrose and lavender in bloom in the spring months

Spring

The blossoming maquis fills the air with its sweet scent. This begins in March with rosemary and lavender and continues in April with the pink and white rockrose flowers that cover entire areas. In mid-May, myrtle begins to blossom. The air is mild and visitors can enjoy a swim in the clear waters. At high altitudes, the snow may last until June and some paths and roads are closed.

March

Our Lady of Mercy Feast *(18 Mar)*, Ajaccio, with a procession and solemn mass.
Olive Festival *(mid-Mar)*, Santa Lucia di Tallano.
Greek Orthodox Procession *(Easter Mon)*, Cargèse. Traditional ceremonies and songs among the Greek community.

Procession de la Cerca *(Maundy Thu, Good Fri)*, Brando, Hameaux de Erbalunga. This 21-km (13-mile) procession begins at 7am and goes through all the towns in the Brando region. At 8pm, there is the *Granitula* procession, with hooded penitents.
Good Friday Procession, Bonifacio. The five city confraternities carry wooden sculptures and walk to the church of Ste-Marie-Majeure to worship the relics of the Holy Cross. The celebrations last throughout the Easter weekend.
Good Friday Procession, Sartène. At 9:30pm, in the city illuminated by candles, there is the *Catenacciu* (Great Penitent) procession.

April

Les Agrumes en Fête *(late Mar/early Apr)*, Bastelicaccia. A festival celebrating locally grown citrus fruit.
Salon de la Bande Dessinée *(early Apr)*, Bastia. Comic books and strips.
Brocciu Day *(date depending on cheese production)*. Festival dedicated to *brocciu* (traditional sheep's-milk cheese).

May

May 1 Fair, Lucciani. Trade show of Corsican handicrafts.
Festimare *(early May)*, L'Île Rousse. A sea festival for young people.
Corsica X-Tri Triathalon *(mid-May)*, Calvi. A variety of regional races for men, women and children.
Ste-Restitude's Feast Day *(late May)*, Calenzana. Pilgrimage, procession.
Régates Impériales *(late May)*, Ajaccio. A regatta on old sailing boats in the Gulf of Ajaccio.

The Orthodox Easter procession at Cargèse

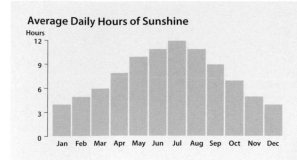

Average Daily Hours of Sunshine

Sunshine Hours
Corsica is well-known as a sunny island, even in autumn and spring, when the weather is still mild due to the many daily hours of sunshine. Along the coast, the warm sun makes swimming possible even into the early autumn.

Summer

During the summer months, the number of visitors to Corsica triples. The hotels, residences and camp sites are all booked up and charge high-season rates. The beaches are constantly packed with bathers, and the harbours are filled with sailing boats and motorboats. At this time, the island also offers many festivals to enjoy.

June

St Erasmus's Feast Day *(2 Jun)*, Ajaccio, Bastia, Calvi. The feast day of the patron saint of fishermen includes a procession in the sea.

Cavall'in Festa *(early–mid-Jun)*, Corte. Horse festival with parades in period costumes, shows, contests, exhibitions and displays

Rencontre d'Art Contemporain *(Jun–Aug)*, Calvi. Exhibition of contemporary art held in the Citadelle.

Fête de St-Jean *(24 Jun)*, Bastia. A traditional celebration held in honour of St John.

Nautival *(end of Jun)*, Macinaggio. Sea festival with stalls, performances, fish tastings and a procession.

July

La Relève de la Garde *(every Thu throughout Jul)*, Ajaccio. Changing of the Guard ceremony, in costume.

Wine Fair *(first weekend of Jul)*, Luri. Enjoy the best Corsican wines at this fair featuring wine tastings, competitions and other fun events.

Jazz in Ajaccio *(early Jul)*, Ajaccio. Corsican and international jazz and blues musicians come together for this annual concert.

La Relève des Gouverneurs *(second Sat in Jul)*, Bastia. Commemoration of an historical event with a procession in the Citadelle.

Music Festival *(Jul)*, Corbara. Concerts and shows.

Calvi on the Rocks *(Jul)*, Calvi. International and local rock and dance music on the Calvi beaches and its Citadelle.

Estivoce *(early Jul)*, Pigna. This celebration of Corsican polyphonic music features folk music, medieval religious songs and theatre.

Olive Festival *(first weekend after 14 Jul)*, Montegrosso. This trade show features the olive oil produced in the Balagne area.

Festival Jacques Luciani *(mid-Jul)*, Corte. Festival of folk dances.

Guitar Nights *(third week of Jul)*, Patrimonio. Folk, jazz and gypsy musicians.

Mediterranean Trophy *(last ten days of Jul)*. Starting from Corsica, this regatta stops at, Maddalena, Elba and Sardinia.

Les Estivales *(Jul–Sep)*, Ajaccio. A traditional music festival also featuring a series of dance performances.

August

Film Festival *(late Jul–early Aug)*, Lama. Featuring showings of European films, as well as Q&A meetings with directors.

Almond Fair *(early Aug)*, Aregno. A celebration of all things almond, with art, cooking demonstrations, children's activities and a market selling local specialities.

Participants in the Mediterranean Trophy regatta

Ballu in Corti *(Aug)*, Corte. Traditional dance with violin accompaniment.

Music Festival *(first week of Aug)*, Erbalunga. Outdoor concerts.

Notre Dame des Neiges *(8 Aug)*, Bavella. Religious procession in honour of the Virgin of the Snows.

Amateur Theatre Festival *(mid-Aug)*, Macinaggio/ Rogliano. Short theatre performances at different venues. Acting workshops for adults and children.

Celebrations in Honour of Napoleon *(mid-Aug)*, Ajaccio. Ceremonies for the birth of Napoleon Bonaparte. Exhibitions and parades in period costumes.

Porto Latino *(mid-Aug)*, St-Florent. Lively festival of Latin-American music.

St Bartholomew Procession *(24 Aug)*, held in Bonifacio.

Average Monthly Rainfall

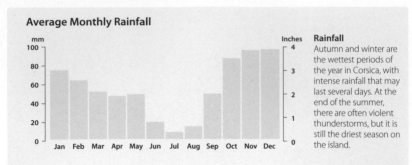

Rainfall
Autumn and winter are the wettest periods of the year in Corsica, with intense rainfall that may last several days. At the end of the summer, there are often violent thunderstorms, but it is still the driest season on the island.

Autumn

The sky is clear, the climate is mild, and until October the temperature of the sea is warm enough for bathing. On the coastline, the maquis begins to blossom again after the summer drought, and the strawberries and black myrtle berries ripen. In the valleys and mountains, the trees take on the colours of the autumn. In the chestnut-grove regions, Castagniccia and Evisa, the earth is carpeted with prickly chestnut burs, and the first rainfall encourages mushrooms to grow.

September

Settembrinu di Tavagna (end of Aug–early Sep), Tavagna. Festival of international music – including Cuban, Corsican, African and Romany.

Procession of the Virgin Mary (7–10 Sep), Casamaccioli. This celebration of the Virgin Mary is the oldest pilgrimage on the island.
8 September Procession, Lavasina. A torch-lit procession and midnight mass.
Fête de Notre Dame (8 Sep), Bonifacio. The Festival of the Virgin Mary, during which a special dish of stuffed aubergines (eggplant) is prepared and eaten.
National Petanque Challenge Pascal Paoli (mid-Sep), Île Rousse. The world's elite players gather to compete in this French game.
Porto-Vecchio Fair (second week of Sep), Porto-Vecchio. This annual trade fair features a complete range of Corsican handicrafts.
Polyphonic Music Week (3rd week of Sep), Calvi. Traditional Corsican music.

The Procession of the Virgin Mary at Casamaccioli

Mele in Festa (Sep), Murzo. A festival to celebrate honey, a Corsican speciality.

October

Rally de France (usually late Sep/ early Oct). Auto-rally champions

One of the public events honouring Napoleon Bonaparte at Ajaccio (see p37)

Average Monthly Temperature

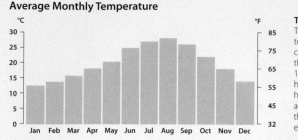

Temperature
Thanks to the sea, the temperature along the coast is mild even in winter, the annual average being 15° C (59° F). Inland, however, the winter is harsh, with heavy snowfall and frequent frost, while the summers are cool, even if the sun is very hot.

compete on the winding roads of Corsica – one of the most interesting stages of this race.
Les Musicales de Bastia *(Oct)*, Bastia. Jazz, dance, theatre and music.
International Festival du Cirque de Corse *(Oct)*, Bastia & Ajaccio. A competition for circus troupes from all over the world.
Le Tour de Corse à la Voile *(late Oct)*. Regatta with start and finish at Bonifacio.
Theatre Festival *(Oct)*, Ajaccio. Actors perform short performances in the street during this festival, concluding with a town ball.

November
Chestnut Festival *(Nov)*, Evisa. Harvest celebrations.
Mediterranean Cultures Film Festival "Arte Mare" *(Nov/ Dec)*, Bastia. Film productions, art and literature from Mediterranean countries.

Winter
The weather becomes colder, partly due to the mistral wind. The mountain tops are covered with snow and the ski-lift facilities are sporadically in operation. At Christmas, Corsican cities are decorated with holiday illuminations, and, in Ajaccio, games are organized and stalls display their wares. At this time of the year, many hotels and

Chestnuts, harvested in late autumn

restaurants are closed, and accommodation can be difficult to find outside the cities and main tourist localities.
However, this can be a very pleasant season; the coastline is green, the streets are lined with flowers, the maquis vegetation retains its foliage, and on sunny days it is possible to forget that it is winter.
In December, the olives are gathered and taken to the presses, and in February the almond trees begin to blossom, allowing for the first taste of spring.

December
Chestnut Festival *(early Dec)*, Bocognano. A popular festival featuring dishes and desserts made from chestnut flour.
Animation de Noël *(Dec)*, Ajaccio. Christmas entertainment in the streets of the capital: bingo contests, games and gig rides.

January
St Anthony Procession *(first Sun after 17 Jan)*, Corbara and Aregno. Procession in honour of St Anthony.

February
Italian Film Festival *(early Feb)*, Bastia. Popular festival featuring screenings of Italian films, themed by director and/or actor, exhibitions, conferences, and Italian cuisine.

The polyphonic music group A Filetta performing at a festival

A Tumbera *(second week of Feb)*, Renno. This festival is inspired by a type of Corsican pig and offers competitions and food stalls.
Spanish and Latin American Film Festival *(Feb)*, Ajaccio. Over 20 films are presented to celebrate the culture and diversity of the different regions.

Public Holidays

New Year's Day (1 Jan)
Easter Sunday and Monday (Mar or Apr)
Labour Day (1 May)
1945 Victory Day (8 May)
Ascension Day (40 days after Easter)
Pentecost Sunday and Monday (mid-May– mid-Jun)
Bastille Day (14 Jul)
Assumption Day (15 Aug)
All Saints' Day (1 Nov)
Armistice Day (11 Nov)
Christmas Day (25 Dec)

THE HISTORY OF CORSICA

Situated near the Tuscan and Provençal coasts, Corsica has been occupied, colonized and fought over for millennia. Its history and culture are the results of the convergence of different civilizations, from the Carthaginians and Romans to the Pisans, Genoese and French. These experiences have given rise to the unique identity of the Corsican nation.

The rock massif that includes the island of Corsica reached its present position in the Tyrrhenian Sea about 18 million years ago.

The exact date of the arrival of people on the island is still shrouded in mystery, but there is evidence that humans settled in Corsica 9,000–10,000 years ago. The most ancient sites excavated are at Macinaggio, Cap Corse and Araguina, not far from Bonifacio. Here, archaeologists found the skeleton of the Dame de Bonifacio, a 40-year-old woman who was buried in 6570 BC; her remains are now kept in the Levie museum.

In the 6th millennium BC, Corsica experienced a considerable influx of migrant populations. The Neolithic inhabitants of this period bred livestock and practised weaving. This growth in population was followed by ever-increasing trade. The mid-4th millennium was the age of megalithic monuments (see p133), the most impressive ruins of ancient Corsica (see pp42–3). During this period, the Corsicans traded mostly with people

on the Italian coast: digs have brought to light Etruscan vases and other items from Magna Graecia.

Around 1500 BC, with the advent of the Bronze Age, the south of Corsica was invaded by a population known as the Torréens, after the towers (torri) they erected in several parts of the island. The Torréens ruled the south until about 600 BC, when infighting between tribes prompted another migration, this time to Sardinia.

In 565 BC, colonists from Phocaea founded the city of Alalia. After Etruscan and Carthaginian rule, the city was conquered by the Romans when Scipio's legions landed in 259 BC and renamed Aléria. During the Pax Romana, the city was developed, first by Caesar and then by the emperors Hadrian, Caracalla and Diocletian. It became the capital of the province of Corsica and remained so until the Barbarian invasions in AD 455. In 100 BC, the Roman general and consul Marius founded the colony of Mariana, just south of present-day Bastia.

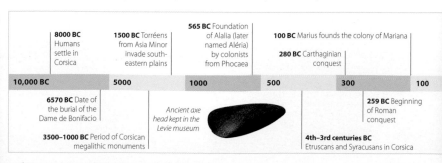

| 8000 BC Humans settle in Corsica | 1500 BC Torréens from Asia Minor invade south-eastern plains | 565 BC Foundation of Alalia (later named Aléria) by colonists from Phocaea | 100 BC Marius founds the colony of Mariana |
| | | | 280 BC Carthaginian conquest |

| 10,000 BC | 5000 | 1000 | 500 | 300 | 100 |

| 6570 BC Date of the burial of the Dame de Bonifacio | *Ancient axe head kept in the Levie museum* | 259 BC Beginning of Roman conquest |
| 3500–1000 BC Period of Corsican megalithic monuments | | 4th–3rd centuries BC Etruscans and Syracusans in Corsica |

◀ "Father of the Nation" Pascal Paoli, portrayed by Richard Cosway

From Megaliths to Romans

Ancient Corsica was an island whose prehistoric populations were extremely dynamic. The most active period of these ancestral cultures began in the Neolithic era, roughly 6000 BC, an epoch when cardial ware was produced. During this time, these populations became more settled, lived on livestock raising, and began to build their dwellings with dry walls, often fortifying them. Towards the end of this period, the megalithic monuments *(see p133)* first appeared. There soon followed invasions, first by the Torréens and then by the Phocaeans and the Etruscans. Lastly, the Romans settled in Alalia, founded by the Phocaeans, renaming it Aléria. Their hegemony extended over most of the island, remaining until the Barbarian invasions.

Anthropomorphic menhirs, with facial features and sometimes warriors' weapons, are unique to Corsican culture.

The alignments of menhirs are a distinguishing element of Neolithic Corsican culture. Many of the arrangements were probably connected to prehistoric religious rituals.

Filitosa has one of the most important alignments of anthropomorphic menhirs on the island *(see p133)*.

• Filitosa

The remains of the past

Most of the menhir alignments and dolmens that are still standing date from the period between the 2nd and 1st millennia BC. They are mainly located in southwest Corsica, while fortified castles can be found on the hills in the eastern sector. The most important Roman ruins lie at the site of Aléria, where the original plan of this ancient city can still be seen.

• Cauria

Cardial ware is a type of pottery dating from the 5th or 6th millennium BC. The name derives from the *Cardium*, or cockle shell, whose jagged lips were used to fashion the characteristic patterns on each piece.

The Cauria plateau has many of the best-preserved menhirs and dolmens, which miraculously avoided destruction by the Christians. Stantari, Pagliaju, Renaggiu and Fontanaccia are the sites to visit *(see p131)*.

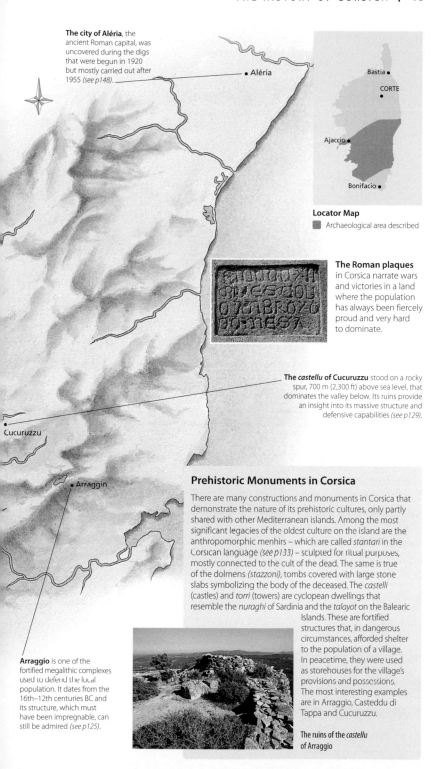

The city of Aléria, the ancient Roman capital, was uncovered during the digs that were begun in 1920 but mostly carried out after 1955 *(see p148)*.

• Aléria

Bastia •

CORTE

Ajaccio •

Bonifacio •

Locator Map

Archaeological area described

The Roman plaques in Corsica narrate wars and victories in a land where the population has always been fiercely proud and very hard to dominate.

The *castellu* of Cucuruzzu stood on a rocky spur, 700 m (2,300 ft) above sea level, that dominates the valley below. Its ruins provide an insight into its massive structure and defensive capabilities *(see p129)*.

Cucuruzzu

• Arraggio

Prehistoric Monuments in Corsica

There are many constructions and monuments in Corsica that demonstrate the nature of its prehistoric cultures, only partly shared with other Mediterranean islands. Among the most significant legacies of the oldest culture on the island are the anthropomorphic menhirs – which are called *stantari* in the Corsican language *(see p133)* – sculpted for ritual purposes, mostly connected to the cult of the dead. The same is true of the dolmens *(stazzoni)*, tombs covered with large stone slabs symbolizing the body of the deceased. The *castelli* (castles) and *torri* (towers) are cyclopean dwellings that resemble the *nuraghi* of Sardinia and the *talayot* on the Balearic Islands. These are fortified structures that, in dangerous circumstances, afforded shelter to the population of a village. In peacetime, they were used as storehouses for the village's provisions and possessions. The most interesting examples are in Arraggio, Casteddu di Tappa and Cucuruzzu.

Arraggio is one of the fortified megalithic complexes used to defend the local population. It dates from the 16th–12th centuries BC and its structure, which must have been impregnable, can still be admired *(see p125)*.

The ruins of the *castellu* of Arraggio

Barbarian Invasions

The fall of the Roman Empire had immediate repercussions for the island, which was soon overrun by Barbarian populations. The Vandals landed in Corsica in AD 455 and were probably the cause of the final abandonment of Aléria. After conquering the North African coastline, the Vandals sent bishops from the conquered cities into exile in Corsica. This was probably a key factor in the evangelization of the island, which had begun a century earlier. In 534, the Byzantines, under Emperor Justinian, took over, but the island remained at the mercy of repeated Barbaric invasions, including those of the Lombards and the Saracens. The Lombards ruled until 774, when they were defeated by the Franks, who had initially been called to support the papacy in Rome against the Lombard threat. The Frankish king, Pepin the Short, donated Corsica to Pope Stephen, a deal that was confirmed by his son Charlemagne 20 years later.

However, a new threat was looming on the horizon for the inhabitants of Corsica. The Arab expansion across the Mediterranean was extensive during this period. A series of landings along the entire coastline of Corsica, particularly in the fertile

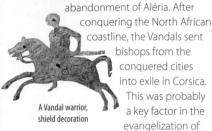

A Vandal warrior, shield decoration

region of Balagne, was so overwhelming that a 15th-century chronicler, Giovanni della Grossa, talked of a mass conversion to Islam.

The many Carolingian expeditions did very little to lessen the pressure of the Saracens, and many Corsicans fled from the island to settle on the nearby Italian coast. Historians mention a flourishing Corsican community in the Roman port of Ostia, the town of Pope Formosus (891–896), who had been born in the Corsican town of Porto.

Feudalism in the Middle Ages

After the year 1000, the influence of the mainland increased, and feudalism developed in Corsica with a structure similar to that prevailing throughout Europe. On the island, however, this political configuration was strongly influenced by the power of the various clans that fought among themselves. These feuds led to the division of the territory into two geographical areas: the *Deça des Monts*, the northeastern half of the island, which was more developed and receptive to trade; and the *Delà des Monts*, the pastoral and "backwards" southwestern sector. Internal struggles prevented the island from strengthening its military force, so the papacy was forced to request that the republics of Pisa and Genoa should step in to defeat the Arabs and bring stability to the island of Corsica.

A 16th-century painting depicting the Arab invasion of Corsica

3rd–5th centuries	5th and 6th centuries		
Evangelization of Corsica	Vandals and Ostrogoths invade	*Carolingian coin*	
AD 200	**400**	**600**	**800**
	420 Aléria falls to the Vandals	**755** Probable donation of Corsica to the pope by Pepin the Short	

Benedictine monks

Pisan Romanesque bas-relief, San Quilico, Cambia *(see p150)*

The Pisan Period

In 1077, the Church granted Corsican rule to Bishop Landolfe of Pisa, thus initiating the period of Pisan domination. There were interesting cultural developments during this time, but it was troubled from a political standpoint. The rivalry with Genoa was at first handled well, thanks to the Holy See, but soon degenerated so much that, in 1133, Pope Innocent II had to divide the island's six bishoprics between Pisa (Ajaccio, Aléria and Sagone) and Genoa (Accia, Mariana and Nebbio).

By 1187, the Genoese, who were becoming increasingly powerful in the Mediterranean, took possession of the harbour of Bonifacio and, in 1268, founded Calvi. The Genoese took control of Corsica in 1284 with the naval battle of Meloria *(see pp46–7)* near the Tuscan coast. There are many traces of Pisan rule on the island, including Romanesque architecture, such as the beautiful

Relief at La Canonica, a church built in the Pisan period

churches of La Canonica and San Michele de Murato, and the development of Cap Corse, where the Pisans created vineyards, small ports and emporia.

Early Genoese Rule

After defeating Pisa, the Republic of Genoa worked swiftly to consolidate its grip on the island by laying out a series of defensive systems along the coastline and creating an administrative structure. However, this proved to be a difficult task. Genoese rule was opposed by some of the local lords, in particular those in Cinarca, who were still faithful to Pisa. With the aim of setting up a Corsican government ruled by the towns (perhaps in the wake of the rise of the Italian city republics), the lords stirred up popular insurrections. In addition, there were repeated attacks by other European nations, often with the backing of the Church. For example, in 1297, Pope Boniface VIII, asserting the rights of the Holy See in the Mediterranean, granted Corsican and Sardinian rule to the Aragonese kings, who sided with the Cinarca lords and remained a thorn in the side of the Genoese republic until the French took over in the mid-18th century.

Boniface VIII (1294–1303)

The citadel of Bonifacio

891–896 Papacy of Formosus, born in Porto

1000

1077 Pope Gregory VII grants Corsica to Pisa

1100

1133 Pope Innocent II divides bishoprics between Pisa and Genoa

1195 Genoese colony is established in Bonifacio

1200

1268 The Genoese found Calvi

6 August 1284 Battle of Meloria

1297 Boniface VIII gives Corsica in fee to kingdom of Aragon

The Battle of Meloria

In the course of its history, Corsica was subject to the rule of two Italian maritime republics, Pisa and Genoa. The event that marked the passage from one ruler to the other was the Battle of Meloria (1284). Both republics had previously helped to free the Mediterranean from the Saracens and the pirates that had been plaguing the region, after which they vied for control of Corsica. In 1077, Pope Gregory VII granted Corsican rule to Landolfe, the bishop of Pisa. This led to an increase in friction: skirmishes, confrontations and treaties became the norm, until the battle. During the first two centuries of Genoese rule, the island continued to be torn by war, pirate attacks and vendettas. Only in the late 1500s did Genoa manage to impose some kind of order.

The coat of arms of the Republic of Pisa displays a ship that is also found on the Leaning Tower in Campo dei Miracoli. It is one of the many iconographic symbols of the city's maritime supremacy.

Oberto Doria

The commander Albertino Morosini was, with Ugolino della Gherardesca and Andreotto Saraceno, the head of the Pisan fleet, which was helpless against the two Genoese fleets.

The Saracens set fire to the towns and massacred the inhabitants or made them their slaves. Pisa in particular was devoted to freeing the island from this scourge.

The Pisan fleet comprised 72 galleys and its defeat was total: 5,000 Pisans died and 11,000 were taken to Genoa in chains.

The Fate of Count Ugolino

After the defeat of Meloria, Ugolino della Gherardesca gave castles and land to the enemy to avoid a siege by the Florentines and Luccans, who were allies of Genoa and therefore enemies of Pisa. Accused of betrayal, he was imprisoned with his sons and grandsons in a tower, where he died. Dante considered him a traitor to his country, and in the *Divine Comedy* had him put in Hell, a curse that accompanied the count for centuries: "Ah, Pisa, scandal to the people / of the beauteous land where the 'yes' is heard, / since thy neighbours are slow to punish thee / let the Caprara and Gorgona move."

Illustration of the *Divine Comedy*

Benedetto Zaccaria led a second group of Genoese ships that arrived by surprise at Meloria at a later stage in the battle, when the Pisans felt they were almost out of danger. His intervention was a key factor in the Ligurian republic's victory.

The chains of the anchors of the Pisan ships were impounded by the Genoese at the end of the battle. Considered a sort of war booty, they were on exhibit in Genoa as a sign of the city's supremacy. Only in the 19th century were they given back to Pisa, where they hang under the loggia of the Camposanto.

The cliffs of Meloria are about 7 km (4 miles) off the coast of Livorno, facing Corsica.

Meloria was the scene of an earlier battle, in 1241, in which the Pisans, aided by the emperor Frederick II, defeated the Genoese.

The wealth of Genoa, which stemmed from commercial trading, made it a political power that dominated the Mediterranean for a long time.

In the thick of the battle

In August 1284, a Genoese fleet led by Oberto Doria sailed into the waters opposite Porto Pisano. Startled by this move, the Pisans attacked from the cliffs of Meloria. The battle was violent and the outcome uncertain, until the arrival of a second group of Genoese galleys, which caught their enemies by surprise and decided the outcome of the fight. Giovanni David's The Battle of Meloria *(left) hangs in the Palazzo Ducale in Genoa.*

The Genoese fleet consisted of 93 galleys.

The Genoese galleys were fast ships, suitable for both cargo transport and naval battles. Largely because of these vessels and their commanders, Genoa prospered and became a power able to defeat its enemies and rivals.

The Genoese fleet near the coast of Corsica on a print kept at the Musée de la Corse

The End of the Middle Ages

The 14th century was a troubled time for Corsica. In 1348, the population was decimated by the Black Death, and difficult living conditions triggered a series of revolts among the islanders. On the one hand, there were the landowners who were keen to maintain the feudal system, and on the other, there were the commoners, who wanted to get rid of the aristocrats.

One of the members of the feudal faction was Arrigo della Rocca, who in 1376 asked the Aragonese to come to his aid. The commoners also boasted legendary figures, such as Sambucuccio d'Alando, a peasant whose famous exploits shook the foundations of local feudalism. The common people established the *Terres des Communes*, a confederation of villages favouring the common use of local land, in opposition to the feudal powers.

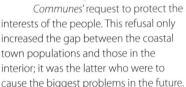

Sambucuccio
d'Alando

organizations that, as well as administering it, also safeguarded Genoa's interests. The first such commercial company to have this assignment was the Maona, in 1378, but it soon went bankrupt, prompting some of the nobles to ask the Aragonese throne for help. One of these nobles was Vincentello d'Istria, a soldier, estate owner and pirate who, in 1420, led a Spanish fleet of 400 ships to the island. Bonifacio resisted, but almost all of Corsica fell into Vincentello's hands. A few years later, Genoa had an opportunity to subdue the feudal landowners but did not make the most of it. The Genoese chose instead to ignore the *Terres des Communes'* request to protect the interests of the people. This refusal only increased the gap between the coastal town populations and those in the interior; it was the latter who were to cause the biggest problems in the future.

Genoese Policy

Occasionally, the Genoese Republic gave control of the island over to private

The Bank of St George

In 1453, Genoa delegated control of Corsica to the Bank of St George, whose

1348 The plague decimates the island population

1376 Arrigo della Rocca asks the Aragonese to support the rebellion

1453 *Capitula Corsorum*: Corsica governed by the Bank of St George

1300   1350   1400   1450   1500

Victims of the plague

1378 Corsica governed by the Maona organization

1358 Revolt of Sambucuccio d'Alando

1420 Revolt of Vincentello d'Istria, who founds Corte

1498 Sampiero Corso is born in Bastelica

power was sanctioned by the *Capitula Corsorum*, the statute of the Genoese government of the island. This Genoese bank ruled Corsica with special powers. It had the right to collect taxes, mint coins and to administer justice, and it had its own army. The bank's activities were many and varied, and were controlled by a series of basic guidelines. One of its primary objectives was to guarantee political control of the land by curbing the powers of the feudal lords. In addition to this, the Genoese promised to make the coastal plains productive in the hope of overcoming the scourge of malaria.

Sampiero and the End of Genoa

Born in 1498 in a hamlet near Bastelica, Sampiero Corso was one of the many islanders forced by poverty and tradition to enlist as a mercenary in the French Army. In 1553, after the momentous clash between France and Spain, the French decided to land on Corsica to gain a solid foothold in the Mediterranean. Sampiero Corso also took part in the French expedition, which was backed by the ships of the renowned pirate Dragut.

The Genoese strongholds fell one after the other – Bastia, St-Florent, Corte, and even the impregnable Bonifacio – until a peace treaty obliged the French to withdraw. Sampiero refused, however, and continued his struggle against the Genoese, even going so far as to ask various European courts to come to his

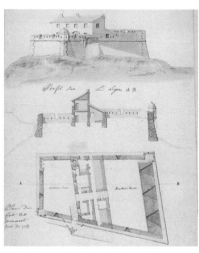

aid. In 1563, a few months after landing once again in Corsica with the hope of stoking the fire of popular rebellion, Sampiero was assassinated. Genoese rule was reinstated in 1569, and for the next 200 years the island swung between insurrections on the one hand and normal colonial administration on the other. Genoa's power was in decline, however, and widespread dissatisfaction smouldered among the Corsicans.

Royal Corsican artillery (1740) In the early 18th century, a series of revolts led first to independence for the island, and then to annexation by France. The only traces of the troubled Genoese rule that future islanders would note would be the chain of coastal towers and some cities with massive walls – the citadels.

Monserrato Fort, in Bastia, in a 1761 drawing

Sampiero Corso

1640–70 Religious revival

1676 Foundation of a Greek colony at Sagone

1729 Revolt of Corte and peasants

| 1550 | 1600 | 1650 | 1700 | 1750 |

1569 Genoa reconquers Corsica

1553 Sampiero Corso's landing with a French expedition

The citadel of Corte

1755–69 Pascal Paoli's government

Revolt and Independence

One key event triggered the Corsicans' fight for independence – the imposition of new taxes by the Genoese rulers in 1729. Many Corsicans refused to pay the taxes and several years of revolts followed. In 1735 in Corte, the Corsicans first drafted a constitution for an independent sovereign state. The following year, Corsica elected a king, Baron Theodor von Neuhof, but he abandoned the throne after only eight months. In 1745, Jean-Pierre Gaffori became the leader of a major insurrection, followed by the 30-year-old Pascal Paoli in 1755. Paoli succeeded in establishing a constitutional state, founded the University of Corte, and created an army. For 14 years, the island was independent, but on 8 May 1769, Paoli lost the battle of Ponte-Novo, and French rule began.

Theodor von Neuhof, a German baron who had taken up the island's cause, was elected king by the Corsicans in 1736 but was forced to flee only a few months later.

The hills of Castagniccia

French army

Jean-Pierre Gaffori was one of the leaders of the 1745–55 revolts and was a member of the triumvirate during that period. He was assassinated in a street in Corte in 1753.

Faustina, Gaffori's wife, also took part in the clashes. She is portrayed in the bas-reliefs on the pedestal of the monument to her husband in Corte *(see p138).*

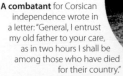

A combatant for Corsican independence wrote in a letter: "General, I entrust my old father to your care, as in two hours I shall be among those who have died for their country."

The End of a Dream

On 8 May 1769, near the bridge at Ponte-Novo, the nationalist Corsican troops led by Pascal Paoli suffered a decisive defeat at the hands of the French army. This event brought to an end 14 years of independence, the only period to date during which the island was free from domination by other peoples or nations.

The Moor's Head has been the symbol of Independent Corsica for three centuries. Used by the Aragonese kings to celebrate the victory over the Moors in the 13th century, it was ceded to local clan leaders, taken up by Neuhof and then adopted by Paoli.

James Boswell and Corsica

The British author James Boswell went to Corsica in 1765 and published his travel journal, *Account of Corsica*, in England three years later, thus spreading the image of Pascal Paoli's democratic government throughout Europe. During the period of the French Revolution, the still-fresh memory of French intervention on the island made the revolutionary politician Comte de Mirabeau express his "regret and sorrow" for having helped to suppress the freedom of such a proud people.

Two thousand Corsican patriots led by Paoli took part in the battle.

Ponte-Novo was named after a new stone bridge built by the Genoese over the Golo river.

The French army surrounding the Corsicans on the bridge

Pascal Paoli was not only a fine military strategist, he was also an educated, enlightened and cultured man. He drafted the only constitution that Corsica ever had and founded the University of Corte, which was reopened in 1981 (*see p140*).

The bridge was a typical Genoese construction, much like those that can still be found on the island.

The Golo river

	1735 Declaration of Independence	**1755** Pascal Paoli is elected General of the Nation		**8 May 1769** Corsicans defeated at Ponte-Novo	
1729 First revolt against Genoa; start of the War of Independence		**1748** Second French intervention		**1765** The University of Corte opened	
1720	**1730**	**1740**	**1750**	**1760**	
	1733 Second revolt headed by Hyacinthe Paoli, Pascal's father	**1745** Third revolt led by Jean-Pierre Gaffori	**1753** French troops leave the island		**1762** The Moor's Head becomes the national symbol
		1738 France intervenes on request by the Genoese			

French Dominion

During Corsica's years of revolt and brief period of independence, France had kept a close eye on the island, intervening on the side of Genoa against the Corsicans. In 1768, the weakened Genoese ceded the island to France, but French rule only started after a final attempt of resistance at the Battle of Ponte-Novo in 1769 *(see pp50–51)*. Corsica was

Napoleon Crossing the St Bernard Pass, Jacques-Louis David, 1800

now governed by a provincial administrator and a military governor, one of whose duties was to repress popular revolts, which from then on were labelled as banditry.

Corsica was divided into provinces, each of which had its own law court. The cities gradually lost the privileges conferred on them by the Genoese, and efforts were made to establish clear-cut limits between private property and the municipalities.

Supporters of French rule were granted a series of benefits, including land, which stirred discontent among the people. Corsican nationalism was by no means dead, as proved by a rebellion that broke out in Niolo in 1774 and by the constant support given to General Paoli during his exile by the French. At the first signs of revolutionary activity in France, Corsicans made it quite clear that they would not be mere spectators to these events. There were differences, however, between the demands made by the French and those of the Corsicans. The latter were not interested

in the struggle against the noble class, but fought for equal rights for French people and Corsicans. In 1790, the people disarmed the garrison in Bastia and political exiles such as Paoli could return to the island.

Sentenced to death by radical French revolutionaries, the Jacobins, Paoli appealed to the English for help. Their intervention led to the birth of the Anglo-Corsican kingdom (1794–6), with Sir George Elliott as viceroy. The sidelined Paoli left for London, where he died in 1807. In 1796, French troops were sent out to retake the island. They were led by a young Corsican-born officer – Napoleon Bonaparte. He would always have close ties with his motherland, and Ajaccio in particular *(see p91)*.

The 19th and 20th Centuries

After Napoleon's fall in 1815, the 19th century in Corsica was fairly calm, and the presence of France took on ever-increasing importance. The decrease in banditry and vendettas, alongside a relatively stable economic and political scene, lent a certain credibility to French rule.

Efforts were made to create a middle class that would support and promote the island's growth. One of the most successful initiatives was the development of an infrastructure on the island, which vastly

Napoleonic crest

1769 Birth of Napoleon Bonaparte in Ajaccio

1775

1790 Paoli returns from exile

1794–96 Anglo-Corsican kingdom

1800

1825

1827 Opening of Ajaccio–Bastia road

1830 First maritime service to Corsica established

1850

1855–70 Repression of banditry and blood feuds

1894 Inauguration of Ajaccio–Bastia railway line

1875

Corsican emigrants waiting to embark

improved communications. The Ajaccio–Bastia road was constructed in 1827 and the railway in 1894, and a permanent ferry service was established in 1830. All this led to an unprecedented population increase, from 150,000 people in 1790 to 300,000 in 1890. There was a parallel development in agriculture, even in the hills and mountain areas inland, and the centralized administration tried to curb the free circulation of transhumance shepherds. Around the mid-19th century, a liberal Corsican middle class was on the rise.

However, a short time later, during the Industrial Revolution, Corsica was affected by decline. The mainly rural and, in comparison, non-modernized society could not compete with agricultural products from the mainland and the French colonies. Despite improvements in living standards, dire poverty once again afflicted the island, forcing thousands of Corsicans to emigrate. Corsica paid a high toll in World War I (20,000 dead), then lost an average of 5–6,000 people annually to emigration.

In 1942, Italian troops occupied Corsica. After the rise of a strong Resistance movement known as the "Maquis", Corsica was the first French *département* to be liberated, in 1943.

The Independence Movement

At the end of World War II, the many Corsicans who had gone abroad were repatriated, and in the 1960s there was a new presence in the elections, the Front Régionaliste Corse (FRC). In 1973, the FRC, together with the Action Régionaliste Corse (ARC), demanded autonomy for Corsica, a decentralized government and protection for Corsican land against tourist developments. In 1975, a series of demonstrations ended in the shooting of two police officers. Following this, the Front de Libération Nationale de la Corse (FLNC) was founded, which committed many acts of terrorism.

While the independence movement rapidly gained popularity, the island was again divided into two *départements*, Haute-Corse and Corse-du-Sud. In 1981, the University of Corte was reopened. The process of establishing a federal statute for Corsica began in 1991. The 1990s saw a boom in tourism, which created no environmental problems, partly because of the islanders' respect for their land. In 2003, separatist tension flared again after voters rejected a referendum to grant Corsica increased autonomy, but today Corsica and the mainland government are working together to build a peaceful future.

Graffiti by the Corsica Independence Movement

1942 Italian occupation

1966 FRC founded

Logo of the University

2003 Referendum to increase regional autonomy is rejected

2013 Corsica hosts the first three stages of the 100th Tour de France for the first time in the event's history

1925	1950	1975	2000	2025

1910–20 Great wave of emigration

1943 Liberation of Corsica

1976 FNLC founded

1981 University of Corte reopens

1991 Regional autonomy law is passed

2009 Expanded low-cost airline services and the launch of modern autorail rolling stock improve travel to and around the island

CORSICA
AREA BY AREA

Corsica at a Glance

Within a distance covered by a short drive, Corsica offers beaches that are not unlike those in tropical countries and wild mountains surrounded by woods. The island boasts extremely varied and fascinating landscapes, such as the coast carpeted with maquis vegetation, the hillside olive and chestnut groves, the valleys where rivers have created deep gorges, the mountains traversed by the GR20 long-distance path *(see pp26–31)*, and the beautiful surrounding waters and seabeds. In this natural setting, man-made splendour can also be found in prehistoric megaliths, Pisan Romanesque churches, Genoese citadels, and villages of old stone houses. The two cities that have played a major role in the history of the island, Ajaccio and Bastia, are joined by the "historical capital", Corte, along with Bonifacio, Calvi and Porto-Vecchio, famous for their beaches.

Calvi's Citadelle
The strongholds of Genoese power, the citadels still dominate the main cities in Corsica, surrounded by massive bastions. Calvi's Citadelle was built in the 15th century.

L'Île-Rc

Calvi

Calenzana

Porto

Cargèse

Vico

Sagone

AJACCIO ANI
THE WEST COA
(see pp86–109)

Ajaccio

Caure

Pointe de la Parata
One of the most common sights along the coastline are the Genoese watch-towers, surrounded by the brilliant colours of the maquis. One such building features at Pointe de la Parata, the famous cape in the Golfe d'Ajaccio.

Porto-Pollo

Propriano

Campomoro

Sartè

Megalithic Monuments
Relics of prehistoric Corsica can still be found in the interior of the island, which has many alignments of menhirs. The menhirs can be dolmens or the so-called *castelli* (castles).

| 0 kilometres | 20 |
| 0 miles | 20 |

◀ The village of Zonza, against the dramatic backdrop of the Aiguilles de Bavella

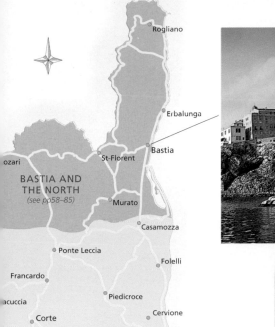

Rogliano

Erbalunga

St-Florent

Bastia

ozari

**BASTIA AND
THE NORTH**
(see pp58–85)

Murato

Casamozza

Ponte Leccia

Folelli

Francardo

Piedicroce

acuccia

Corte

Cervione

**CORTE AND
THE INTERIOR**
(see pp134–55)

Vivario

cognano

Aléria

Ghisonaccia

Cozzano

Travo

Solenzara

Zonza

NIFACIO AND
HE SOUTH
(see pp110–33)

Porto-Vecchio

ari

nifacio

Vieux Port, Bastia
Like so many other ports, the Vieux Port of Bastia, dominated by the Citadelle, exudes the spirit of the island's past. Hundreds of years ago, the foundations of the present-day cities rose up around natural harbours that were used for merchant vessels.

Rocks and Rivers
In the untamed Corsican interior, rugged mountains and deep valleys crossed by violent torrents offer an exciting and challenging landscape for hikers.

The Cliffs of Bonifacio
The white limestone cliffs in the Bonifacio area are perhaps one of the most famous sights in Corsica. The cliffs are also geologically interesting, since limestone is an unusual presence in this mostly granitic island.

BASTIA AND THE NORTH

Bastia has a charm of its own, which can be found in the Citadelle and the historic centre, with its narrow alleys reminiscent of Italian villages. Indeed, the town owes its development and commercial success to Genoa. To get a true sense of Bastia, the best thing to do is join the locals in their rituals: a coffee in Place St-Nicolas, a *pastis* at the Vieux Port and shopping at the Sunday market.

Geographically closer to Italy than to France, Bastia aims to become a regular stopover port for Mediterranean cruises and a base for ecological tourism thanks to its proximity to the mountains inland. Cap Corse is nearby, with villages squeezed between the sea and mountains and small harbours protected by old watch-towers. This region is a world unto itself and has always been more similar to Pisa, Marseille, Genoa and Livorno than to the rest of the island.

With their sailing prowess, the inhabitants of this peninsula made it a port for the shipment of wine, firewood, oil, cork and other local products. Thanks to their farming traditions, they transformed the steep mountainsides into cultivable terraces. This can be seen in the Rogliano and Patrimonio vineyards, among the best on the island. The proximity to and close relations with Italy have left their mark on the language, with its Tuscan influence, and on the architecture, which resembles that of Italy's Ligurian coast. In fact, the islands in the Tuscan archipelago are visible from the east coast of Corsica.

The other "microregion" in the north is sunny Balagne, famous for its beaches and hamlets nestled in productive olive orchards. The history of this region is linked with that of Pisa, which developed Balagne's agriculture. Beautiful Pisan churches can be found in Aregno, Lumio and Calenzana. When the Genoese arrived, they built the citadels of Calvi and Algajola, exploited the cork oak groves, and planted the olive trees that still surround the old stone villages.

A small harbour at Porticciolo, near Macinaggio, along the eastern coast of Cap Corse

◀ Detail of the 12th-century Église de la Trinité et San Giovanni at Aregno, in the Balagne

Exploring Bastia and the North

The main tourist localities in the northern region lie along the west coast, beyond the Col de Teghime. St-Florent boasts a lovely yacht harbour and boat service to the wild beaches in the Désert des Agriates. Calvi is renowned for its nightlife and its beach – a long stretch of white sand under the shade of a pine grove. The relatively short distances between interesting sights in this area make it possible to organize one-day excursions inland through Balagne or Nebbio. These villages have preserved their centuries-old architecture, including stunning Pisan Romanesque churches. The Cap Corse peninsula is for those who love cliffs or small pebble beaches. Visitors may also enjoy hikes along the coast or among the maquis to villages where time seems to have stood still.

A slope in the Désert des Agriates covered with maquis undergrowth

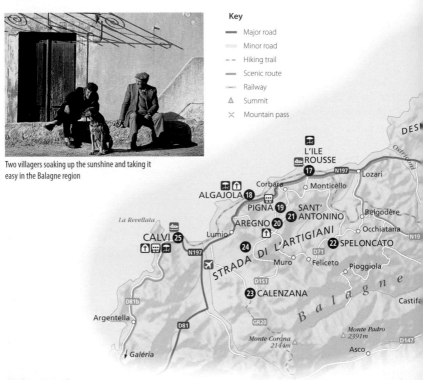

Two villagers soaking up the sunshine and taking it easy in the Balagne region

Key

— Major road

═══ Minor road

-- Hiking trail

— Scenic route

▬▬ Railway

△ Summit

✕ Mountain pass

Sights at a Glance

CAP CORSE 5
Tollare
Barcaggio
D253
SENTIER DES 7
DOUANIERS
Ersa
Rogliano
CENTURI 6
MACINAGGIO 4
D80
D80
PINO 8
Tour de Sénèque
Luri
Minervio
Marine
de Porticciolo
PIETRACORBARA 3
CANARI 9
Marine de
Pietracorbara
Sisco
Albo
Marine
de Sisco
*Monte Stello
1307m*
NONZA 10
Castello
ERBALUNGA 2
*Golfe de
St Florent*
San Martino
di Lota
*Plage de
Saleccia*
D80
*Plage de
Loto*
*Serra di Pigno
950m*
AGRIATES
PATRIMONIO 11
BASTIA 1
16
ST-FLORENT
12
D81
D81
*Col de
Teghime*
D82
D62
N E B B I O
14
*onte Asto
1530m*
OLETTA
15
*Col de
San Stefano*
Rapale
N193
Murato
SAN MICHELE 13
DE MURATO
*Etang di
Biguglia*
Lama
Borgo
D5
N1197
Pietralba
D107
La Canonica
Lento
Casamozza
Golo
N193
Aléria
Ponte
Leccia
Corte

0 kilometres   10
0 miles   10

Getting Around

The most convenient means of travelling is by car, which allows access to the most isolated villages. The main roads from Bastia to Bonifacio, Calvi and Corte are wide and well paved. The same cannot be said for the minor roads, however, such as those in Balagne or along Cap Corse. Those on the west coast have a seemingly endless number of curves and a surface that is not always in good condition.

For this reason, it can be easier, although not as safe, to get around by motorcycle. Always keep an eye on the petrol gauge – petrol stations are few and far between. Bicycles are popular and are available for hire, but they should only be used by experienced cyclists, and cycling is not advisable in the summer. The main road network is good. It runs from Bastia to Aléria, Porto-Vecchio, Bonifacio, Corte and Ajaccio. The CFC train links Bastia, Calvi and Ajaccio, via Ponte Leccia. There are also bus services connecting the main localities.

Picturesque Macinaggio harbour, with its colourful boats and nets

❶ Bastia

With its colourful houses overlooking the sea, Bastia is the second-largest city in Corsica and is considered its economic capital. This is because of the port and the industrial zone that extends south of the old centre. Although the ancient Romans founded the city of Mantinon, mentioned by the Greek geographer Ptolemy, on the hills, Bastia was for centuries only the small port of the village of Cardo in the neighbouring hinterland. Wine was loaded on to ships here in the Middle Ages and taken to Pisa. It was not until the 15th century that the Genoese began to construct a tower and enlarge the fortress that protected the port (*bastiglia* in Italian, hence the name of the city). Genoa was responsible for the prosperity of Bastia and left its mark there – including a certain coldness towards foreigners. With a little time and patience, however, this city can provide many surprises.

The simple, elegant façade of the Chapelle St-Roch

🏛 Place du Marché

Dominated by the old Mairie (town hall) and a lovely fountain shaded by plane trees, this square is the heart of Terra Vecchia (the ancient port area), with streets winding around the Vieux Port, or old harbour. The name "marché" (market) derives from the stalls, which, especially on Sunday mornings, make for a colourful and noisy scene. As well as the stands with fruit, vegetables, cheese and charcuterie, there are those that make a sort of pancake with *brocciu*, the local sheep's-milk cheese.

Detail of the fountain in Place du Marché

🏛 St-Jean-Baptiste

4 Rue du Cardinal Viale Prela, Place de l'Hôtel-de-Ville. **Tel** 04 95 55 24 60. **Open** daily (10:30am Sun for mass only).

The largest church in Corsica is flanked by two bell towers and has an imposing, austere façade that rises majestically among the roofs of the Terra Vecchia area. It was built in the mid-1600s and redecorated in the following century in Baroque style. The façade stands on a narrow alleyway and is one of the most recognizable images of the island. The two-aisle nave displays marble decoration, gilded stucco work and trompe-l'oeil decorations. The high altar,

pulpit and font are made of polychrome marble.

🏛 Oratoire de l'Immaculée Conception

Rue Napoléon. **Open** daily. Constructed in 1611, this chapel reveals a rich Baroque interior. Wooden panels and red Genoese velvet cover the walls, and there is a fresco on the central vault representing the Immaculate Conception. On the small square outside, black and white pebblestones are laid out in the shape of a sun.

🏛 Chapelle St-Roch

Rue Napoléon. **Tel** 04 95 32 91 66. **Open** Mon–Sat.

This chapel was dedicated to the saint who protected the

population from the plague. It was built in 1604 for the St Roch Confraternity, founded in 1588 *(see p65)*. The work of Ligurian architects and artists, the chapel has 18th-century, Genoese-style wooden panelling and features a statue of St Roch, which is borne in local processions. The organ was made in 1750 and is housed in an interesting tribune made of sculpted, gilded wood.

🏛 St-Charles

Rue du Général Carbuccia. **Closed** to the public.

Preceded by a stairway, this church with its impressive façade was constructed in 1635 for the Jesuits' college and dedicated to St Ignatius Loyola, the founder of the order. When the Jesuits were driven out of Corsica in 1769, the church became the seat of the St Charles Borromeo Confraternity *(see p65)*.

The rooftops of the Terra Vecchia quarter

The jetty known as Môle Génois, on the north of the Vieux Port

Inside are several restored paintings, an altarpiece of the miraculous *Virgin of Lavasina* and a statue of the *Virgin Mary and Child*.

Vieux Port

Nestled between Terra Nova, the Citadelle and the Terra Vecchia quarter, which frames it with its old buildings, the small cove of the medieval port has retained the atmosphere of an old maritime village. It was once the marina of Cardo, and fishermen still mend their nets here in the blue-and-white wooden boats that are flanked by luxury yachts. Lining the quays are cafés and restaurants where the locals spend their evenings. In the summer, the road is closed to traffic and the old port is transformed into a large and lively pedestrian precinct, excellent for people watching.

The tall façades lining the port have suffered erosion from the sea wind and salty air. Walks along the outer jetties are spectacular: the Môle Génois to the north, and the Jetée du Dragon to the south, ending at the 1861 lighthouse.

VISITORS' CHECKLIST

Practical Information
Road map D2. ⛰ 44,000.
ℹ Place St-Nicolas (04 95 54 20 40). 🎬 Italian Film Festival (Jan–Feb); Black Christ (3 May); St John's Feast Day (24 Jun); Relève des Gouverneurs (mid-Jul), Les Musicales (Oct).
🌐 bastia-tourisme.com

Transport
✈ Poretta, 25 km (16 miles) (04 95 54 54 54). 🚌 🚆 Place Maréchal Leclerc (04 95 32 80 61). 🚢 from Genoa, Savona, Livorno, La Spezia, Nice, Marseille, Toulon.

◖ Jardin Romieu

Open daily; gates close at 6pm.
At the right-hand jetty of the Vieux Port are steps up to the Citadelle along a winding – but not particularly steep – path. It crosses over the Jardin Romieu, an oasis of tranquillity. With palm, pine and laurel trees and succulent plants, it offers a splendid view of the city.

The Centre of Bastia

1. Place du Marché
2. St-Jean-Baptiste
3. Oratoire de l'Immaculée Conception
4. Chapelle St-Roch
5. St-Charles
6. Vieux Port
7. Jardin Romieu
8. Quai des Martyrs de la Libération
9. Place St-Nicolas
10. Citadelle pp64–5

0 metres 180
0 yards 180

Bastia: the Citadelle

This impressive structure was built by the Genoese in the 15th–16th centuries. It is still surrounded by the original ramparts and lies in the Terra Nova quarter, which is quite different from Terra Vecchia. Unlike the ancient port area, which grew up almost at random, the Citadelle was laid out in keeping with rigorous town-planning principles, with houses of the same height and broad squares. After decades of neglect, a restoration campaign was initiated in the 1980s. The first houses to regain the original pastel colours typical of Ligurian tradition were those on Rue St-Michel, which has a splendid view of the Terra Vecchia quarter.

The Citadelle seen from the sea, with the Jetée du Dragon in the foreground

★ **Ste-Marie**
The cathedral in Bastia has a majestic yellow façade built in 1604–19. The bell tower is 71 m (233 ft) high. Ste-Marie was consecrated in 1570, when Bastia became a bishopric.

KEY

① **The rampart walls** of the Citadelle were built between 1480 and 1521 by the Genoese governor Tomasino da Campofregoso. This section of the walls extends furthest into the sea.

② **Pavillon des Nobles Douze**

③ **The glacis** of the Citadelle offers the best panoramic view of Terra Vecchia and the old port.

④ **Place Guasco** is a square among the old houses, protected by trees.

Oratoire Ste-Croix
This gem of Rococo architecture boasts the *Christ des Miracles*, the protector of fishermen, which is borne in procession every third year on 3 May. Other sculptures include this angel.

Louis XVI Gate
The monumental entrance to the citadel that directly connects Rue du Colle and Place du Donjon was built in the late 18th century.

Palais des Gouverneurs
From the 15th to the 18th centuries, this palace was the residence of the Genoese governors. It is now home to the Musée de Bastia, which covers the history and art of Bastia.

Religious Brotherhoods

Religious brotherhoods, or confraternities, are groups that carry out charitable works and organize religious celebrations, such as processions on Christian holidays and feast days. They grew up in the 17th century and many are still quite active throughout the island. At Bastia, there are also brotherhoods of people with a common profession (artisans, fishermen) that meet in oratories decorated with stucco work, sculptures, fabrics and paintings of high artistic value. The chapels of the local confraternities are in the side aisles of the Bastia cathedral.

Singing during a religious procession

Luthiers in Bastia
In his workshop in Place Guasco, Christian Magdeleine makes stringed instruments, such as this cittern, decorated with wooden inlay.

Exploring Bastia

The centre of Bastia, facing the commercial port, can easily be explored on foot. Those travelling by car can park in the garage under Place St-Nicolas, the heart of the city and the junction between Terra Vecchia and the modern area. Bastia is relatively small, but for those who would rather not walk, there is a small electric train that starts off from the square, a short distance from the tourist information office, and arrives at the Citadelle via the Quai des Martyrs and the tunnel under the Vieux Port. Guided tours of the Old Town are available, as is a tour of the outlying villages.

Bric-à-brac for sale on Sundays in Place St-Nicolas

The Quai des Martyrs de la Libération

🏛 Quai des Martyrs de la Libération

This quay, enlivened by cafés and restaurants, provides a pleasant walk along the seaside from Place St-Nicolas to the Vieux Port. One of the buildings on the quay is the Palais Monti Rossi, a residence of one of Corsica's old families and one of the finest 19th-century constructions in the city. The building miraculously remained intact after the American bombings that destroyed 90 per cent of the Terra Vecchia quarter in the late summer of 1943. Its façade boasts a pediment, arches and pilasters.

This street is known for its lively nightlife during the summer.

🏛 Place St-Nicolas
Maison Mattei

Tel 04 95 32 44 38 for tastings.
Facing the new port and shaded by the old palm and plane trees, this 300-m (980-ft) long square occupies the site of an old hospital for the poor that was destroyed in the early 19th century. In the middle of the square is a music pavilion where concerts are held on summer evenings.

On the south side of the square stands the white marble

statue of Napoleon in the guise of a Roman emperor, while on the opposite side is a bronze sculpture group dedicated to widow Renno, a Corsican heroine who lost her sons in the wars of independence, and to all those Corsicans who lost their lives in war.

On the west side of the square are the bars and cafés where locals and visitors alike sit at alfresco tables. It is worth trying a glass of Cap Corse, the unique apéritif of the Maison Mattei, the historic establishment located on the square (see opposite).

Every Sunday morning, Place St-Nicolas is enlivened by dozens of market stalls offering goods of every kind, and even some interesting antiques. Behind the charming cafés, there are some elegant 19th-century buildings.

🏛 Musée de Bastia

La Citadelle, Place du Donjon.
Tel 04 95 31 09 12. **Open** May–Sep: 10am–6:30pm; Oct–Apr: 9am–noon & 2–5pm. **Closed** Sep–Jun: Mon; Oct–Apr: Sun; public holidays. 🖼
🔲 musee-bastia.com

Housed in the majestic 16th-century fortress known as the Governors' Palace, this state-of-the-art museum offers an eclectic collection of historical and ethnological items, plus a number of Corsican artworks, including several Renaissance pieces from the Fesch collection. The displays illustrate Bastia's development as a trade and political capital, as well as highlighting its importance as a cradle of intellectual and artistic movements.

🚢 Port de Toga

When the Vieux Port proved unable to take the number of pleasure boats arriving there in the high season, an area was created between Bastia and Pietranera to cope with all this heavy traffic.

Panorama of Bastia's Port de Toga, also known as Port de Plaisance

For hotels and restaurants in this area see pp162–3 and pp172–4

The Port de Toga is a long quay that has become a lively, trendy place frequented by young people, especially on summer evenings. The restaurant and disco bar tables almost touch the sea, their multicoloured lights reflected in the water. Some of the best nightspots that are open until late are Le Bounty, Le Café Cézanne and Le Maracana.

Façade of the church of St-Étienne in Cardo

⌂ Cardo

Today a chic suburb in the hills above Bastia, Cardo used to be a fishing village. Its marina, Porto Cardo, was the original nucleus of Bastia in the Middle Ages. It became a municipality in its own right in 1844, by order of Louis Philippe. Cardo offers a spectacular view of the coastline, and there are many paths popular with hikers and cyclists.

The Neo-Classical church of **St-Étienne** has painted wooden statues from the 17th century and a Neo-Gothic organ tribune. From Cardo, the D231 and then D31, the **Route de la Corniche Supérieure** is a panoramic road running at around 300 m (980 ft) above sea level. It goes through the village of Pietrabugno and proceeds to San Martino di Lota and Miomo. In clear weather, the islands of the Tuscan archipelago can be seen on the horizon.

✽ Étang de Biguglia

Lido de la Marana, Furiani. **Tel** 04 95 33 55 73. ▣ (summer only). Eco Museum Route de l'étang. **Open** Tue–Sat; Jul–Aug: 9am–4pm; Sep–Jun: 9am–noon & 1–5pm.

On the southern outskirts of the city, between the airport, the industrial area and the strip of Marana coastline, is the Étang

de Biguglia, a lagoon designated as a reserve to conserve the largest wet zone in Corsica. The lagoon consists of 18 sq km (7 sq miles) of pools and rivers that are part of the mouth of the Golo river and is connected to the sea in its northern part.

The scourge of malaria, which was an endemic disease in Corsica for centuries, was finally eliminated after World War II. The land was reclaimed and partly used for farming. Now the canebrakes and grassland are the ideal habitat for

A flamingo in the wet Étang de Biguglia

100 species of birds, including the great cormorant, the purple heron and the flamingo. Other inhabitants of the lagoon are marsh tortoises. The reserve is also a habitual stopover for birds migrating from Europe to Africa. The best seasons to observe the

60 or more species of migrators are spring and autumn.

The water, which used to be polluted, has been purified, resulting in the return of the mullet and eel populations. They are caught using traditional methods by a local fishermen's cooperative.

Since 1994, the Étang has been a regional reserve, with nature walks, a cycling path, and guided tours. An old fort now houses an **Eco Museum** dedicated to the history and evolution of the area. The town of Biguglia, which overlooks the lagoon, was the capital of the island under the Pisans and the residence of the Genoese governors until 1372. The sandy belt that separates the sea from the lagoon is one of the loveliest beaches in Bastia.

The Maison Mattei in Bastia

This renowned firm makes tobacconist's products, cork objects and, above all, liqueurs distilled from muscat grapes and flavoured with maquis herbs and quinine, including the famous Cap Corse (see pp170 and 181). The Maison was established in Bastia in 1872 by Louis-Napoléon Mattei. Almost immediately the firm became a symbol of the spirit of enterprise, and its so-called "products of nostalgia" were exported throughout the world, especially where there were many Corsican emigrants. While the

The stone sign on the façade of the Maison Mattei

original cigarette factory at Toga closed in 1977, when the company was sold to a large group, the shop is still in Place St-Nicolas.

Étang di Biguglia from the sea

The bay of Calvi, viewed from the battlements of the Citadelle ▶

White houses surrounding the small harbour of Erbalunga

❷ Erbalunga

Road map D1. 🗻 400. 🚌
ℹ️ Place de St Nicolas, Bastia
(04 95 54 20 40). 🎭 Procession de la Cerca (Maundy Thu & Good Fri); Music Festival (early Aug).

A Genoese tower protects the small harbour lined with old stone houses and fish restaurants. Erbalunga, the marina of the district of Brando, was for centuries the port where Pisan ships landed to be loaded with local wine.

At the start of the village is the church of **St-Erasme**, home to the crosses of the Cerca procession: the men's crucifix weighs 60 kg (132 lb); the women's is 30 kg (66 lb). On the evening of Maundy Thursday, the procession winds through the streets to the Benedictine nuns' convent. On Good Friday, it leaves early in the morning and proceeds for 7 km (4 miles), visiting the hamlets of Pozzo, Poretto and Silgaggia.

In Erbalunga, as in many other locations around Cap Corse, there are sumptuous country mansions known as *Maisons d'Américains*. These were built by Corsicans who had returned home wealthy after emigrating to Latin America. Rich families also had impressive mausoleums built, which can be seen from the D32 all over the cape *(see p33)*.

Environs

In **Castello**, 3 km (2 miles) inland, there is a 13th-century fortress. A 15th-century Italian nobleman murdered his wife here, and she is said to haunt Castello. The chapel of **Santa Maria di e Nevi** lies a short walk south towards Silgaggia. It houses the oldest frescoes in Corsica, dating from 1386. **Pozzo** is the starting point for the path to **Monte Stello** (1,307 m/4,288 ft), which takes 6 hours to walk.

North of Erbalunga, along the D80, is the **Sisco Valley**. In Sisco is the Chapelle de St-Martin, housing a precious 13th-century silver mask of St John Chrysotom. From the main road, a path leads to the Romanesque Chapelle de San Michele, built by the Pisans. Closer to the coast is the former Couvent de Santa Catalina, famous for once having housed relics of a fantastic nature, such as a lump of clay from which Adam was made and almonds from Paradise.

🏛️ Santa Maria di e Nevi

Castello. **Tel** 04 95 33 20 84. 🎟️ Visits by guided tour only. Book one day in advance (06 86 78 02 38).

❸ Pietracorbara

Road map D1. 🗻 600. 🚌 ℹ️ Port de Plaisance, Macinaggio (04 95 35 40 34); Town Hall (04 95 35 20 59).
🌐 pietracorbara.fr

A broad, cultivated valley behind a long, sandy beach enclosed by a canebrake protects

The Genoese Tour de l'Osse near Pietracorbara

the village of Pietracorbara. A skeleton found here in 1990 and dating from 6000 BC is proof of the prehistoric origins of the site, which was later used by the Greeks and Romans as a base.

Environs

Northwards, along the coast, is the 16th-century **Tour de l'Osse** (Bone Tower), one of the best preserved in the area, and **Porticciolo**, a tiny marina with houses grouped around a pier.

Fishing boat in Macinaggio's busy harbour

❹ Macinaggio

Road map D1. 🗻 480. 🚌 ℹ️ Port de Plaisance (04 95 35 40 34), Harbor Masters office (04 95 35 42 57).
🎭 Amateur Theatre Festival (Aug).
🌐 **macinaggiorogliano-capcorse.fr**

Fishing boats are anchored next to the yachts that stop at Macinaggio after sailing across from Italy. The most popular tourist harbour in Cap Corse, it has always been a military and commercial port. Controlled by the Genoese for a long time, it was liberated by Pascal Paoli, after years of struggle, in 1761 *(see pp50–51)*. Plaques on the quay mark Napoleon's landing, as did the empress Eugénie on her return trip from the Suez Canal inauguration in 1869, and that Paoli also stopped here. The port is divided into three basins that can take in over 500 boats and is surrounded by visitors' facilities.

Environs
Around the village are vineyards, extending as far as **Rogliano**. Inhabited in Roman times, from the 12th to the 16th centuries it was ruled by the da Mare family, which had trade relations with Genoa.

At **Bettolacce**, the area's main village, a round tower bears witness to its former splendour. The church of Sant'Agnellu boasts a beautiful altar of white Carrara marble.

Île de la Giraglia, opposite the tip of Cap Corse

❺ Cap Corse

Road map D1. ⛰ 480. ℹ Port de Plaisance, Macinaggio (04 95 35 40 34); Ersa Town Hall (04 95 35 69 06). 🌐 **macinaggiorogliano-capcorse.fr**

On the northern tip of the peninsula are some villages that have retained the spirit of the past. One of these is **Barcaggio**, which has a beautiful beach where cows go to graze and a small harbour where time seems to have come to a halt.

The road leading here, the D80 followed by the D253, is simply spectacular. It descends among the maquis, holm oak groves and pastures covered in white asphodel, offering a fine view of the **Île de la Giraglia**. The northernmost part of Corsica, this green serpentine rock island is separated from the coast by 2 km (1 mile) of

treacherous, fast-flowing sea. This island has a square 16th-century Genoese tower and a lighthouse built in the 1940s that, until 1994, was inhabited by a keeper; now it is wholly automatic. Giraglia is famous because the sailing regatta that goes from Sanremo, in Liguria, to Le Lavandou, Provence, and back passes by here.

About 2 km (1 mile) west of Barcaggio is **Tollare**, another small harbour with a tuna fishery. From here, a small road winds back to the D80 and **Ersa**, whose church of **Ste-Marie** has a 17th-century wooden tabernacle. West of here, on Col de Serra is **Moulin Mattei**, an old, round mill offering a fabulous panoramic view. In a poor state of preservation, it was restored in the past by the Maison Mattei, the renowned apéritif makers (*see p67*).

❻ Centuri

Road map D1. ⛰ 215. ℹ Port de Plaisance, Macinaggio (04 95 35 40 34); Town Hall (04 95 35 60 06). 🌐 **macinaggiorogliano-capcorse.fr**

A narrow inlet lined by ochre, grey and white houses with green serpentine roofs is an apt description of the small port of Centuri, which for centuries was

A fisherman from Centuri making a lobster pot

a loading point for wine, wood, oil and citrus fruits that were then shipped to Italy and France. Today, Centuri, the ancient Roman Centurium mentioned by Ptolemy, is in fact the leading fishing centre in Cap Corse. The docks are covered with fishing nets and lobster pots that are still handmade. The port is full of the typical double-ended fishing boats that return laden with lobsters (3,000 kg/ 6,600 lb a year) that can be enjoyed in the local restaurants.

The sea floor here is a paradise for scuba divers, especially around the islet of Centuri, at the mouth of the bay, which was fortified in the 13th century.

From the port, an hour's walk up a path leads through luxuriant vegetation to the village of **Cannelle** (also accessible by car from the D80 road). Its simple stone houses hugging the mountainside are rich in bougainvillea, and its narrow streets and covered passageways offer views of the sea. On the D80 road, 3 km (2 miles) from Centuri, is the16th-century **Couvent de l'Annonciation** dedicated to Our Lady of the Seven Sorrows. The church is considered the largest in Cap Corse. The monastery is not open to the public, except when it hosts temporary exhibitions.

Fishing boats anchored in the Centuri harbour

❼ Tour of the Sentier des Douaniers

Once used by customs officers to control smuggling activities (hence the name, "path of customs officers"), this coastal footpath runs along the tip of Cap Corse, in places offering stunning views. Similar paths run along the entire perimeter of Corsica, but the Sentier des Douaniers, going from Macinaggio to Centuri – among the junipers, mastics and asphodels, and over beaches and craggy cliffs – is simply breathtaking. This tour can be divided into three stages: Macinaggio–Barcaggio, Barcaggio–Tollare and Tollare–Centuri. It is not particularly difficult, but watch out for bush fires, especially in the summer. Drivers can reach the separate sights via inland paved roads.

③ **Barcaggio**
Past the Punta d'Agnello tower and promontory – one of the most panoramic spots in Cap Corse – is Barcaggio (see p71). This is the first stage of the tour that is directly accessible by car, from the D253. The water in the bay is crystal clear.

④ **Tollare**
Tollare, a tiny port with a Genoese tower, is another stage in the tour that can be accessed by car, from the D153 road.

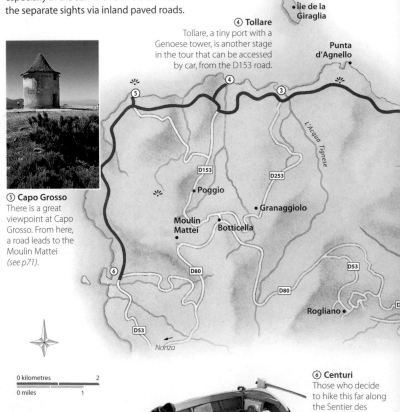

⑤ **Capo Grosso**
There is a great viewpoint at Capo Grosso. From here, a road leads to the Moulin Mattei (see p71).

⑥ **Centuri**
Those who decide to hike this far along the Sentier des Douaniers will have a challenging but interesting day. At Centuri (see p71), delicious seafood makes for an excellent reward.

Key

— Tour footpath

— Motorable road

TIPS FOR HIKERS

Practical Information
ℹ️ Port de Plaisance,
Macinaggio (04 95 35 40 34).
Length of tour: 26 km (16 miles).
Duration: Macinaggio–Barcaggio
3 hours; Barcaggio–Tollare 45
minutes; Tollare–Centuri 4 hours.
Footpath: of average difficulty;
it can be taken all year long.
Stopping-off points:
Macinaggio, Barcaggio, Tollare
and Centuri.

② Chapelle de Santa Maria

Further along the path is the
chapel of Santa Maria, built
in the 12th century over an
early Christian church. The
ruins of a Genoese tower
can be found on the coast
along Santa Maria bay.

① Macinaggio

The tour begins at
Macinaggio *(see p70)* and leads to the
beautiful beach
of Tamarone,
the entrance
to a reserve
opposite the Îles
Finocchiarola. These
craggy rocks with a
watchtower inhabited by
colonies of marine birds are
also a nature reserve. The
path then skirts the high
coastline, with continuous
fine views of the sea and
the coves below, where it
is possible to take a swim.

Cap Corse and Patrimonio Wines

Appreciated since ancient times, the white wines of Cap Corse
come from terraces carved out of the mountainside. The two
AOC *(appellation d'origine contrôlée)* labels here are Coteaux du
Cap Corse and Muscat du Cap Corse *(see p171)*. They produce
Malvasia, Muscat and Sciaccarellu wines, and Rappu, a sweet
white wine that can be purchased only at the wineries. Among
the most famous wineries
is the Clos Nicrosi, which
produces one of the best
Corsican whites. Another AOC
area is Patrimonio *(see p74)*;
Domaine de Pietri at Morsiglia
has been in business since
1786 and at St-Florent there
is the Domaine Gentile. Both
make reds and whites, as well
as Rappu and Muscat.

A wine label of Patrimonio,
a famous AOC region

❽ Pino

Road map: D1. 🗺️ 150. ℹ️ Port de
Plaisance, Macinaggio (04 95 35 40
34); Town Hall (04 95 35 12 70).
🌐 **macinaggiorogliano-capcorse.fr**

This small village at the foot of
Col de Ste-Lucie lies in the midst
of luxuriant vegetation. Umbrella
pines protect the Maisons
d'Américains *(see p70)*, including
the Maison Savelli and the family
mausoleum. Other monumental
tombs surrounded by cypress
trees lie at the junction of the D80
and D180 roads. The church of
Ste-Marie has a Baroque façade
and, inside, two fonts decorated
with fish, salamanders and lions.
The **Couvent St-François**, built
in 1486 in Marina di Scalu, is
flanked by a Genoese tower.

Environs

About 5 km (3 miles) from Pino,
on the D180 road going up to Col
de Ste-Lucie, is the footpath for
the **Tour de Sénèque**. The tower
is at the top of **Monte Ventiggiola**,
564 m (1,850 ft) above sea level,
where the great Roman play-
wright Seneca is said to have
been exiled. In reality, the tower
is medieval. It can be reached
after a steep climb through the
maquis that can take over an hour.
The view is well worth the climb.

🏠 **Ste-Marie**
Tel 04 95 35 12 32. **Open** contact the
Town Hall for details.

🏠 **Couvent St-François**
Tel 04 95 35 12 70.
Closed to the public.

❾ Canari

Road map: D1. 🗺️ 326. ℹ️ Port de
Plaisance, Macinaggio (04 95 35
40 34); Town Hall (04 95 37 80 17).
🎭 St Thomas's and St Erasmus's feast
days (Jul). 🌐 **canarivillage.com**

Rather isolated from the D80
highway and divided into various
hamlets, the medieval fiefdom
of Canari boasts two interesting
churches. The 12th-century
Pisan Romanesque **Santa Maria
Assunta** has a cornice decorated
with animal heads and human
figures. This church is open only
on 15 August. **St-François** was
built in 1506 and then rebuilt
in Baroque style.

From 1932 to 1966, Canari
grew significantly due to a local
asbestos mine. Though this was
closed when this mineral was
found to be toxic, it has left an
ugly scar on the landscape.
The **Marine d'Albo**, protected
by a watchtower, is where, in
1588, Hassan Pasha's fleet landed
and his men sacked the area.

🏠 **St-François**
Tel 04 95 37 80 17 or 04 95 37 13 90.
Open ask for the keys at the Town Hall.
Rooms are available for short stays.

The old watchtower at Marine d'Albo

Panoramic view of Nonza, dominated by the cliff overlooking the sea

⓾ Nonza

Road map D1. 🏔 70. 🛈 Bâtiment
Administratif, Route du Cap Corse,
St-Florent (04 95 37 06 04); Town Hall
(04 95 37 82 82). 🎭 Cultural Festival
(2nd week of Aug).

One of the most fascinating
villages in Corsica, Nonza clings
to a black rock falling steeply
down to the sea. Its old, pastel-
coloured stone houses are
surrounded by terraces and
gardens, and many are reached
by steps rather than streets.

Steps also lead up to the
church of **Ste-Julie**, built in the
16th century but enlarged in
the 19th. Inside is a Baroque
altar, a chapel dedicated to
St Erasmus, patron saint of
sailors, and a painting of St Julia,
one of Corsica's patron saints.
According to legend, this girl
was crucified by a Roman
prefect after refusing to take
part in some pagan revelry.
Nearby, 54 steps lead down to
the **Fontaine de Ste-Julie**,
which is said to have sprung
up as she was martyred and
to have miraculous water.

More steps lead down to the
beach, 160 m (525 ft) below the
village. Until the early 19th
century, the inhabitants left
from here in boats every morning
to reach the then-fertile Désert
des Agriates (see p76). Today, the
beach offers an awe-inspiring
view up to the village and its
18th-century green schist tower
built by Paoli. The dark colour of
the sand is the result of pollution
from an asbestos mine up the
coast that was closed in 1966. It
is safe to walk here, but bathing
is not allowed. On the D80 road

to Albo, there are many mortuary
chapels and mausoleums (see
p33). These belonged to Corsican
families that emigrated to find
their fortunes and returned rich
enough to have elaborate
tombs built for themselves.

⓫ Patrimonio

Road map D2. 🏔 680. 🚍
🛈 Bâtiment Administratif, Route
du Cap Corse, St-Florent (04 95 37
06 04); Town Hall (04 95 37 08 49).
🎭 Guitar Nights (3rd week Jul).

At the foot of the Col de
Teghime and the Serra di Pigno,
this village in the heart of the
Nebbio region is one of the
main wine-producing centres
on the island (see p73). The
vineyards, which all belong to
small, family-owned wineries,
dot the limestone hills that
dominate Patrimonio.

While driving along the
highway, it is worth stopping at
one of the many wineries to
taste and purchase the white
Vermentino, or a fine red wine
made from the Niellucciu grape.
The latter is the ideal
accompaniment for
charcuterie and game.

Overlooking the village
is the church of **St-Martin**,
built in 1570 and reached
by a stairway. At sunset, its
façade takes on golden
hues. Just down the lane,
next to the church, is a
megalithic menhir with
a carved face.

ⓘ St-Martin
Tel 04 95 37 08 49. **Open** daily;
make enquiries at the Town Hall.

⓬ St-Florent

Road map D2. 🏔 1,650. 🚍
🛈 Bâtiment Administratif, Route du
Cap Corse (04 95 37 06 04). 🎭 Porto
Latino: Latin-American music (mid-
Aug). 🌐 **saint-florent.fr**

At the end of a long gulf, the
village of St-Florent sits with
its brightly coloured houses
along the harbour and a lively
promenade with boutiques,
restaurants and cafés. In summer,
these are open till late at night.

Although it was inhabited in
the Neolithic era and was an
ancient Roman base, the village
only really developed in the
15th century around the
Genoese fort. The area was
marshy and unhealthy, however,
and was abandoned between
the 17th and 19th centuries
because of malaria.

The homes in the old town
surround the parish church,
which houses a statue of
St Florent the Martyr.

At the edge of the village is
Santa Maria Assunta, the old
cathedral of the Nebbio region.
This splendid Romanesque
church dates back to 1140.
Made of pale limestone, its
façade has two superimposed
tiers of blind arches and a niche
with a Virgin Mary and Child
statue. The basilica-style interior
has pillars and pilasters whose
capitals are decorated with shells
and animal figures. In a glass
case are the remains of St Flor,
a Roman soldier mummified in
the 3rd century AD.

ⓘ Santa Maria Assunta
Open Jun–Sep: Mon–Sat & pm Sun;
Oct–May: by appt (04 95 37 06 04).

The quay at the port of St-Florent

⑬ San Michele de Murato

This 12th-century church is one of Corsica's best examples of Pisan Romanesque architecture. It lies just north of Murato village, 475 m (1,560 ft) above sea level, dominating the valley of the Bevincu river and the Nebbio region. San Michele de Murato has a simple structure, with a rectangular nave ending in a small semi-circular apse. The porticoed bell tower is set against the middle of the façade. The materials used were white limestone and green serpentine. All around the church are tiny blind arches. The consoles and cornices of the small windows have bas-reliefs with animal and plant motifs, as well as allegorical scenes, such as Eve taking the forbidden fruit or the Lamb attacked by other animals.

VISITORS' CHECKLIST

Practical Information
Road map D2. **Open** May–Oct: pm daily or ask for the keys at the Mairie (Town Hall) in Murato (04 95 37 60 10).

The central window of the apse with green serpentine decoration

The square bell tower in the middle of the façade was rebuilt and enlarged in the 19th century. It is the truly original element in this church, forming a colonnaded portico around the entry door.

Consoles
The blind arches lie on consoles with various sculpted nature motifs.

Façade
Dominated by the bell tower, the façade has one entrance and three blind arches on the consoles of which are bas-relief sculptures of animals.

The sculpture decoration in the church includes geometric patterns and scenes with birds and human figures.

A feature of the Pisan Romanesque style is the irregular checkerboard arrangement of different-coloured stone blocks.

On the two columns framing the portal, the limestone and serpentine alternate in irregular bands.

Capitals
A garland surrounds the columns at the base of the capitals, which are carved in the shape of two simple volutes.

Symbols
The two figures flanking the three blind arches may be symbols of the political and religious power in Murato during that time.

The village of Oletta, perched on the slopes of the Nebbio hills

⓮ Nebbio

Road map D2. 🚌 ℹ️ Bâtiment Administratif, Route du Cap Corse, St-Florent (04 95 37 06 04).-

Called the Golden Shell (Conca d'Oro) for its fertile land, the Alisu basin is an area with vineyards and olive and fruit orchards. Via the D38, D82 and D62 roads, there is a semi-circular route that departs from St-Florent, passing through the Nebbio region's main towns, from Oletta up to Rapale. The roads lead to the passes of Col de Teghime (a small road goes up to Serra di Pigno, for an even better view) and Col de San Stefano. From here, the stretch of D62 known as Défilé de Lancone descends to the coast in dangerously steep curves. A 30-minute walk from Rapale is the 13th-century **Chapelle de San Cesario**, with its green shale and white limestone façade. The parish church of **Murato** has a painting attributed to Titian, but the village is famous for the Romanesque church of San Michele (see p75).

⓯ Oletta

D2. 🔼 1,400. 🚌 ℹ️ Bâtiment Administratif, Route du Cap Corse, St-Florent (04 95 37 06 04).

Immersed in the greenery of the hills of Nebbio is the small village of Oletta. It seems to be clinging to the hillside and is characterized by simple houses of white, ochre and pink. Oletta offers spectacular views of the Golfe de St-Florent and the Nebbio region, including the bell tower of the old **Couvent St-François**, the only remaining architectural element from the original complex. Dominating the view towards the hilltop is the **Mausoleum of Count Rivarola**, governor of Malta, one of the many monumental family tombs in this region. The 18th-century parish church of **St-André** has a bas-relief of the Creation on its façade and a wooden triptych inside dating from 1534.

Detail of a monumental tomb in the Nebbio area

The area around Oletta is renowned for its sheep's-milk cheese, which was once used to make Roquefort.

⓰ Désert des Agriates

Road map C–D2. ℹ️ Route du Cap Corse, St-Florent (04 95 37 06 04).

Situated between St-Florent and the mouth of the Ostriconi river, this 160 sq km (60 sq miles) of green desert is virtually uninhabited. Only some shepherds and a few people in the hamlet of Casta live here. Until the mid-19th century, however, this area was the "bread basket" of Bastia and Cap Corse, and it produced wheat, olives and olive oil, wine and fruit. The farmers arrived by boat from Nonza, Canari and St-Florent to work the land. Today, the only remains of this area's fertile past are the barns and stone granaries. The fields are abandoned and the maquis has invaded the terrain.

The panoramic D81 highway crosses this sweet-smelling desert, which is extraordinary in spring. There are also two detours, negotiable only by four-wheel drives, that lead to the beaches of **Saleccia** (see p25) and **Guignu**. It is worth spending a few days on the 35-km (22-mile) coastal path, taking lodgings in the renovated barns. Boats also sail from the St-Florent port to the **Loto** beach, which is a 30-minute walk from Saleccia. The lovely, white-sand beach of **Ostriconi**, bounded by sand dunes and a pool, is more convenient and accessible.

Spring blossoms on the slopes of the Désert des Agriates

Mediterranean Maquis

Known in the Corsican language as *macchia*, maquis is one of the most luxuriant types of vegetation in southern Europe. The low, thick undergrowth and bushes occupy vast areas along the coast and in the interior, covering a surface area of about 2,000 sq km (770 sq miles). The maquis is spectacular in spring, when it blossoms covering entire hills with white and pink rockrose flowers and yellow broom. The flowers are used to produce essences, as well as honey with a particular aroma. Despite the frequent fires, the maquis manages to grow back in a relatively short time compared to trees and tall shrubs. Besides rockrose, other herbaceous plants are asphodel thistle, cyclamen, lavender, heather and sarsaparilla. Typical shrubs include rosemary, juniper, myrtle, mastic shrub, phillyrea and strawberry trees. Among the trees are two kinds of oak – the cork oak and evergreen holm oak.

Wild fennel has umbrella-shaped flowers that look like small white or yellowish clouds. It also has a strong, almost oleaginous scent that is quite characteristic of the maquis. It can be used for pot-pourri after being dried.

Cistus, or rockrose, is a typical maquis plant that can also grow in the mountains, up to an altitude of 1,200 m (3,950 ft). This is a low-growing shrub with slightly fleshy leaves. Its five-petalled flowers frame a centre of golden-yellow stamens.

Wild rosemary exudes an intense scent that infuses the entire maquis. Its aromatic leaves are used to flavour food and as a perfume and a medicine.

Myrtle is considered a sacred plant, the symbol of fertility. It has aromatic leaves, white flowers and dark berries from which a liqueur is distilled.

Broom inflames the sides of hills and mountains from April to late summer with its dazzling yellow flowers, which cover the green, arched and spiny stems.

The red granite rocks around the bay of L'Île Rousse

⑰ L'Île Rousse

Road map C2. 🏛 3,100. 🚌 🚉 Route du Port. 🚢 from Genoa, Savona, Marseille, Nice, Toulon. 🛈 Ave Calizi (04 95 60 04 35). 🎭 Festimare (early May), Petanque Challenge (mid-Sep). 🌐 **ot-ile-rousse.fr**

A busy beach with fine sand, a pleasant, Riviera-style promenade, shops and a lively port sum up L'Île Rousse. It was founded in 1758 by Pascal Paoli, who had the port built to counter the presence of the Genoese at Calvi and Algajola. L'Île Rousse revolves around Place Paoli, with its mix of cafés, shops and *pétanque* players in the shade of palm and plane trees. In the middle of the square is a fountain with the statue of Paoli.

The square is the starting point for the little train that skirts the bay and goes to Isola di La Pietra. This islet is linked to the mainland by a pier with a tower and a lighthouse built by Paoli in 1857.

At one end of Place Paoli is the covered market, a 19th-century structure similar to a Greek temple, which sells charcuterie, vegetables, cheese, maquis-flower honey, fish and home-made bread. For shops and restaurants, try the old quarter north of the square, with its well-kept houses and paved streets that descend to the seaside.

Outside the town is the popular but less urban Bodri beach, which can be reached by a dirt track.

L'Île Rousse is the starting point for excursions in the Balagne region *(see pp80–81)*. This area of Corsica boasts the island's best artisans, whose products are exported all over the world.

The area is also renowned for its idyllic villages surrounded by olive groves, such as **Monticello**, overlooked by the 13th-century Castel d'Ortica. Further inland, the road climbs up to **Santa Reparata di Balagna**. Here, the church of Santa Reparata, with its origins in the 11th century, offers a great view from its terrace.

⑱ Algajola

Road map C2. 🏛 300. 🚉 🛈 Place de la Gare (04 95 62 78 32). 🌐 **balagne-corsica.com**

Fringed by a beach of golden sand some 2 km (1 mile) long, Algajola makes an excellent base for water sports, especially windsurfing.

Founded by the Phoenicians, Algajola was used by the Romans as a base for their legions, and then chosen by the Genoese because of its central position in the region. Sacked repeatedly by the Saracens, the village enjoyed a period of splendour in the 1600s, when the bastions were built.

Fortified after a Barbary pirate raid, the church of **St-Georges** houses a 17th-century painting of the Deposition attributed to the Italian artist Guercino.

Music box by Scat'a Musica in Pigna

🏛 St-Georges

Tel 04 95 62 78 32. **Open** for religious services only.

⑲ Pigna

Road map C2. 🏛 100. 🛈 Ave Calizi, L'Île Rousse (04 95 60 04 35). 🎭 Estivoce (Jul).

This thriving hamlet in the Balagne is perched on a slope alongside olive orchards. It has retained its charming medieval character, with stepped paths, narrow alleys and vaulted passageways. By the tree-lined central square stands the local church with two bell towers.

Pigna, a centre for traditional Corsican music, is famous for its handicraft workshops. The **Casa Musicale** (Music House), which also has hotel facilities and a restaurant, is the centre for the safeguarding of Corsican music and the island's major traditions. In the workshops, ancient instruments, including various types of cittern, are built in traditional style. **Scat'a Musica** sells musical boxes and, in summer, the Estivoce festival celebrates traditional songs. The Corsican restaurant A Merendella Citadina is also worth a visit.

🏛 Casa Musicale

Place de l'Église. **Tel** 04 95 61 77 31. **Closed** Jan–mid-Feb.

Environs

The Franciscan **Couvent de Corbara**, 2 km (1 mile) from Pigna, was founded in 1456, destroyed during the French Revolution and rebuilt by the Dominicans in the 1800s. To arrange a visit or stay the night, call 04 95 60 06 73.

The sea wall at Algajola protecting the port at the foot of the citadel

For hotels and restaurants in this area see pp162–3 and pp172–4

⑳ Aregno

Road map C2. 🏛 600. 🛈 Port de Plaisance, Calvi (04 95 65 16 67). 🎪 Almond Festival (early Aug).

The village of Aregno, surrounded by olive and citrus-fruit trees, should be visited for its two churches: the Baroque parish church of **St-Antoine** and the Pisan Romanesque church of the **Trinité et San Giovanni**. Built in 1177 of green, white and pink granite, the latter has a façade with four blind arches over the portal. It also has a pediment decorated with small arches, in the centre of which is a statue of a man holding his foot while pulling a thorn from it – an allegory for the knowledge of man. The chapel interior has two 15th-century frescoes: *St Michael and the Dragon* and *The Four Doctors of the Church*.

🔼 **Trinité et San Giovanni**
Tel 04 95 61 70 34. **Open** Jul–Aug; during other months, ask for the keys at the Mairie (Town Hall).

㉑ Sant'Antonino

Road map C2. 🏛 100. 🛈 Port de Plaisance, Calvi (04 95 65 16 67). 🌐 **santantonino.fr**

An eagle's nest 447 m (1,467 ft) above sea level, this hamlet overlooks the Regino and Tighiella river valleys. Its unique position affords a magnificent view, from the snow-capped mountains to the sea. Sant'Antonino is laid out in a circle and was one of the fiefdoms of the Savelli family.

Steps going up to the village of Sant'Antonino

The Baroque church and campanile at Feliceto, near Sant'Antonino

It was an impregnable fortress that took in the entire valley population when Saracen pirate ships appeared on the horizon. Along the alleys of this hamlet, which are for pedestrians only, there are steps and passageways. The dark-granite houses have been restored and now contain shops selling locally made handicrafts.

Environs
About 10 km (6 miles) along the D663 road is **Feliceto**, which has a Baroque church and a mill producing olive oil.
In the opposite direction is the Giussani region, with the villages of **Pioggiola** and **Olmi-Cappella**, linked by a number of footpaths. The latter is known for its olive oil.

㉒ Speloncato

Road map C2. 🏛 300. 🛈 Ave Calizi, L'Île Rousse (04 95 60 04 35); Town Hall (04 95 61 59 00).

Perched on a spur of Monte Tolo, the small village of Speloncato offers wonderful views of the surrounding Balagne region. It is named after the *spelunche*, the caves in the vicinity, which include the 8-m (25-ft-) long **Pietra Tafonata**. Supposedly, twice a year, on 8 April and 8 September, the setting sun is visible through the tunnel, briefly illuminating the village square with the Baroque church of **San Michele**.

㉓ Calenzana

Road map C2. 🏛 2,300. 🛈 Port de Plaisance, Calvi (04 95 65 16 67). 🎪 Ste-Restitude's Feast Day (end of May). 🌐 **balagne-corsica.com**

Olive oil, wine and honey are still the mainstays of the economy of this town, one of the liveliest in the Balagne region. It is also the starting point of the GR20 long-distance path *(see p26)*.
The Baroque collegiate church of **St-Blaise**, designed by the Milanese architect Domenico Baina, was built in the late 17th century. The ceiling over the nave has an 18th-century fresco, *St Biagio Healing a Child*. At the foot of the campanile, a plaque commemorates the battle of Calenzana, fought on 14 January 1732 between Corsican nationalists and the Genoese Republic, in which 700 German mercenaries lost their lives.
About 1 km (half a mile) away is **Ste-Restitude**, a 12th-century church built over a Roman necropolis. It is dedicated to a martyr killed in Calvi in the 3rd century and venerated in the entire region. Her story is told in two 14th-century frescoes, and her sarcophagus is in the crypt.

Environs
A short way along the D151 is **Montemaggiore**. This village, built on a promontory, has a lovely Baroque church and views of the Golfe de Calvi.

㉔ Tour of the Strada di l'Artigiani

The "Artisans' Road" is a route that covers the most characteristic craftsmen's workshops in Balagne, the fertile region behind Calvi and L'Île Rousse. These shops are located in villages perched on hilltops and are a popular tourist attraction thanks to their handicraft production. The main centre is Pigna *(see p78)*, with its Casa Musicale, an organization committed to safeguarding the island's rich cultural heritage. The road signs indicate different ways to reach Calenzana, Corbara, Santa Reparata, Feliceto, Pigna, Lumio, Monticello, Occiglioni, Lozari, Palasca, Olmi-Capella, Cateri and Occhiatana, all of which are fascinating villages thanks to their architecture and panoramic views.

④ Pigna
Musical instruments, music boxes and pottery, along with many natural products such as wine, honey, olive oil and cheese, can be found in Pigna. This village is the leading handicraft centre in the region, with all kinds of work-shops – as if the best artisans in Corsica had decided to settle here.

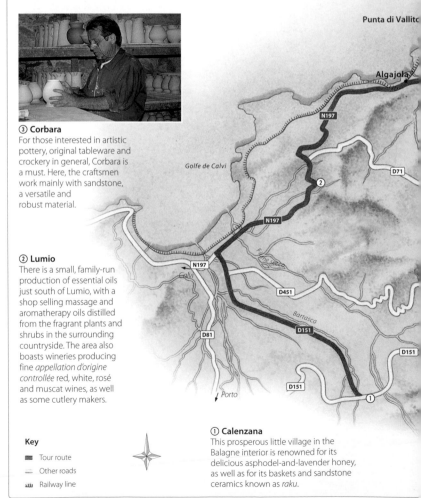

③ Corbara
For those interested in artistic pottery, original tableware and crockery in general, Corbara is a must. Here, the craftsmen work mainly with sandstone, a versatile and robust material.

② Lumio
There is a small, family-run production of essential oils just south of Lumio, with a shop selling massage and aromatherapy oils distilled from the fragrant plants and shrubs in the surrounding countryside. The area also boasts wineries producing fine *appellation d'origine controllée* red, white, rosé and muscat wines, as well as some cutlery makers.

① Calenzana
This prosperous little village in the Balagne interior is renowned for its delicious asphodel-and-lavender honey, as well as for its baskets and sandstone ceramics known as *raku*.

Key

- ▬ Tour route
- – Other roads
- ⏚ Railway line

Punta di Vallitc

Algajola

Golfe de Calvi

Porto

Olive Oil in Balagne

Olive harvesting

Among the many local gastronomic specialities in the Balagne region, the extra-virgin olive oil is outstanding. Olive trees and their products are an integral part of Corsican tradition. It has been proven that the trees are endemic to the island, as are myrtle and the Corsican pine, and many of them are over 500 years old. The olives are gathered by setting large nets under the trees and shaking the branches. The olives are then pressed in hydraulic presses. Olive oil is a true "fruit juice", wholly natural, with many nutritious qualities.

Tips for Drivers

ℹ️ Calvi tourist information, 97 Port de Plaisance (04 95 65 16 67), or any other in the Balagne region have leaflets about the tour.
Length of tour: 50 km (30 miles).
Duration: one day for the route suggested here, while more time will be needed for an extended tour to take in other localities in the area or to make an additional gastronomic tour.
Stopping-off points: there are many in all the localities.

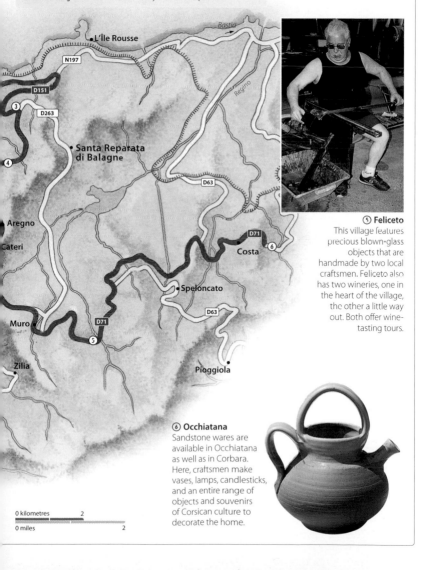

⑤ **Feliceto**
This village features precious blown-glass objects that are handmade by two local craftsmen. Feliceto also has two wineries, one in the heart of the village, the other a little way out. Both offer wine-tasting tours.

⑥ **Occhiatana**
Sandstone wares are available in Occhiatana as well as in Corbara. Here, craftsmen make vases, lamps, candlesticks, and an entire range of objects and souvenirs of Corsican culture to decorate the home.

0 kilometres 2
0 miles 2

㉕ Calvi

Situated on a rocky promontory, the 15th-century Genoese Citadelle dominates the yacht harbour and the promenade of Calvi. Massive bastions protect it on all four sides, three of which overlook the sea. In 1794, the Citadelle was bombarded by 30,000 cannon shots fired by the British fleet. Inside, there is a quiet atmosphere, which contrasts with the liveliness of the rest of the town. A series of alleys leads to the Palais des Gouverneurs Génois and the cathedral of St-Jean-Baptiste. The latter was almost destroyed in 1567, when an arsenal of gunpowder exploded. A walk along the ramparts, including the Tour de St-Antoine and the Teghiale and Malfetano bastions, offers magnificent views.

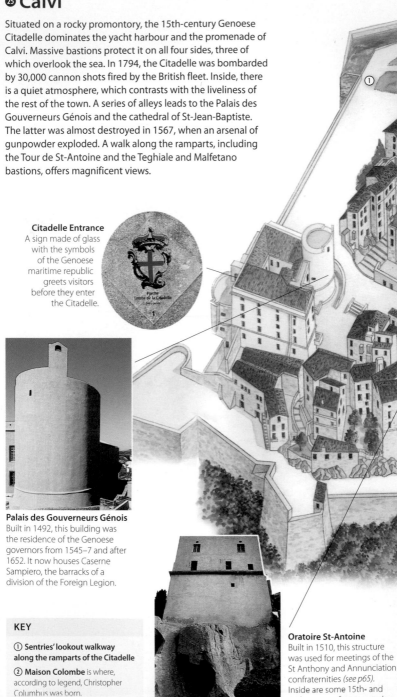

Citadelle Entrance
A sign made of glass with the symbols of the Genoese maritime republic greets visitors before they enter the Citadelle.

Palais des Gouverneurs Génois
Built in 1492, this building was the residence of the Genoese governors from 1545–7 and after 1652. It now houses Caserne Sampiero, the barracks of a division of the Foreign Legion.

KEY

① **Sentries' lookout walkway along the ramparts of the Citadelle**

② **Maison Colombe** is where, according to legend, Christopher Columbus was born.

③ **Teghiale Bastion**

Oratoire St-Antoine
Built in 1510, this structure was used for meetings of the St Anthony and Annunciation confraternities *(see p65)*. Inside are some 15th- and 16th-century frescoes and an ivory statue of Christ attributed to the Italian artist Sansovino.

VISITORS' CHECKLIST

Practical Information
Road map B2. ⚅ 5,600. ℹ 97
Port de Plaisance (04 95 65 16 67).
Maison Colombe: open by appt
(04 95 65 16 67). 🎭 La Granitula
(Holy Week); Corsica X-Tri (May);
Polyphonic Music (Sep); Festiventu
(Oct). 🆆 balagne-corsica.com

Transport
✈ Ste-Catherine, 4 km (2 miles)
(04 95 65 88 88). 🚍 🚉 Avenue
de la République (04 95 65 00 61).
⛴ from Marseille, Nice, Toulon
and Savona.

★ **St-Jean-Baptiste**
Calvi's cathedral *(see p84)*
houses a 15th-century ebony
crucifix known as *Christ des
Miracles*, and the *Virgin of
the Rosary*. Carried in
processions, she is
dressed differently for
each religious festival.

Holy Week

The Holy Week celebrations are among the most
fascinating and beautiful in Corsica. They begin
on Maundy Thursday in the church of Ste-Marie-
Majeure *(see p84)*, with the benediction of the
canistrelli (biscuits made from chestnut flour).
Another benediction of *canistrelli* takes place in
the Oratoire St-Antoine after a procession of
penitence by Calvi's two confraternities,
St Erasmus and St Anthony. On Good Friday
evening, the Granitula procession starts off from
St-Jean-Baptiste and winds through the streets
of the lower city and the Citadelle. Members of
the confraternities carry the statues of the *Christ
des Miracles* and the *Virgin of the Rosary*, who
is dressed in black. Some penitents follow the
procession barefoot, wearing a white habit
and carrying wooden crosses.

View from the Bastions
The impressive Citadelle walls and Tour de
St-Antoine overlook the yacht harbour and
the lower city.

The Holy Week Procession

Exploring Calvi

The capital of Balagne is one of the most beautiful seaside resorts in Corsica, partly because of its long beach. Calvi was founded by the Romans in the 1st century AD. From 1278 onwards, it was the main Genoese stronghold – the wealthy capital of the island governed by this maritime republic. It comprises the upper sector, the Citadelle with its centuries-old Genoese ramparts, and the lower town, with houses overlooking the harbour and the animated atmosphere typical of seaside resorts. Calvi claims to be the real birthplace of Christopher Columbus.

Sunbathers enjoying the white-sand beach paradise at Calvi

🏛 St-Jean-Baptiste

Perched in the centre of Calvi's towering citadel is the St-Jean-Baptiste cathedral, whose foundations date from the mid-13th century. Boasting a dramatic history, the original church burned down in 1481, was heavily damaged in a Turkish siege in 1553, and, just 14 years later, was virtually destroyed when a nearby gunpowder store exploded. In 1576, the cathedral was rebuilt in its present Greek cross form.

Stop in for a peek at the *Christ des Miracles*, the consecrated crucifix that sits to the right of the marble altar. During the 1553 siege, locals paraded through the streets carrying the ebony sculpture, which according to legend, caused the Turks to hastily abandon the city.

🏛 Place Christophe Colomb

At the foot of the Citadelle is a square linking the old and new towns, the ideal starting point for a walking tour of the city (partly thanks to the large car park). In the middle of the square is a bronze statue commemorating those who died in World War I, while a stone pays homage to the first battalion of the French Liberation Army, which liberated Corsica in 1943. A stairway descends to the Rue Clemenceau, a pedestrian precinct with restaurants and shops selling beach accessories.

The Calvi War Memorial

🏛 Ste-Marie-Majeure

Rue Clemenceau.
Open daily.
This rose-coloured church can be found on a small square next to Rue Clemenceau, in the heart of the lower city. Begun in 1765, with the bell tower added in 1838, it is Baroque in style, with a softly rounded dome. It houses some statues, including one of St Erasmus, the fishermen's patron saint who is popular here, and an *Assumption* that is carried through the city in a procession. The chapel in the choir has a 15th-century oil painting on leather from Cordoba.

Marina

The marina in Calvi is one of the loveliest in all Corsica, with luxury yachts berthed next to simple fishing craft and other small boats. The marina is the starting point for day-long boat tours of the west coast

that go to the Scandola Nature Reserve *(see pp108–9)*, the Calanques de Piana *(see pp104–5)*, continuing even as far as Ajaccio. Much of this coast, with its fascinating red granite rock formations, can be seen up close only from the sea.

The harbour also hosts the boats that belong to the diving centres. These take scuba divers to the best spots, such as those around the nearby Pointe Revellata promontory *(see p191)*, where short courses for beginners are available.

🏛 Quai Landry

This promenade, with its hotels, cafés and restaurants shaded by palm trees and colourful awnings, is the liveliest spot in Calvi. Many relaxing hours can be spent at one of the tables, enjoying a refreshing drink, watching the boats anchoring or setting off or observing the passers-by along the quay.

The lively Quai Landry, with Ste-Marie-Majeure in the background

For hotels and restaurants in this area see pp162–3 and pp172–4

Under the Citadelle at the end of the quay is the **Tour du Sel**, a medieval lookout post once used as a salt storehouse. Further along is the lighthouse, which dominates the entrance to the harbour.

🏖 The Beach

Calvi's beach is 4.5 km (3 miles) long, from the marina to the mouth of the Figarella river. It is bordered by a pine grove that was laid out in the 19th century, when the marshland was reclaimed. It has fine white sand and low dunes protected

The Chapelle de Notre-Dame-de-la-Serra, with views of the bay

View of the Pointe Revellata promontory, a popular site for divers

by fencing. The sea is shallow and free from rocks. Campsites and establishments offering deckchairs and other beach items can be found among the pines. It is also possible to swim and sunbathe off the rocks at the foot of the Citadelle.

Environs

About 4 km (2 miles) along the Ajaccio road leading south out of Calvi, there is a steep road on the left that climbs into the maquis among rocks sculpted by wind

erosion. From here, there is a fine view of the **Pointe Revellata** promontory, a scuba divers' paradise (see p191). The road ends at **Notre-Dame-de-la-Serra**, a 19th-century chapel built over the ruins of a 15th-century complex destroyed during the 1794 siege, when British and Corsican troops surrounded Calvi. This is a popular picnic spot. The terrace with the statue of Notre-Dame-de-la-Serra affords a fabulous view of the bay and the city below.

Calvi

① *Citadelle (see pp82–3)*
② St-Jean-Baptiste
③ Place Christophe Colomb
④ Ste-Marie-Majeure
⑤ Marina
⑥ Quai Landry
⑦ Beach

For keys to symbols see back flap

AJACCIO AND THE WEST COAST

A rugged, craggy coastline beaten by the wind, white sandy beaches and red granite cliffs: Corsica's west coast offers no end of grand, natural scenery. This stretch of land has three gulfs – Porto, Sagone and Ajaccio – that highlight the jagged nature of the western coastline, which is so different from the rather straight profile of eastern Corsica.

The Golfe de Porto has retained its wild beauty thanks to the regional nature reserve that protects the Scandola peninsula and the smaller Golfe de Girolata, which can be reached only on foot or by sea.

The sandy beaches of the gulfs of Ajaccio and Sagone have led to the creation of tourist facilities, which fortunately have not altered the beauty of the area. Most of this coastline can also be explored on foot by following the shrub-lined mule tracks that go to Girolata or traverse the rock formations of the Calanques, between Piana and Porto.

Just outside Ajaccio, there are other panoramic footpaths, ending opposite the Îles Sanguinaires and the beaches of Capo di Feno. The capital of Corse-du-Sud *(see p53)*, Ajaccio owes its foundation and prosperity to the Genoa Maritime Republic *(see pp45–9)*, but it is linked mostly to Napoleon Bonaparte, who was born here. Ajaccio jealously preserves Napoleon's memory: his name and effigy are everywhere to be seen in the city, on plaques, statues and souvenirs.

As well as a stunning coastline and some of the most interesting sea beds in the Mediterranean, Corsica offers valleys full of olive, pine and chestnut trees. Some mountain villages have maintained their old pastoral traditions, linked to wild-pig breeding and the exploitation of the woods. The rivers have created deep and spectacular canyons, such as the Gorges de Spelunca at Evisa and the Gorges du Prunelli near Bastelica. On the old stone bridges, the sounds of sheep and mules have been replaced by those of hikers on the panoramic *Mare a Mare* (Sea to Sea) and *Mare e Monti* (Sea and Mountains) paths.

The Genoese tower, dominating the Golfe de Porto, still seeming to be defending the city

◄ Typical rock formations and shrub vegetation at the Calanques de Piana

Exploring Ajaccio and the West Coast

The west coast of Corsica, with the gulfs of Porto, Sagone and Ajaccio, offers spectacular marine landscapes, from the porphyry cliffs in the Scandola Nature Reserve *(see pp108–9)* to the white beaches of Porticcio. Apart from Ajaccio, with its museums and stylish streets, the most interesting sights in western Corsica are nature-based. Some of them are part of the Parc Naturel Régional de la Corse *(see p103)*: Evisa and the Forêt d'Aïtone, the Vallée du Fango, the Gorges de Spelunca, the Calanques de Piana, the Gorges du Prunelli and the Golfe de Girolata. This area is ideal for hiking, especially the region around Porto, which offers numerous waymarked routes of varying degrees of difficulty.

Plage de Verghia, a cove with a sandy beach and transparent sea in the Golfe d'Ajaccio

Key

— Major road
═ Minor road
--- Hiking trail
— Scenic route
— Main railway
✕ Mountain pass

A natural arch of typical red rock in the Scandola Nature Reserve

For additional map symbols *see back flap*

0 kilometres 10
0 miles 5

Sights at a Glance

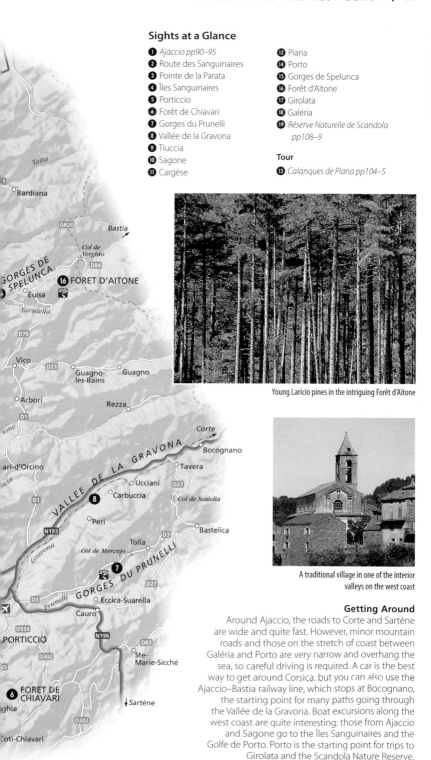

Young Laricio pines in the intriguing Forêt d'Aïtone

A traditional village in one of the interior valleys on the west coast

Getting Around

Around Ajaccio, the roads to Corte and Sartène are wide and quite fast. However, minor mountain roads and those on the stretch of coast between Galéria and Porto are very narrow and overhang the sea, so careful driving is required. A car is the best way to get around Corsica, but you can also use the Ajaccio–Bastia railway line, which stops at Bocognano, the starting point for many paths going through the Vallée de la Gravona. Boat excursions along the west coast are quite interesting: those from Ajaccio and Sagone go to the Îles Sanguinaires and the Golfe de Porto. Porto is the starting point for trips to Girolata and the Scandola Nature Reserve.

❶ Ajaccio

The largest city in Corsica, as well as the island's political centre, Ajaccio has a typically Mediterranean look. It is divided into three sectors: the old Genoese town, with its narrow streets and houses with pastel-coloured façades; the modern city, with tree-lined avenues and outdoor cafés; and the outskirts, which extend up to the hills and offer a marvellous view of the gulf, dominated by the Citadelle. A Roman settlement during the Imperial Age, Ajaccio began to develop in 1492 thanks to the Genoese. In 1553, the city was conquered by Sampiero Corso *(see p49)* for the French, but in 1559 it was returned to the Genoese as part of the treaty of Cateau-Cambresis. Under Genoa, Ajaccio prospered, thanks to commerce, agriculture and coral fishing, but not until 1592 were the locals granted the right to live here. In 1723, the city became the capital of West Corsica. Ajaccio is famous because Napoleon Bonaparte was born here on 15 August 1769.

The Tino Rossi harbour, bordered by the Jetée de la Citadelle

🎥 Citadelle

Closed to the public.
The construction of the Citadelle, on a rocky spur jutting over the sea, began in 1554, by order of the French Marshal de Thermes, and was completed by the Genoese in 1559. The building faces the innermost part of the gulf and overlooks the Jetée de la Citadelle, a jetty that encloses the Tino Rossi harbour. With its sentry walkways, walls and ramparts, the Citadelle towers over the old Genoese quarter.

As a military zone, the Citadelle is not open to the public, but its majestic profile can be admired from the beach, from the breakwater or from Boulevard Danielle Casanova,

named after the Ajaccio-born French-Resistance heroine who died in Auschwitz in 1943.

🏛 Ajaccio Cathedral

Rue Forcioli-Conti. **Tel** 04 95 21 07 67.
Open 8–11:30am & 2:30–5:45pm Mon–Sat.
Dedicated to the Virgin Mary, the cathedral of Ajaccio was built in 1582–93 by Giacomo della Porta in Venetian Renaissance style, but has Baroque elements. The simple façade contrasts with the lavish interior, which features polychrome marble and gilded decoration. In July 1771, when he was almost two, Napoleon was baptized at the font.

The first chapel on the left has a painting by Eugène Delacroix,

the *Madonna of the Sacred Heart*. The next chapel, dedicated to Our Lady of Mercy, the patron saint of Ajaccio (celebrated on 18 March, *see p36*), contains an impressive 18th-century statue of the Virgin Mary. The high altar, made of white marble with black tortile columns, was donated to the cathedral in 1811 by Elisa Bacciochi, Napoleon's sister and princess of Lucca and Piombino.

🏛 St-Erasme

Rue Forcioli-Conti.
Founded in 1617 as the chapel of the Jesuit College, St-Erasme later became the chapel of the Royal College. During the French Revolution, the church was closed to the public and turned into a city office. In 1815, it was reconsecrated and dedicated to the sailors' patron saint, Erasmus. Inside are model ships, three processional crosses and a statue of St Erasmus with angels. On 2 June, the statue is carried in a procession down to the seaside.

🏚 Rue Bonaparte

This street was the old *carrugio dritto* (straight alley) of the Genoese city, inhabited by merchants and leading citizens. During Genoese rule, Rue Bonaparte divided Ajaccio into two quarters: to the north was the Macello, where the poor lived, and to the south was the area of the upper middle classes. Today, this is a pleasant, lively street with antique shops and boutiques catering to all tastes.

The simple façade of Ajaccio Cathedral, built in Venetian Renaissance style

The study of Napoleon's father, furnished in the style of a bedroom of the late 1700s

🏛 Maison Bonaparte Museum

Rue St-Charles. **Tel** 04 95 21 43 89. **Open** Tue–Sun. **Closed** 1 Jan, 25 Dec. 🅿 📷 📹 **w** **musees-nationaux-malmaison.fr**

The house that belonged to the Bonaparte family from 1682, and where Napoleon was born, features an austere façade overlooking the small, tree-lined Place Letizia, where there is a bust of the emperor's son.

In 1793, Napoleon and his family were forced to flee the house (through a trap door) by supporters of Pascal Paoli *(see pp50–51)*. The Paolist mob was seeking revenge because Napoleon (then an officer in the French army) had ordered his troops to fire at a local rally. The house was then impounded by the British (1794–6) and partly used as an arsenal. In 1797, Napoleon's mother, Letizia, returned to Ajaccio and obtained compensation to refurbish the house. Maison Bonaparte is now a state-managed museum illustrating the turbulent history of the Bonaparte family. A modern-day restoration has revealed Second Empire artworks under layers of wallpaper.

🏛 Place Foch

The true heart of Ajaccio, this square is lined with cafés with tables outside in the shade of the palm and plane trees. Formerly called Piazza Porta, it used to be the only gate to the Citadelle. Place Foch has a marble statue of Napoleon as First Consul, in the middle of the Four Lions Fountain, which was sculpted by Jérôme Maglioli. Due to the restoration of the market square, Place Foch is currently home to Ajaccio's farmers' market.

Marble bust of Napoleon

Ajaccio City Centre

① Citadelle
② Ajaccio Cathedral
③ St-Erasme
④ Rue Bonaparte
⑤ Maison Bonaparte
⑥ Place Foch
⑦ Salon Napoléonien
⑧ Marina
⑨ Boulevard du Roi Jérôme
⑩ Cours Napoléon
⑪ Chapelle Impériale
⑫ *Palais Fesch – Musée des Beaux-Arts pp94–5*
⑬ Bibliothèque Patrimoniale (City Library)

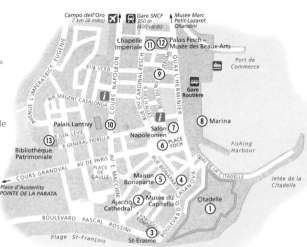

0 metres 400
0 yards 400

Exploring Ajaccio

Ajaccio is a relatively small town and can easily be explored on foot. One of its main thoroughfares, Rue Cardinal Fesch, is a pedestrianized area with craft shops and boutiques. In Cours Napoléon and along the seafront, on the Quai Napoléon and Quai l'Herminier, it is quite enjoyable to sit at one of the outdoor cafés and watch the world pass by. Ajaccio can also be discovered by *Petit Train (see p184)*. It leaves from Place Foch for a tour of the city (45 mins) or goes to the Pointe de la Parata (90 mins).

The *Petit Train* leaving Place Foch for a tour of the city

🏛 Salon Napoléonien
Place Foch. **Tel** 04 95 51 52 53.
Open Mon–Fri (summer: daily).
Closed public hols. 🖼

Housed on the first floor of the town hall (Hôtel de Ville), the rooms of the Napoleonic Museum are accessed via a grand staircase. The museum displays documents and paintings relating to the life of Napoleon and his family. In the Grand Salon, under the large Bohemian crystal chandelier donated for the 200th anniversary of the birth of Napoleon, there are large portraits of the family and several busts, including one of Napoleon's mother, Letizia. A painting by Domenico Frassati celebrates the *Glory of the Emperor* (1840). Other interesting items are Napoleon's baptism certificate and a replica of his bronze death mask. The Hall of Medals features a fine collection of coins and gold, silver and bronze medals.

First Consul Bonaparte,
detail

🚢 Marina
At the foot of the Citadelle, a long breakwater protects this harbour from the west wind. Next to the passenger terminal of the port, where the large ferries land, are the yacht harbour and the fishermen's port, with many brightly coloured boats filled with fishing nets. Every morning from 7am, in the open space in front of Place Foch, there is an animated market offering fresh fish. This quay is also the departure point for the boats taking visitors on excursions to the Îles Sanguinaires, the Golfe de Porto and Porticcio.

🏛 Boulevard du Roi Jérôme
Lined with hotels and restaurants, this boulevard is a favourite with locals, who gather here to have a *pastis* or play a game of *pétanque*. Every morning, the area behind the town hall facing the sea becomes a colourful open

market offering typical Corsican products: *brocciu* cheese, *lonzu* (smoked fillet of pork), *coppa* (pork neck), *prizuttu* (cured ham), pâtés, honey, fig jam and myrtle liqueur. Vegetables and flowers also fill the market with their scents and colours.

The hubbub and gaiety invade the adjacent streets, as well as the pedestrianized Rue Cardinal Fesch, once the main thoroughfare in the Genoese quarter, which from the 16th century onwards grew outside the city walls. Halfway down this street is the Palais Fesch, built by Cardinal Fesch, one of Napoleon's uncles, in 1827–37 and now a museum containing part of his huge fine art collection *(see pp94–5)*.

🏛 Cours Napoléon
The main street in Ajaccio crosses the city from northeast to southwest. It is intersected by smaller streets that go down to the sea or up to the hills. Cours Napoléon is lined with cinemas, shops, banks and cafés, including the famous Café Napoléon, built in 1821 by the architect Carrayol. Towards the railway station, the street becomes wider, forming Place Abbatucci, which was once the border between the old town and the countryside.

About halfway down Cours Napoléon is the Chapelle de St-Roch, built in the late 1800s,

Typical Corsican products for sale on Boulevard du Roi Jérôme

Detail of the statue of Napoleon on horseback in Roman dress

while towards the southern end of the street is the **Palais Lantivy**, now home to the prefecture and the General Council. The street ends at Place de Gaulle, a large square dominated by a statue of Napoleon in the guise of a Roman emperor on horseback, surrounded by his four brothers.

🔼 Chapelle Impériale
50 Rue du Cardinal Fesch.
Tel 04 95 26 26 26. **Open** call for details. 🅿

In 1857, Emperor Napoleon III had Cardinal Fesch's palace restored by the architects Corona, Casanova and Paccard; the project was completed in 1860. Napoleon III decided to use the right-hand wing as a chapel to house the remains of the nine members of the Bonaparte family, including Napoleon I's parents – Carlo Bonaparte and Letizia Ramolino (Napoleon's tomb is in Les Invalides, Paris), and Cardinal Fesch himself. The sober Renaissance exterior is made of light St-Florent limestone.

Inside, the trompe-l'oeil dome was painted by the Ajaccio-born architect Jérôme Maglioli, and is decorated with the cardinal's insignias, which are also on the stained-glass windows. On the high altar is a gold crucifix that Napoleon gave to his mother when he returned from his campaign in Egypt. The remains of the ten family members are all in the round crypt under the dome.

🏛 Palais Fesch – Musée des Beaux-Arts
See pp94–5.

📖 Bibliothèque Patrimoniale
50 Rue Cardinal Fesch.
Tel 04 95 51 13 0. **Open** 10am–noon & 2–7pm Tue–Fri, 2–6pm Sat
W bibliotheque.ajaccio.fr

The brainchild of Lucien Bonaparte (Napoleon's younger brother), this listed library and monument was founded in 1801 and inaugurated in the Palais Fesch in 1868. Alongside its stunning 30 m (98 ft) long and 10 m (32 ft) high reading room, the library contains 40,000 volumes, including 29 incunabula, alongside rare historical, medical and theological books. The oldest manuscript is a didactic poem from the Norman poet Gace de la Bigne, dating from c. 1379.

The library is currently undergoing a conservation project, which aims to protect more than 18,000 ancient books. Some 100,000 pages of their oldest collections are now digitally available, enabling members of the public to enjoy them without damaging the precious texts.

📖 Place d'Austerlitz
At the western end of Place Foch begins Cours Grandval, a street running parallel to the sea in the direction of the Pointe de la Parata *(see p96)*. Cours Grandval ultimately leads to Place d'Austerlitz, a square dominated by an imposing structure, known as U Casone, which features a statue of Napoleon. Preceded by two eagles and a stone that commemorates his victories and exploits, this monument represents the emperor in a riding coat and wearing his famous two-cornered hat as he looks towards Ajaccio, his native town.

To the left of U Casone is the cave where, according to one legend, Napoleon pretended he was an emperor when he was a child. Every year, around 15 August, his birthday, Ajaccio commemorates Napoleon's imperial period with impressive parades in period costumes *(see pp37–8)* during the lively *Journées Napoléoniennes*.

📖 Musée Marc Petit–Lazaret Ollandini
Route d'Aspretto 20090.
Tel 04 95 10 85 15. **Open** Mon–Thu (summer: also Sat pm).
🅿 **W** lelazaret-ollandini.fr

Built in the mid-1800s, the Lazaret originally served as the quarantine for the port of Ajaccio. It was classified as a national historic monument in 1977, and opened to the public as a museum in 2008. The museum houses 32 large-scale sculptures by Marc Petit in its permanent collection, as well as other drawings and sculptural works. The building is also open for cultural events throughout wthe year.

The monument to Napoleon in Place d'Austerlitz

Palais Fesch – Musée des Beaux-Arts

Cardinal Fesch, Napoleon's uncle, had this palace built between 1827 and 1860. He dedicated three wings to housing works of art, which were donated to the city when he died, in 1839. The main building has the most important collection of Italian paintings in France after the Louvre, as well as works by Spanish, Flemish and Dutch artists. The second floor contains 13th–17th-century Italian paintings, including many depictions of the Virgin Mary and Child and a fine collection of still lifes. On the first floor are works dating from the 17th and 18th centuries. The ground floor is given over to Napoleon, with statues, paintings and various other objects bearing his image, as well as temporary exhibitions. The basement contains modern Corsican art. The left wing houses the City Library, founded by Napoleon's brother Lucien.

Holy Family
This detail of a painting by 17th-century Italian artist Benedetto Gennari shows the attention he paid to minutiae.

The Grande Galerie contains large-scale Italian paintings.

Jesus and the Samaritan
This work is by Étienne Parrocel, an 18th-century French artist. Above is a detail of the Samaritan.

Cardinal Fesch

Cardinal Fesch

Joseph Fesch (1763–1839) was Napoleon's uncle, but he was only six years older than the emperor. He was the archdeacon of Ajaccio and archbishop of Lyon. In 1803, he became a cardinal and moved to Rome, where he collected 16,000 works of art; some of these are on display in the museum, while others were donated to many churches in Corsica. However, the main part of the collections, including the masterpieces, were sold in Paris, Rome and London after his death. It was thanks to his diplomatic intervention that Pope Pius VII agreed to go to Paris in 1804 to crown Napoleon emperor. In 1811, Fesch fell into disgrace for siding with the Church in the conflict between the Pope and Napoleon.

The collection of Italian Renaissance paintings is the core of the museum.

★ Virgin Mary and Child with Angel
This early masterpiece by the Italian artist Sandro Botticelli (1445–1510) is one of the loveliest works in the museum. It is innovative from an iconographic point of view because the Virgin is standing, and also because of her open display of affection.

★ **Portrait of a Man with a Glove**
This work by Titian (1485–1576), depicting an unknown Venetian aristocrat, is the twin of a portrait kept in the Louvre, Paris.

VISITORS' CHECKLIST

Practical Information
50–52 Rue du Cardinal Fesch.
Tel 04 95 26 26 26. **Open** May–Sep: Wed–Mon; Oct–Apr: Mon, Wed–Sat; 3rd Sun of month.
Closed Tue & national holidays. Note that as a result of the renovation of the museum, some works of art may have moved rooms or may not be available to view. 🅿 📷 ♿ 🅦 **musée-fesch.com**

Second floor

First floor

Landscape
Matthijs Brill, a late 16th-century Flemish painter, makes surprising and refreshing use of cool colours highlighted by brilliant ochre hues. His works helped to revolutionize landscape painting.

Visitors' entrance to the museum

The Chapelle Impériale
(see p93) occupies the right wing of the palace.

Visitors' entrance to the Chapelle Impériale

The statue of Cardinal Fesch in the museum's court of honour is by Vital-Dubray.

Entrance from Rue Fesch

The City Library is on the ground and first floors in the left wing of the complex.

Entrance to the Library

Key

- ▨ Italian "Primitive" and early Renaissance paintings
- ☐ Florentine paintings
- ▨ Venetian paintings
- ☐ Paintings from the end of the 16th century
- ▨ Bolognese paintings
- ▨ Paintings from the School of Caravaggio
- ▨ Roman 17th-century paintings
- ☐ Paintings from the School of Giaquinto
- ☐ Italian 18th-century paintings
- ▨ Temporary exhibitions

One of the many beaches on the Route des Sanguinaires

❷ Route des Sanguinaires

Road map B4. **i** 3 Boulevard du Roi Jérôme, Ajaccio (04 95 51 53 03).
w ajaccio-tourisme.com

This panoramic road, the D111, runs along the northern shore of the Golfe d'Ajaccio, passing by the locals' favourite sandy beaches. There are also many cafés and restaurants with terraces from where it is possible to admire the cormorants in flight and, with a bit of luck, see dolphins playing.

As well as by car or bicycle, this coastline can be explored by bus or by the *Petit Train* (departure from Place Foch in Ajaccio, *see p92*).

The coastal route begins at Boulevard Lantivy and continues along Plage St-François, the most central beach in Ajaccio, at the foot of the walls of the Citadelle. It then proceeds along Boulevard Pascal Rossini, where every Sunday from 8am to noon there is a colourful flea market in front of the Fesch Lyceum, with second-hand objects and antiques.

The road continues through residential quarters, which offer a view

of the gulf and are surrounded by lush Mediterranean gardens.

At the edge of the city, at Place Emmanuel-Arène, is the **Chapelle des Grecs**, a small Greek Orthodox church built in 1632 and used by the Greek community that had fled from the Peloponnese seeking political asylum. Not far from the main road is the cemetery, with Baroque and Neo-Classical chapels.

Some 5 km (3 miles) from the heart of town, the road skirts the beaches of Scudo, with bathing facilities and restaurants, the beautiful Marinella cove, and Vignola beach. The latter also marks the end of the **Chemin des Crêtes**, a popular, easy-to-follow ridge path with a superb view of the gulf. Waymarked with spots of paint, it starts in the centre of Ajaccio, at Bois des Anglais, behind Place d'Austerlitz (*see p93*), and takes about three hours. The number five bus travels back into town.

❸ Pointe de la Parata

Road map B4. 🚌 from Place de Gaulle, Ajaccio. **i** 3 Boulevard du Roi Jérôme, Ajaccio (04 95 51 53 03).
w ajaccio-tourisme.com

A black granite headland, the Pointe de la Parata makes for a dramatic end to the D111 road. The cape is dominated by the **Tour de la Parata**, a tower built by the Genoese in 1608 to defend the island from pirate raids. A path leads to the end of the cape (about 30 minutes there and back). From here, the view of the red Îles Sanguinaires is grandiose, especially at sunset. Another, longer route

starts about 500 m (1,600 ft) before the restaurant at the Pointe de la Parata. Once on the far side of the headland, a path winds through tall maquis to a lovely beach at Anse de Minaccia (90 mins), also accessible via the D111-B road from Ajaccio. From here, it is possible to continue to windswept Capo di Feno, with its Genoese watchtower (60 mins).

❹ Îles Sanguinaires

Road map B4. 🚤 from Ajaccio. **i** 3 Boulevard du Roi Jérôme, Ajaccio (04 95 51 53 03).
w ajaccio-tourisme.com

The red rock seems to have been the reason behind the name ("sanguinary") of the maquis-covered cliffs that emerge from the sea a short distance from the Pointe de la Parata. However, because the islands mark the southern border of the Golfe de Sagone, some people claim that the name derives from the Latin *Sagonares Insulae*, or Islands of the Gulf of Sagone.

The largest of the islands is the Grande Sanguinaire, also called Mezzumare. There is a lighthouse, built in 1840, as well as the ruins of the Genoese tower and a leprosy hospital. In spring, this island is clad in white thanks to Montpellier rockrose in bloom. The Grande Sanguinaire is home to cormorants, herring gulls and other birds.

In 1863, the French author Alphonse Daudet lived in the lighthouse. He described the Sanguinaires as wild islands populated by wild goats, Corsican ponies and an osprey.

The other three islands are very small, little more than cliffs emerging from the sea.

The rocky terrain of the Îles Sanguinaires

The long beach at Porticcio, with its fine white sand

❺ Porticcio

Road map B4. 🏔 320. 🚌 from Ajaccio. 🚌 *i* Les Echappes, BP 125 (04 95 25 10 09).

Just opposite Ajaccio, on the southern coastline of the gulf, is Porticcio. This resort is filled with hotels, residential complexes and lovely beaches with fine sand and facilities for water sports, from sailing to diving.

The beach with the best facilities is **La Viva**, while the most spectacular are **Agosta** and **Ruppione**, separated by the Isolella peninsula, which has coves with turquoise water.

On the headland is an old Genoese tower called Tour de l'Isolella. Another tower, Tour de Castagna, is further south, at Punta di a Castagna. Built in 1584, it is now off limits, since it stands in a military zone. The headland can be reached by taking the D55 road, past the Port de Chiavari and the little Portigliolo cove. From here are fine views of the Golfe d'Ajaccio and of Île Piana, a maquis-covered island.

❻ Forêt de Chiavari

Road map B5. *i* Parc Naturel Régional de la Corse, 2 Rue Major Lambroschini, Ajaccio (04 95 51 79 00/08).

The large Forêt de Chiavari extends for 18 sq km (7 sq miles), from the coast to an altitude of about 600 m (1,970 ft) on top of the hills separating the Golfe d'Ajaccio from the Golfe de Valinco. The forest consists

mainly of holm oaks, eucalyptus (imported from Australia in the 19th century to reclaim the land and help eliminate malaria), maritime pine and shrubs such as strawberry trees, mastic trees, ruscus and thyme. It also has many footpaths and mountain-bike paths of all levels of difficulty and for all tastes. One of the most pleasant is the Sentier de Myrte ("Myrtle Path"), which starts and ends at Plage de Verghia, a beach with a café.

At 485 m (1,600 ft), perched on a hill at the edge of the forest, is the hamlet of **Côti-Chiavari**, with a tree-lined terrace offering a splendid panoramic view of the gulf. Destroyed in the 16th century by

Barbary pirates, this village was repopulated in 1713, when the Genoese government decided to transfer here the inhabitants of Chiavari, a locality in the Gulf of Tigullio, in Liguria, hence the name.

Not far from Côti-Chiavari, there are interesting viewpoints that take in both sides of the surrounding hills and the two large gulfs on the west coast, Golfe d'Ajaccio and Golfe de Valinco.

On the narrow D55 road that leads up to Côti-Chiavari from Verghia is the old agricultural penal colony that was constructed in 1855. The mortality rate of the prisoners who worked the land here was very high because of malaria and the unhealthy climate. The prison was therefore abandoned in 1906 and the inmates were transferred to Cayenne.

A village at the edge of the Forêt de Chiavari

The Coastline Towers

As well as the fortified cities that defended their ports, the Genoese rulers left another symbol in Corsica: the series of 67 coastline towers that were constructed in the early 16th century along the entire perimeter of the island. Built to spot pirates and, in some cases, to afford refuge for the populations of the small seaside villages, these towers are either square or round and their size differs to quite an extent. Some, such as the towers of Girolata (*see p107*) or Campomoro (*see p132*), were the centres of true fortresses, while in other cases the towers were merely outposts built on sites that could easily be seen from the villages or from the neighbouring towers. Normally, a tower contained storehouses and a cistern to collect rainwater, since sources of drinkable water were very scarce so close to the sea.

Round watchtower

The interior of the Catholic church of Cargèse ▶

❼ Gorges du Prunelli

Road map C4. **ℹ** Parc Naturel Régional de la Corse, 2 Rue Major Lambroschini, Ajaccio (04 95 51 79 00/08). **W** parc-corse.org

The Prunelli torrent flows from Monte Renoso, which stands 2,352 m (7,716 ft) high, to the Golfe d'Ajaccio. The torrent has carved a deep canyon, or gorge, partly irrigated by the water from an artificial lake created by a dam.

From Ajaccio, the D3 twists along the north bank of the torrent. At the village of **Eccica-Suarella**, a stone commemorates the site where Sampiero Corso, the enemy of Genoa in the 16th century (*see p49*), was killed.

A little further along the D3, at the pass of **Col de Mercuju**, 716 m (2,349 ft) above sea level, a path begins. It leads to a belvedere with great views.

Overlooking the lake is **Tolla**, a small village surrounded by orchards. From here, the road joins the D27 leading up to **Bastelica**. This hamlet on the slopes of Monte Renoso is known for its wild-pig charcuterie and for being the birthplace of Sampiero Corso. The national hero is portrayed in a bronze statue in front of the parish church. The house he was born in is in Dominacci, a nearby hamlet.

If driving back towards Ajaccio, it is possible to

Convolvolus berries

follow the D27 along the south side of the gorge. Here, between Col de Cricheto and Col de Marcuggio, is the **Forêt de Pineta**, with pine, beech and chestnut trees. A footpath descends from the road towards the Èse torrent and the Genoese bridge of Zipitoli.

Environs
Continuing north from Bastelica, the D27 first ascends to Col de Scalella, then descends to Tavera, a village in the Vallée de la Gravona. Another panoramic road from Bastelica is the D27-A, leading southeast to the Val d'Èse ski resort, 1,700 m (5,577 ft) above sea level.

❽ Vallée de la Gravona

Road map C4. **ℹ** Parc Naturel Régional de la Corse, 2 Rue Major Lambroschini, Ajaccio (04 95 51 79 00/08). **W** parc-corse.org

This wide valley is traversed by the N193 highway, one of Corsica's main roads, which leads to Corte and Bastia. Parallel to the N193, but further up on the slopes, are the winding and panoramic roads leading to the villages of **Peri**, **Carbuccia**, **Ucciani** and **Tavera**, on the south side of the Vallée de la Gravona.

At the hamlet of Carbuccia is **A Cupulatta**, a reserve for 166 species of tortoise and the largest of its kind in Europe. **Bocognano**, the main village in the valley, lies at the foot of Monte d'Oro and is surrounded by chestnut trees. The village marks the start of many paths. The most popular begins 4 km (2 miles) southwest of the village, down the D27, and leads to the Cascade du Voile de la Mariée ("Bride's Veil Falls").

The beautiful coves and beaches en route to Tiuccia

❾ Tiuccia

Road map B4. **⛰** 150. **🚌** **ℹ** BP 05, Sagone (04 95 28 05 36). **W** golfdesagone.net

On the Golfe de Liscia, between the Genoese towers of Ancone and Capigliolo, is Tiuccia. This small seaside resort is dominated by the ruins of the Capraja Castle, which once belonged to the Counts de la Cinarca. In the 13th–16th centuries, this family resisted Genoese rule and established its hold over the south of the island.

The mouths of the Liscia river and, further north along the coast, of the Liamone river have created long, sandy beaches surrounded by hills covered in maquis. These secluded beaches and coves can be reached via the Ancone footpath along the coast.

Tiuccia is also the starting point for boat excursions towards Girolata (*see p107*), the Calanques de Piana (*see pp104–5*) and Capo Rosso.

Environs
The valley of the river Liscia forms **La Cinarca**, a fertile area covered with woods, olive and orange trees and vineyards. Livestock raising is the main activity here. At an altitude of 400–600 m (1,300–2,000 ft) are villages with splendid views of the coast, such as Sari d'Orcino and Calcatoggio.

This area was once the home of some famous bandits, including Spada, also known as "the Tiger of Cinarca".

The dam at Gorges du Prunelli

Corsican Charcuterie and Cheeses

The gastronomic products *prisuttu* (cured ham), *lonzu* (smoked pork fillet), *coppa* (smoked pork shoulder) and *figatellu* (smoked liver sausage) are typical of Corsica. They are prepared by hand and smoked on the *fucone,* an open fireplace that burns chestnut wood and grapevine stumps. The wild pigs used for these products are allowed to roam freely, a factor reflected in the meats' unique flavour. Other typical products are cheeses made of goat and sheep's milk. They are named after their areas of production, such as Niolo, Balaninu, Orezzincu, Bastelicaccia and Venaco. Niolo is one of the best-known strong, aged cheeses. Usually, cheese is eaten with fig preserves and nuts. *See also pp168–9.*

Sheep can be found almost anywhere, especially in upper Corsica. Their milk is used to make a variety of cheeses, including *brocciu* and *toma*. Goats are common above all in the Balagne and Castagniccia regions.

There are about 45,000 wild pigs in Corsica. They live in woods along the roads, feeding on chestnuts, acorns and aromatic herbs that give their meats a special flavour.

Salsiccia

Partly aged cheeses

Goat's milk cheese

Lonzu

Cheese with herbs

Fresh herbs

Lonzu is raw pork fillet rolled with salt and pepper, tied into thick sausages and smoked.

Corsican Flavours
In tourist resorts, there is no shortage of delicatessens selling gift baskets filled with tempting food items. But produce can also be purchased directly from the farmers.

Prisuttu is a very savoury cured ham. It is best when it is cut by hand in thick, compact slices, so that its taste can be enjoyed to the full.

Brocciu is a ewe's- or goat's-milk cheese similar to ricotta, prepared with whey and heated milk. It can be fresh or salted to last longer. Since 1983, its trademark has been registered.

Boats moored in the Golfe de Sagone

❿ Sagone

Road map B4. 🏔 250. 🚌
ℹ️ BP 05 (04 95 28 05 36).
🌐 golfedesagone.net

The wide Golfe de Sagone, between Punta di Cargèse to the north and Capo di Feno to the south, has long, sandy beaches formed by the silt carried by the Liamone, Sagone and Liscia rivers.

The small village of Sagone was once a major Roman city and owed its prosperity to timber from the Forêt d'Aïtone. In the 6th century AD, it became a bishopric, and, in the 11th century, the cathedral of **Sant'Appiano** was built near the port. Its ruins can still be seen there. In the Middle Ages, however, the town declined because of malaria from the stagnant river water.

Thanks to land reclamation, Sagone is now a pleasant seaside resort. Among the activities on offer are sailing, scuba diving and boat trips to Scandola and Girolata.

Environs
A beautiful 15-km (9-mile) road goes up the Liamone river valley to **Vico**, a large, hilly village with narrow houses packed around two squares. Until the 18th century, Vico was the residence of the bishops of Sagone.

The church of the Couvent St-François has a lovely wooden crucifix; sculpted in the 15th century, it is considered one of the oldest in Corsica.

The road continues through lush vegetation to **Guagno Les Bains**, a tiny spa with two springs: the Occhiu (37°C/98.6°F),

Sign for the spa of Guagno Les Bains

which is used to cure eye and throat ailments, and the Venturini spring (52°C/125.6°F), used by those afflicted by sciatica, rheumatism and obesity. Among the illustrious guests at this spa were Pascal Paoli and Napoleon's mother, Letizia. Further along the road is the village of Soccia, the starting point for a footpath to the **Lac de Creno**, a lake surrounded by Laricio pines (2 hours return trip).

⓫ Cargèse

Road map B3. 🏔 1,300. ℹ️ Rue Dr Dragacci (04 95 26 41 31).
🎭 Byzantine countryside blessing and procession (Easter Monday).
🌐 cargese.net

In the mid-17th century, a group of Greek families that had fled from the Peloponnese following the Turkish invasion asked the Genoese for political asylum. First they settled at Paomia, 50 km (31 miles) from Ajaccio, and then at Cargèse, where they were allowed to retain their traditions and religion. To this

day, this village, which is about 100 m (330 ft) above sea level, reflects its Greek history. Two churches, both from the 19th century, stand opposite each other: a Greek-Orthodox church, with Byzantine-style icons and a 13th-century double-sided panel of the *Deposition of Christ*; and a Latin church, with a Neo-Classical interior. The terraces of both offer fine views of the gulf.

⓬ Piana

Road map B3. 🏔 500. 🚌 ℹ️ Place de la Mairie (09 66 92 84 42). 🎭 Broddiu Day (Apr). 🌐 otpiana.com

With its white houses, large Baroque church and the granite formations of the Calanques in the background, Piana occupies a panoramic position overlooking the Golfe de Porto. Often called 'Plus beaux villages de France', the village is the ideal base for excursions along this stretch of coastline, which has many beaches and is one of the most fascinating in Corsica.

Among the beaches is the **Anse de Ficajola**, situated among red rocks at the end of a winding road descending to the sea. The panoramic D824 road leads to **Plage d'Arone**, a pretty, undeveloped beach surrounded by maquis.

A difficult hike (4 hours return trip) from the roadside 2 km (1 mile) above the beach leads to **Capo Rosso** and the Tour de Turghiu, which, from its position 300 m (1,000 ft) above sea level, offers a great view of the area.

Panoramic view of Piana, surrounded by forest

Parc Naturel Régional de la Corse

With a surface area of 3,300 sq km (1,274 sq miles) and 143 towns, this park occupies nearly two thirds of Corsica, including the peaks of Monte Cinto, Rotondo, d'Oro, Renoso and Incudine, up to the Aiguilles de Bavella and the Massif de l'Ospédale. The park was founded in 1972 to support the mountain economy and protect the island's natural wonders: its forests (Aïtone, Valdu-Niellu, Vizzavona, Bavella and Ospédale), its rugged gorges (Spelunca, Restonica, l'Asco), the Calanques, and lakes such as Creno and Nino. The park is traversed by all the main hiking paths, including the GR20 long-distance path *(see pp26–31).*

Cork oak is one of the most widespread species of trees in Corsica and is protected in the park.

Locator Map
■ *The park area*

Elderly Corsican women are often dressed in black clothes.

Wheel to untangle the wool

The wheel is fastened to a chair

Traditions and Nature

The Parc Naturel Régional was established not only to protect the Corsican flora and fauna, but also to safeguard the traditional activities of the hill and mountain environments. Most of the inhabitants in the park area are people whose families have lived and worked here for centuries and have forged the region's history and traditions.

The Gorges de l'Asco are a stunning example of the many deep canyons created by the rivers that flow from inland Corsica to the sea.

The donkey is one of the many domesticated or semi-domesticated animals linked to the economic activities of mountain life.

This bergerie at Cagna exemplifies mountain architecture. *Bergeries* are used in the summer for transhumance (the movement of livestock). In 1973–8, Father Doazan wrote about 20 notebooks describing this activity and the life of Corsican shepherds.

⓭ Tour of the Calanques de Piana

The granitic rock formations known as the Calanques de Piana feature sensational colour changes from gold to pink to bright red depending on the time of day. The wind and water have sculpted the granitic rock, creating awesome cavities, known as *tafoni*, and intriguing formations. Although it is possible to cover this whole route in half a day, or a full day with a lunch break, it might be more relaxing to explore the Calanques in the course of two separate walks, especially during the hottest period of the year. For those who are driving, this stretch of the D81 road is at its most beautiful and impressive at sunset.

① **Tête du Chien**
The "dog's head" rock, eroded by the sea and wind, is one of the many intriguing shapes in the Calanques. It is near the parking area on the D81 road and is the starting point for many excursions.

② **Château Fort**
This massive block of granite that looks like a fortress forms a panoramic terrace overlooking the gulfs of Porto and Girolata and Capo Rosso. It can be reached on foot in 30 minutes from the Tête du Chien through a maze of sculpted rocks, cavities and pinnacles that in spring are covered by flowering shrubs.

④ **Café les Roches Bleues**
In one of the most spectacular spots along the D81 highway is the Roches Bleues café. Drinks are served on the terrace overhanging fantastically shaped rocks: to the left is the Tortue ("turtle", seen here), and to the right the Aigle ("eagle").

⑥ **The D81 Road**
Once back on the D81, walk about 500 m (500 yards) towards Piana. Along this stretch of road, the Calanques can be appreciated at their most beautiful. Turn back and follow the D81 all the way back to the parking area.

Dardo

Mezzanu

Piana ← D81

Key

▬ Tour route
═ Other roads

The Tafoni

In Corsican, *tafone* means a large hole, and this term is used to indicate a natural cavity in the rock of areas where the dry season is very long and the terrain is steep. Erosion begins

when even just one crystal of granite is corroded by the humidity and swings in temperature that occur in this area. The shapes the rock then takes on are truly astonishing. The *tafoni* became part of the Corsican way of life in ancient times, when these holes were used as burial sites or as primitive dwellings.

A *tafone* formation in the Calanques de Piana

Tips for Drivers

i Place de la Mairie, Piana (09 66 92 84 42).
Length of tour: 3 km (2 miles).
Duration: about four hours, without stops, to do the paths, plus 45–60 minutes to get back to the parking area.
Difficulty: average. Wear comfortable shoes and carry a hat and sunglasses, a supply of water and a detailed map of the area (free from local tourist offices).
Stopping-off point: Café les Roches Bleues.
W otpiana.com

③ Corniche

Once back at the Tête du Chien, a path east of the D81 road zigzags through the Laricio pine forest for about an hour before returning to the road a short distance from the Café les Roches Bleues. Marked with blue dots, the strenuous path offers splendid views of the rocks and the Golfe de Porto.

Forêt Domaniale de Piana

| 0 metres | 400 |
| 0 yards | 400 |

⑤ Chemin des Muletiers

Just after the café, near a small shrine to the Virgin Mary, begins the Chemin des Muletiers. This was the old mule track that connected Porto and Piana. A short but tough climb leads to the path, which runs through rocks and scented woods. One hour of easy walking leads back on the D81.

For additional map symbols *see back flap*

The Genoese watchtower at Porto

⓮ Porto

Road map B3. 🚗 460. 🚌
ℹ️ Quartier La Marine (04 95 26 10 55). 🌐 porto-tourisme.com

A modern seaside resort with facilities for water sports of every kind, Porto is also an ideal base for visitors who want to make inland excursions. Its favourable geographic position was providential for Porto, which, during the Genoese period, was the only outlet to the sea in the agricultural zone of Ota.

On either side of the village are tall cliffs that conceal enchanting beaches. Overlooking the village's harbour is the impressive Genoese tower that defended the small port, the river and the valley. This quadrangular construction was built in 1549 on levelled red-granite cliffs and offers magnificent views of the gulf, where the red rock contrasts with the blue sea.

Next to the village, with its many hotels, cafés and boutiques, is the **Marina**, which has a wide beach of grey pebbles backed by a large grove of centuries-old eucalyptus trees. The Marina can be reached via a charming wooden footbridge leading over the estuary of the little river where fishing boats and yachts are anchored. This tiny port is the departure point for many excursions by boat along the entire coastline. The Golfe de Porto, part of the Parc Naturel Régional *(see p103)*,

can be seen in all its splendour from the sea – the tourist boats go as far as the Scandola Nature Reserve *(see pp108–9)* and the Calanques de Piana *(see pp104–5)*.

Environs
South of Porto loom the magnificent Calanques, which reach an altitude of 1,294 m (4,245 ft) at Capo d'Orto. North of Porto, among the coast's granite cliffs, are some beautiful beaches that can be reached either by car (by taking turn-offs from the D81 road) or by boat. Among the most scenic are the pebble beaches of **Bussaglia** and **Gradelle**, the latter on the way to Osani; and the **Caspiu** beach, with its dark rocks. Caspiu can be reached by taking the detour after the village of Partinello.

A strawberry tree laden with fruit

The stretch of the D81 road to Galéria is arguably the most difficult and spectacular in all Corsica. This high, narrow road with numerous bends offers wide-ranging views of the Golfe di Porto and coast. Small lay-bys along the road make for good viewpoints, as does the **Col de la Croix**, from which a path leads to the beaches of Tuara (75 minutes return) and Girolata (3 hours return; also accessible by boat).

⓯ Gorges de Spelunca

Road map B3. ℹ️ Quartier La Marine, Porto (04 95 26 10 55).
🌐 porto-tourisme.com

Behind Porto is a splendid valley from where it is possible to admire this gorge, formed by the Aïtone and Tavulella torrents. Fine views of the Gorges de Spelunca (also known as Evisa-Ota) can be had from the D84 road that goes up to Evisa on the south side of the valley.

On the north side of the valley, at an altitude of 310 m (1,017 ft), is **Ota**, a mountain village with simple stone houses that was once famous for its citrons, which were exported to Europe. Today, the orchards are partly overrun by scrub. Ota is one of the stops on the *Mare e Monti* path *(see p31)* in the Parc Naturel Régional *(see p103)*.

Interesting sights in this area are the Genoese bridges, about 2 km (1 mile) along the road to Evisa. The first of these, at **Pianella**, is a perfect arch. The nearby bridge of **Ota** lies where the Aïtone and Tavulella torrents meet and passes over both of them. This point also marks the start of the old mule track that once linked Ota and Evisa through the gorges, passing over the **Vecchju** and **Zaglia** bridges (90 minutes return). The latter, built in 1745, is one of the gems of Genoese architecture.

The entire area is reminiscent of American canyons. A ravine can be followed along the path hewn out of the rock.

The Genoese bridge of Ota, with its characteristic arch

Laricio pines in the Forêt d'Aïtone

⓰ Forêt d'Aïtone

Road map C3. ℹ️ Quartier La Marine, Porto (04 95 26 10 55); Parc Naturel Régional de la Corse, Ajaccio (04 95 51 79 00/08). 🆆 **parc-corse.org**

With the atmosphere of an enchanted forest, the Forêt d'Aïtone can be explored through its easy, enjoyable and well-marked footpaths.

An ancient forest, its name seems to have derived from the Latin word *abies*, meaning fir tree. The forest covers an area of 24 sq km (9 sq miles) at an altitude of 800–2,000 m (2,600–6,500 ft). The Genoese used the wood to make their ships and, in the 16th century, built a road to transport the trunks to Sagone *(see p102)*. The forest is made up mostly of Laricio pines, a sweet-scented variety of *Pinus nigrus* that can grow to more than 45 m (150 ft) high and live for 200 years. There are also maritime pines, firs, beeches and larches that protect the rich undergrowth and its wild fruit and mushrooms. The forest is inhabited by foxes, wild boars and mouflons.

Just west of the forest, at 830 m (2,723 ft) above sea level, is **Evisa**. Surrounded by chestnut groves that yield high-quality fruit, this village plays host to a famous chestnut festival in November. Evisa is

situated at the junction of the *Mare a Mare* and *Mare e Monti* footpaths *(see p31)* and is therefore a great starting point for excursions.

About 4 km (2 miles) from Evisa, on the road to Col de Verghio *(see p155)*, is the starting point of the path that leads to the **Cascades d'Aïtone** (30 minutes return), a series of waterfalls formed by the Aïtone torrent, at the foot of which are limpid pools perfect for a swim.

The **Sentier de la Sittelle** (the French word for the nuthatch, a local bird) is a path beginning by the park information centre of **Paesolu d'Aïtone** and going through the forest along the **Sentier des Condamnés** (2 hours 30 minutes), a circular path named after convicts who, in the 19th century, felled the trees for firewood.

The ramparts and keep of the Genoese fort at Girolata

⓱ Girolata

Road map B3. 🚗 100. ℹ️ La Marine, Porto (04 95 26 10 55). 🆆 **port-girolata.com**

A fishermen's hamlet facing a splendid cove sheltered from the wind, Girolata can be reached only on foot (90 minutes from Col de la Croix, *see p106*) or by one of the boats that offer excursions from Porto in the summer. On the headland is the majestic square Genoese fort, which is protected by a

defensive wall. It was in the sea in front of Girolata, that, in 1540, the Genoese led by Andrea Doria captured the infamous Turkish pirate Dragut Rais.

In the summer, the bay area becomes crowded with yachts and loses much of its charm, even though the sea beds and red cliffs are still beautiful.

⓲ Galéria

Road map B3. 🚗 330. 🚌 ℹ️ Carrefour du Fangu (04 95 62 02 27). 🆆 **ot-galeria.com**

The only residential area of any importance between Calvi *(see pp82–4)* and Porto, this isolated village is a great base for visits to the Scandola Nature Reserve *(see pp108–9)*, dives and water sports in general. Galéria is also the departure point for excursions along the coast, where a panoramic path that also penetrates the maquis skirts the Golfe de Galéria from Punta Ciuttone to the north to Punta Stollu to the south.

Just behind Galéria is the **Vallée du Fango**, created by the river Fango, the mouth of which forms a vast pebbled beach. The valley was a transhumance route along which flocks of sheep from the mountains above the Vallée de Niolo were moved to the sea for winter. They stayed there until spring, when they made the return trip.

The D351 road penetrates the valley for about 10 km (6 miles), traversing the Forêt du Fango. Here, the Fango river flows between low rock faces, creating transparent water holes ideal for a swim. Shortly before the village of Barghiana is the spectacular meeting point of the Fango and the Taita torrent.

The Taita torrent in the Vallée du Fango

⑲ Réserve Naturelle de Scandola

Red granite cliffs plunge into the sea at the Scandola Nature Reserve, while cormorants perch on the rocks and ospreys circle in the sky. Under the water's surface is a blaze of colours created by sponges, anemones and corals. Along with the Calanques de Piana and the Golfe de Girolata, the reserve forms the Golfe de Porto, a UNESCO World Heritage site that protects 9.2 sq km (3½ sq miles) of land and 10 sq km (4 sq miles) of sea between Punta Mucchilina to the south and Punta Palazzo to the north. The park's unparalleled wealth of flora, rare bird species and underwater fauna (including 450 species of algae and 125 species of fish) is protected by bans on fishing, on mooring for more than 24 hours, and on gathering marine fauna and flora.

Cliffs of beautiful red volcanic rock

Volcanic Rock
The entire Scandola peninsula is part of a volcanic complex, the rocks of which date back to the Upper Permian era (248 million years ago). Among these are porphyry flows at Cala Ficaccia, the lava and rhyolite domes at Punta Palazzo, and the prismatic organ-pipe shapes at Elbo, shown above.

KEY

① **Clinging to the volcanic rocks**, at the water's surface, are sea urchins and anemones, as well as numerous crustaceans.

② **Algae platform**

③ **The nest** of the osprey, a large white bird of prey with brown wings, is one of the features of these cliffs. After being close to extinction, there are now about 20 pairs of ospreys in the Scandola Nature Reserve.

④ **Over 450 species** of algae live here as a result of the exceptional clarity of the water.

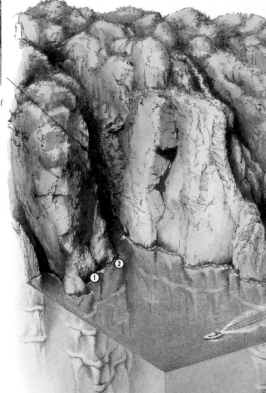

The Algae Platform

Lythophyllum is a calcareous algae forming encrustations that hang over the surface of the water and are often as thick as 30 cm (12 in). At Punta Palazzo is the largest algae platform in the Mediterranean, about 100 m (330 ft) long and 2 m (6½ ft) wide. Though they seem robust, algae platforms are extremely fragile.

Algae platform above the water

Underwater layers

Euphorbia Dendroides
Growing as much as 1 m (3 ft) high, this shrub is one of the most common in the reserve. It blossoms in May, when it tinges the cliffs yellow; at the end of spring, as it becomes dry, it takes on a bright brown hue. Only in late summer, with the first autumn rain, does it become green again.

Fauna in the Reserve

The Scandola Nature Reserve is above all the domain of marine birds and fish. Here, the birds find shelter and food in the crevices of the rocks, where they nest. Cormorants, peregrine falcons and ospreys can all be observed here, as can a species of bat. The pure water also favours underwater life: flora lives as deep as 45m (150 ft) down and the range of sea creatures is truly exceptional.

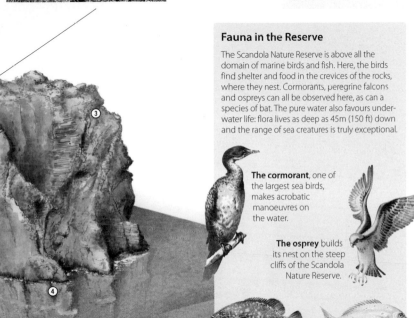

The cormorant, one of the largest sea birds, makes acrobatic manoeuvres on the water.

The osprey builds its nest on the steep cliffs of the Scandola Nature Reserve.

The grouper is a large fish that can be as much as 1.5 m (5 ft) long. It is recognizable by the light spots on its brownish dorsal portion.

The sea bream is highly prized and much in demand for its tasty meat, but in this park it is protected by the ban on fishing.

Panorama
The coast along the Scandola Nature Reserve is one of the most evocative in Corsica. Here, steep red rock formations plunge into the crystalline sea.

BONIFACIO AND THE SOUTH

The fortified city of Bonifacio, with its narrow streets from which Sardinia can be seen on the horizon, is one of the most ancient on the island. But long before the Pisans, Genoese and Spanish fought for control here, southern Corsica was the centre of a prehistoric indigenous population that left amazing traces of its presence in the alignments of menhirs and *casteddi*.

The inlet of Bonifacio, on the cliffs of which are the defensive walls of the old Genoese city, is an ideal starting point for boat excursions along the precipitous white coastline. The menhirs at Filitosa are among the best-known aspects of Corsican history, but this is only one of the many sites where it is possible to admire Neolithic architecture. North of the Golfe de Porto-Vecchio are the impressive walls of the *casteddu* (castle) of Araggio, while south of Sartène the alignments of menhirs at Palaggiu, Stantari and Renaggiu are eloquent reminders of Corsica's early history.

The natural scenery in this area is quite varied and splendid: from the forests around the Aiguilles de Bavella to the white rocks on the islands of Lavezzi and Cavallo – protected by an international marine park that extends over the Straits of Bonifacio – the landscape offers incomparable views. There are many walking tours, and indeed the interior of southern Corsica should be explored, at least to some degree, on foot. A series of small villages occupies the most protected part of the mountain valleys, where olives and chestnuts grow and where traces of Corsica's medieval past can be found.

Amid small churches and old houses there is still an atmosphere of peace and quiet – the region is far removed from the world most of the year, becoming animated with tourists only in the summer. A low-season visit is highly recommended.

Three of the best-known anthropomorphic megaliths at the prehistoric site of Filitosa

◀ The dramatic cliffs of Bonifacio

Exploring Bonifacio and the South

Southern Corsica is divided into two adjacent areas that are quite different to one another. Starting off from Bonifacio, two main routes are worth exploring. Along the south coast there are many small coves, peaceful beaches and sheer rocks overlooking the sea. This is the area with the most popular tourist resorts, such as Bonifacio, Propriano, Solenzara and Porto-Vecchio, which in summer all become crowded. The inland route, after crossing the Alta Rocca region, leads to the Col de Bavella zone, which offers wonderful spots for nature hikes and many small secluded villages. The best-preserved prehistoric sites in Corsica – Filitosa, Palaggiu, Renaggiu, Fontanaccia and Stantari – are only a short driving distance from the town of Sartène, while near Levie, the sites of Cucuruzzu and Capula are also worth a visit.

Above the citadel of Bonifacio

Menhirs at Palaggiu, one of the prehistoric sites on the Cauria plateau

Getting Around

The main communication routes on the south coast of Corsica are the N196 and N198 roads, connecting Bonifacio to Propriano and Sartène, and Porto-Vecchio respectively. The N198 then proceeds northwards towards Bastia. The D368 road, with its many hairpin bends, goes from Porto-Vecchio into the mountains; in the village of Zonza, it merges with the D268 road and leads to Col de Bavella. To explore the prehistoric sites, it is necessary either to take minor roads, some of which are unpaved, or to go on foot. The main coastal towns are connected to Ajaccio and Bastia by bus service, while Bonifacio is a stopover for the ferries from Sardinia.

For additional map symbols *see back flap*

Sights at a Glance

Characteristic granitic rocks on Îles Lavezzi, shaped by the wind and sea

Key

— Major road
═ Minor road
--- Hiking trail
— Scenic route

0 kilometres   10
0 miles   5

Transparent water and wild beauty on the exclusive Île Cavallo

❶ Bonifacio

This stunning medieval town on a striking limestone promontory was developed by Bonifacio, Marquis of Tuscany, who passed by upon his return from an expedition in Africa in 828. For three centuries, the fortified harbour lived on fishing and piracy and was partly under the rule of Pisa. In 1195, Bonifacio became a Genoese colony and took in a number of immigrants from Liguria. At about the same time, it became a republic, was granted the right to mint its own money and began construction of the massive walls. Bonifacio was conquered in 1553 by the French before being recaptured by the Genoese, and in the 17th century it was fortified with modern military structures. Although the town fell definitively under French rule in the 18th century, it has kept an Italian flavour and a certain sense of isolation from the rest of Corsica.

Outdoor cafés along the Marina

🍴 Marina

The quays of the old port of Bonifacio are now a popular promenade filled with cafés and restaurants. This is the departure point for cruises to the Grotte du Sdragonatu (see p118) and the Îles Lavezzi (see p121). In the summer, this area remains quite lively until late at night.

Further along, towards the mouth of the inlet, is the commercial port with the Gare Maritime (passenger terminal). In the Middle Ages, the port was entrusted to the benevolence of St Erasmus, the patron saint of sailors and fishermen who is celebrated on 2 June (see p37) and honoured by a church named after him in the Marina.

To the Haute Ville

The old town can be reached by walking up the stairs known as Montée Rastello, next to St-Érasme, and then up Montée St-Roch, which leads to the old Porte de Gênes. It is also possible to drive along the road that goes past the Porte de France. This road skirts the foot of the Bastion de l'Étendard and a war memorial that consists of an ancient Roman column found on a nearby islet, and leads to the car park in the upper town (haute ville), next to the monument to the Foreign Legion soldiers.

🏛 Bastion de l'Étendard

Open May–Sep: daily; Oct: Mon–Fri. 🖼
The silhouette of this massive bastion towering over the quays of the Marina and the port is one of the most famous features of the city. The bastion was built in the 16th century by modifying the existing fortifications, and its function was to house the powerful heavy artillery that at that time was bringing about a drastic change in military architecture. Along with the Porte de Gênes, it was the strong point of the walls of Bonifacio, which proved impregnable on several occasions.

The upper platforms of the bastion afford a magnificent panoramic view of the narrow inlet of Bonifacio and the Marina below.

Four halls in the interior are now a small museum featuring reconstructions of significant moments in Bonifacio's history.

🏛 Porte de Gênes

During Genoese rule, the Porte de Gênes was the only entrance to Bonifacio's upper town. Surrounded by tall ramparts, the gate gave access to the Place d'Armes, beyond the walls. These walls were so thick that, to get to the square, one had to pass through eight successive barriers made of wood reinforced with iron.

In 1588, a drawbridge was added at the end of these barriers. The drawbridge was raised and lowered by a complex system of counterweights that can still be seen inside the structure.

The massive Bastion de l'Étendard towering over the Marina

Open and blind double lancet windows,
Ste-Marie-Majeure

🏛 Ste-Marie-Majeure

Rue de la Loggia and Rue du
St-Sacrement. **Open** daily.

Bonifacio's cathedral was the
heart of the city's religious and
cultural life for centuries. At the
front of the building is a vast
loggia with porticoes, which, in
the past, was the meeting point
for the town notables and the
seat for administering justice.
The structure was built over a
large cistern that is now used as
a conference room. Construction
of Ste-Marie-Majeure was
begun in the 12th century,
before the Genoese conquered
the city, by Pisan artisans, and
was completed a century later.
This extremely long delay has
led to a mixture of styles that
does not, however, diminish
the beauty of the whole. The
first floor of the bell tower, for
example, is Romanesque, while
the upper three are Gothic
with some Aragonese relief
decoration. The three-aisle
interior is partly Baroque.

Inside, to the left of the
entrance, is a 3rd- or 4th-century
Roman sarcophagus surmounted
by a magnificently wrought
tabernacle executed by Genoese
masters in the mid-1400s. The
high altar dates from 1624 and
is clearly Baroque in style. In the
sacristy is a relic of the True
Cross. In the past, during
particularly dangerous times
and when there were heavy
storms, the curate and mayor
carried the Cross in a procession
through the streets of Bonifacio.

The loggia of Ste-Marie-Majeure

Bonifacio Old Town

① Marina
② Bastion de l'Étendard
③ Porte de Gênes
④ Ste-Marie-Majeure
⑤ Porte de France
⑥ St-Dominique
⑦ Escalier du
  Roi d'Aragon

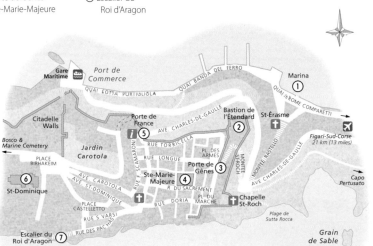

Exploring Bonifacio

The heart of Bonifacio is the *haute ville* (upper town), which perches on the promontory high above the fjord-like inlet that forms Bonifacio's harbour. Bordered by Avenue Charles-de-Gaulle and the massive ramparts, this is the oldest section of the city. Around the cathedral, tall, narrow houses line the streets, the outer rows balancing dangerously on the cliff's edge. Further out on the promontory, west of the city walls, the wind-battered Bosco area stretches out towards the sea, offering panoramic views from the Esplanade St-François.

🏛 Porte de France

In addition to the Porte de Gênes, a second entrance to the *haute ville* was created in 1854, when the French Army Engineers' Corps built a road to the St-Nicolas fort. This new gate also featured a draw-bridge. Within the city walls around the Porte de France, traces of the oldest quarters of Genoese Bonifacio can still be seen. These include the Fondaco, or staple (commercial warehouse), that once stood in the Place Montepagano area.

The bell tower of St-Dominique

⬆ St-Dominique

Haute Ville, near Place Birhakeim.
Open Jul–Aug.

Outside the city walls, but inside the fortifications that once protected the Pisan quarter, is this church dating from 1343. It stands on the site of an earlier Romanesque church, which was begun by the Pisans and finished by the Knights Templars. The present church was built by the Dominicans and, until the French Revolution, was part of a monastery complex.

The Gothic bell tower is unusual: its square base is surmounted by an octagonal section topped with battle-ments, and the white limestone façade is decorated with an ogival portal. Inside are groups of statues depicting Mary and the other holy women at the foot of the Cross and an image of St Bartholomew. Opposite the church doorway are the Montlaur barracks, which were built by the Genoese. Later this building became the home of the Foreign Legion troops.

Next to the church is the Mairie (Town Hall), which is linked to St-Dominique by an arch that was once part of the old Dominican monastery.

🏞 Bosco

At the tip of Bonifacio's promontory is the Bosco area. Here, there is a cemetery, with many small, light-coloured mortuary chapels. Near the edge, the structure of the St-Antoine battery was constructed in the period between the two World Wars. The position of the battery allowed complete control of the maritime traffic in the Straits of Bonifacio.

🏛 Escalier du Roi d'Aragon

Rue des Pachas. **Open** Apr–Nov. 🅿

On the west side of the head-land, where the craggy cliff is at its most precipitous, this steep rock-cut stairway descends to sea level. According to legend, its 187 steps were hewn in only one night, during the Aragonese siege of 1420. It is, in fact, more likely that the stairway was built in a much earlier period and served as access to a well with good drinking water.

The Escalier could be clearly monitored from above, and was never used by any of the foreign troops that tried to storm Bonifacio.

The impressive Escalier du Roi d'Aragon

The Trinite Processions

When heading out of Bonifacio on the D196 road towards Sartène, after about 3 km (2 miles) there is a junction, the left branch of which leads to the Ermitage de la Trinité. A narrow road winds between two walls of maquis to the open space in front of this little church, which affords a magnificent view towards Bonifacio and the Anse de Paragnano. On 13 May (feast day of Our Lady of Fatima) and on 8 September *(see p38)*, the inhabitants of Bonifacio come here in procession, creating such a traffic jam that it is advisable to go to the Ermitage on foot. The small church dedicated to the Trinity contains offerings and vows left by people who survived dangerous trips in the Straits of Bonifacio during heavy storms.

View from the hermitage

Parc Marin International des Bouches de Bonifacio

To preserve the coastal habitats of southern Corsica, the first marine reserves were established in the early 1980s. They now include the islands of Lavezzi, Bruzzi, Monaci and Cerbicale. Underwater fishing was prohibited and rigorous regulations were applied even to professional fishermen. In 1986, the idea for an international marine park in the Straits of Bonifacio – the stretch of sea between Corsica and Sardinia – started to take shape. In 1992, the Italian and French ministers of ecology decided to work together for the park. Although they could not block shipping of loads that could cause damage in case of an accident, the authorities did restrict the limits of the navigable channel and set up an emergency plan that goes into effect whenever the wind, which is quite strong in this part of the sea, blows at more than 4 or 5 knots. Because the wind is never lacking here, the straits are a paradise for yachtsmen, whose boats can always be seen slicing through the frothy waves, often during a regatta. The website www.parcmarin.com has more information on this nature reserve.

The Corsican Coast

The French side of the Straits of Bonifacio has one of the best-known coasts in the Mediterranean, characterized by tall white cliffs in which layers of limestone are clearly visible. The profile is extremely jagged and the tiny coves squeezed between the craggy rocks can often be reached only by boat. One of the problems of the marine park is how to limit the damage to the environment caused by mass tourism.

Red coral, according to popular legend, originated from the blood of Medusa after Perseus cut off her head and tossed it into the sea.

Lobsters, crustaceans with highly prized meat, find refuge in this area, where fishing is strictly regulated.

The sea anemone is an inhabitant of the coast of the straits. Although it seems to be an immobile plant, the sea anemone is an exceptional predator.

The Sardinian Coast

On the other side of the Straits of Bonifacio, the Sardinian coastline is as jagged as Corsica's, but generally much lower, with beautiful sandy coves and colourful sea beds. Not far away to the east is the Maddalena archipelago, made up of seven main islands, including La Maddalena and Caprera, and several smaller islets, such as Isola Budelli, famous for its pink-sand beach.

Bonifacio: the Coast and the Cliffs

Perched on its promontory, keeping guard over the deep inlet below, the fortified city of Bonifacio owes its charm and importance to the sea, fishing and commerce. Only an exploration from beneath the cliffs, at sea level, reveals all of Bonifacio's particular beauty and the reason why it has been likened to a ship carved out of rock. On the jetties of the Marina, many companies offer boat tours of the coastline as far as the sea caves, the Grain de Sable and to the open sea, skirting the headlands and coves that lead to the Îles Lavezzi.

The houses of Bonifacio on the steep cliffs overlooking the sea

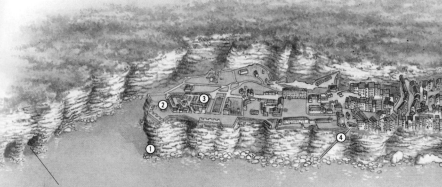

Grotte du Sdragonatu
Created by water erosion, this sea cave is illuminated by the sun, which penetrates through a crack in the vault. The local tourist guides claim that this long, narrow opening resembles the shape of Corsica.

A Geological Anomaly

Typical layers of limestone in the cliffs

The coast around Bonifacio is made up of a chalk outcrop that created the famous cliffs. Extending as far south as Capo Pertusato and towards Pointe de Sperone, these cliffs are friable sedimentary rocks that over time have been sculpted by the wind and sea to create this much-admired craggy coastline. The presence of limestone here is a geological anomaly on an island mostly made up of magmatic rocks, in particular granite (Col de Bavella and the Calanques de Piana) and volcanic rhyolite (Scandola Nature Reserve).

KEY

① **Grotte de St-Antoine**

② **Esplanade de St-François**

③ **The marine cemetery**, with its aligned mortuary chapels surrounded by greenery, is a fine panoramic viewpoint.

④ **Escalier du Roi d'Aragon**

⑤ **The *haute ville*** of Bonifacio dominates the port situated in the inlet.

Grain de Sable
This solitary stack, which now has the curious nickname of "grain of sand", broke off from the cliff 800 years ago. It is one of the most recognizable cliffs around Bonifacio.

VISITORS' CHECKLIST

Practical Information
Road map C6. ℹ️ 2 Rue Fred Scamaroni, Bonifacio (04 95 73 11 88). 🌐 **bonifacio.fr**

Transport
🚢 Apr–Oct: excursions leave from the Marina of Bonifacio every 15 minutes for the sea caves and the Grain de Sable (duration: 1 hour).

Capo Pertusato Lighthouse
Clearly visible at night from the coast of Sardinia, this lighthouse was built on the southernmost point of Corsica.

Craggy Cliffs
The cliffs near Bonifacio have many fine belvederes from which the beauty of this splendid coastline can be fully enjoyed. Among the birds that nest in this wild stretch are shags, herring gulls and the rare Andouin's gull.

Capo Pertusato
Viewed from the sea, the southernmost point of Corsica appears quite rugged and shaped by the waves. A view from the land highlights a colossal cave carved out of the limestone. Capo Pertusato was named after this natural opening – in Genoese dialect, the language of the former rulers of Bonifacio, the word *pertusato* means "perforated".

Bonifacio: the Îles Lavezzi

Continuing along the coast after Capo Pertusato, the cliffs remain quite high, and the few beaches here can only be reached via steep paths. Past the Pointe de Sperone, the view opens on to the group of the Îles Lavezzi and Île Cavallo. This fascinating archipelago is made up of granitic-rock islands fringed by small sandy beaches. Inland, although the scenery appears to be extremely barren, there are plenty of endemic plant species. The Îles Lavezzi lie in the middle of a large marine reserve and mooring is strictly regulated. Today, there are about 20 people working here, including park wardens and marine biologists.

Aerial view of Île Cavallo, with its runway in the middle

The *Sémillante* Shipwreck

The Straits of Bonifacio have been the dramatic scene of many shipwrecks. One of the most famous was that of the *Sémillante*, a French frigate that set sail from Toulon in February 1855 with a crew of 301 to take 392 French soldiers to Crimea. On the night of 15 February, a terrifying storm caused the ship, which was full of gunpowder, to explode on the rocks of Île Lavezzi. The *Sémillante* sank quickly and there were no survivors. The bodies found were buried in the two small cemeteries of Lavezzi. A year after the tragedy, a monument commemorating the victims of this shipwreck was built on one of the island's promontories.

Granite and Limestone
Shortly after Pointe de Sperone is the "border" between granite and limestone formations. Here, the layers of white rock are lined with pink granitic crevices. The vegetation also changes, with limestone shrubs giving way to maquis.

KEY

① **Capo Pertusato**

② **An exclusive golf club,** the Sperone *(see p193)*, is situated on the Bonifacio promontory.

③ **The islet of San Bainsu** was used by the ancient Romans as a granite quarry.

④ **Cormorants** and Corsican gulls find ideal nesting places among the rocks of Lavezzi.

⑤ **The flora on Lavezzi** includes endemic species, the presence of which is somewhat of a mystery. Some of these exist only here, in Australia and in South Africa.

The monument to the victims of the *Sémillante* shipwreck, on a promontory of Lavezzi

Pointe de Sperone
This wind-beaten, maquis-
covered promontory is a perfect
example of the untamed nature
of this stretch of coast. Many sea
birds nest and live here.

Île Cavallo
This beautiful island is private property.
Hidden among the rocks and low
vegetation are luxury villas, and there is
even a small airport. Mooring is forbidden
along the entire coastline.

Île Lavezzi
Like the rest of the archipelago,
this island is a nature reserve.
Little more than a rock, it is full of
fascinating stone formations but
also has a range of flora and
fauna that is interesting from a
scientific point of view.

The crystal-clear waters at Palombaggia beach ▶

❷ Casteddu di Tappa

Road map C6. ℹ️ Rue Général Leclerc, Porto-Vecchio (04 95 70 09 58). **Open** daily.
🌐 ot-portovecchio.com

The impressive Neolithic site, just (4 miles) from Porto-Vecchio on the D859, is found in the village of Ceccia. Consisting of fortified dwellings built around two gigantic structures, it has been through some difficult times, having been treated as an open-air quarry. Tappa was saved from a worse fate by a private citizen who bought the land to protect it.

From above, the plan of the site reveals stretches of walls that were added to fortify the natural defence of the small settlement. On the basis of their finds, archaeologists have established that Tappa was already inhabited by the Torréens *(see p41)*, so called because of their tower structures, in the second millennium BC, which makes this one of the most ancient settlements in Corsica.

On the southwestern side of the settlement is a round, non-fortified monument dating from 1350 BC. Access was gained via a steep rock-cut stairway. A round cell in the interior was used to preserve foodstuffs and other valuable materials. Besides serving as a store-house, this monument was probably also used as a place of worship and as a watchtower.

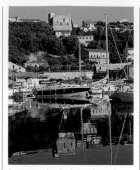

Boats moored in the sheltered port of Porto-Vecchio

❸ Porto-Vecchio

Road map C6. 🔼 10,230. 🚌 from Marseille, 04 95 70 06 03. ℹ️ Rue Général Leclerc (04 95 70 09 58). 🌐 ot-portovecchio.com

It was the Genoese governors of the Bank of St George *(see pp48–9)* who decided, in the early 16th century, to found Porto-Vecchio. Its function was to fill a long gap in the series of strongholds on the coastline between Bastia and Bonifacio. Porto-Vecchio was also known as the "City of Salt" after its most precious natural resource. However, due to its proximity to the marshes created by the Stabiacciu and Osu rivers, Porto-Vecchio was plagued by malaria for centuries.

Around 1553, the period of the revolt headed by Sampiero Corso *(see p49)*, Porto-Vecchio became a refuge for pirates; then, until the mid-1900s, the town lived off

the cork industry and the local salt works.

At the end of World War II, land reclamation stemmed the danger of malaria, paving the way for future development, such as tourism, commerce and small industries. Porto-Vecchio is now an important town, famous above all for the lovely beaches in its vicinity. In the upper part of town, there are still traces of the Genoese fortifications and in the historic centre, in the summer, tourists flock to the many outdoor cafés and restaurants.

Environs
Along the southern coast of the Golfe de Porto-Vecchio, there is a series of very popular tourist resorts. Past the watershed that ends at **Punta di a Chiappa** are the famous white sand beaches of **Palombaggia** and **Santa Giulia** *(see p25)*, which face the Îles Cerbicale reserve.

The beach at Palombaggia, south of Porto-Vecchio

❹ Massif de l'Ospédale

Road map C5. ℹ️ Rue Général Leclerc, Porto-Vecchio (04 95 70 09 58). 🌐 ot-portovecchio.com

Behind the town of Porto-Vecchio is a large wooded and rocky region that offers panoramic views of the sea and many fine footpaths.

The village of **Ospédale** lies 800 m (2,600 ft) above sea level, halfway up the mountain of the same name. It may owe its name (hospital) to the fact that, in the past, affluent Porto-Vecchio families used to come here to spend the hot season away from the unhealthy marshes.

The panorama from here includes a broad section of

The ruins of the *casteddu* at Tappa, a prehistoric settlement

The artificial lake below the peaks of the Massif de l'Ospédale

the coastline below. One of the recommended hikes starts from the hamlet of **Cartalavonu**, 4 km (2 miles) further up the hill, and leads to the 1,315-m (4,300-ft) high **A Vacca Morta** peak, which offers marvellous views.

Beyond Ospédale, a maritime pine forest spreads out, covering the entire massif and surrounding the artificial lake of Ospédale. The whole area is part of the Parc Naturel Régional (see p103).

❺ Araggio (Araghju)

Road map C5. **ℹ** Rue Général Leclerc, Porto-Vecchio (04 95 70 09 58). **W** araggio.com

North of Porto-Vecchio, towards the interior and the hills, the small hamlet of Araggio is the departure point for a steep walkway leading to the nearby casteddu (see p43). This mule track is quite narrow and hard to climb, ascending without a break along a stony ridge. Then, suddenly, the loose stones and sheepfolds

are interrupted by the light-coloured walls of a massive fortress standing on a rocky spur. The walls of the casteddu of Araggio are about 4 m (13 ft) high and 2 m (6 ft) thick. The megalithic complex inside the fortifications consists of a series of rooms that in prehistoric times (16th–12th centuries BC) served as living quarters, kitchen and storehouse for foodstuffs. Close-up, these structures are reminiscent of the great prehistoric nuraghi complexes in Sardinia. From here, there is a splendid view of the gulf and the countryside around Porto-Vecchio.

❻ Punta Fautea

Road map D5. 🚌 from Porto-Vecchio (in summer). **ℹ** Vechja Scola, Sari-Solenzara (04 95 57 43 75). **W** cotedesnacres.com

North of the low coastline of the gulf of Porto-Vecchio is the Cala Rossa promontory, which marks the beginning of a rocky stretch interspersed by a few beaches, including the beautiful **Plage de Pinarellu**.

About 20 km (12 miles) from Porto-Vecchio, towards Solenzara, is the turn-off for Punta Fautea. Here, not far from the main road, is a restored **Genoese watchtower** built in the late 16th century and partly destroyed by fire in 1650.

From here to Solenzara is the **Côte des Nacres**, a rocky coast with many coves, crystal-clear waters and fascinating sea floors. The name of this coast derives from the large triangular shells that can be found locally. They are as much as 50 cm (20 in) long and the inside is covered by a thin layer similar to mother-of-pearl (nacre in French).

Mermaid mural at the port of Solenzara

❼ Solenzara

Road map D5. 🏛 1,200. 🚌 from Porto-Vecchio. **ℹ** Vechja Scola, Sari-Solenzara (04 95 57 43 75). **W** cotedesnacres.com

What was once a tiny hamlet at the mouth of the Solenzara torrent has become one the most lively tourist resorts in southeast Corsica. Solenzara has a port that can take in about 450 boats and a sandy beach bounded by eucalyptus trees. **Sari-Solenzara**, a tiny hamlet above Solenzara, overlooks the plain and is worth visiting for the splendid views of the Bavella.

The restored ruins of the 16th-century Genoese watchtower at Punta Fautea

❽ Col de Bavella

The jagged pinnacles of the Aiguilles de Bavella make for one of the most thrilling landscapes in Corsica. This group of needle-shaped peaks lies at the foot of the Monte Incudine massif, which, at 2,134 m (7,001 ft), is the highest mountain range in south Corsica. The road going over the Col de Bavella passes through rocks that glow red at sunset, pine groves and meadows covered with thyme flowers in spring, and offers one of the most breathtaking views in Corsica. The area boasts many footpaths, including the southernmost stretch of the GR20 *(see pp26–31)* and the more demanding alpine route through the Aiguilles themselves.

One of the marvellous views from the Trou de la Bombe

Laricio pines are very tall. They often live for a considerable time; many are three or four centuries old and some have even reached the venerable age of 800 years. In the past, the pine trunks were used to build ships.

Calamint in Bloom
When spring arrives, the meadows lining the road and the footpaths take on the pink colour of calamint flowers, which bumblebees love for their abundant nectar.

The Trou de la Bombe

There are several holes *(tafoni, see p105)* created by wind erosion in the hard rocks of Corsica. Expertise in hiking or climbing is not necessary to get to the Trou de la Bombe, a hole about 9 m (30 ft) high at the Punta Tafonata of Paliri. The walk, which takes a couple of hours there and back, starts off from the U Canone fountain, a short distance beyond the Col de Bavella in the direction of Solenzara. A forest road, then a footpath with red markings lead to a rocky amphitheatre and onwards to the base of the huge *tafone*. From here, the view of Monte Incudine and of the pines among the rock crevices is remarkable.

Approaching the Trou de la Bombe

Aiguilles de Bavella
The rugged needles of these peaks are a real favourite with hikers and rock climbers. Those with no head for heights can enjoy the spectacular beauty of the Aiguilles while travelling along the D268 road.

VISITORS' CHECKLIST

Practical Information
Road map C5. 🛈 BP 07, Office du Tourisme de l'Alta Rocca, Zonza. **Tel** 04 95 78 56 33. **Open** May–Oct. GR20 long-distance path: 🛈 Parc Naturel Régional de la Corse, 2 Rue Major Lambroschini, Ajaccio (04 95 51 79 10). 🅦 parc-corse.org
🅦 alta-rocca.com
🅦 ot-portovecchio.com

The Aiguilles massif is the habitat of many species of birds of prey. Mouflons (called *muvrini* in the Corsican language) can also be spotted.

Paths and Signs
The many hiking itineraries in this area are all well marked. Easy-to-read wooden signs show the altitudes and distances of the hikes, while other markings painted on rocks or trees indicate the direction to take.

The shrubs are a sign that the wooded area is ending to give way to alpine meadowlands.

Inspiring Landscape
The Bavella area has always been popular, even at the time when tourism was only for the privileged few. Edward Lear, the English artist and traveller, depicted the region in this 1870 watercolour called *Forest of Bavella, Corsica.*

The village of Zonza; in the background, the famous profile of the Aiguilles de Bavella

9 Zonza

Road map C5. 2,500. Town Hall, Sainte-Lucie village (04 95 71 48 99). **w** zonza-saintelucie.com

In the middle of the Alta Rocca region, among pine and oak forests and high along the course of the Asinao river, is Zonza. During the summer, this small town, with the bulk of the Aiguilles de Bavella in the background, is a magnet for those who love outdoor activities. Along the main street are shops selling guides with descriptions of climbing, rafting, trout fishing and hiking itineraries. There are also many associations of tourist guides.

In 1953, the sultan Mohammed V of Morocco lived in Zonza in exile, but the climate proved too harsh for him, and he asked to be transferred to L'Île Rousse (*see p78*), on the north coast.

10 Cascade Piscia di Ghjaddu

Road map C5. Town Hall, Sainte-Lucie village (04 95 71 48 99).

Although the Cascade Piscia di Ghjaddu can only be reached on foot, it is possible to park in the vicinity, near the top of the D368 road leading to the pass of the Massif de l'Ospédale.

After some streams is a larger watercourse, where, over time, the current has sculpted large round pools, commonly known as **Marmitte dei Giganti**.

Further along the path, the river suddenly rushes through a narrow rock crevice, creating a waterfall that is about 46 m (150 ft) high. The best viewpoint for the Cascade Piscia di Ghjaddu can be reached by following the path that goes around the rocks and then descends to the right. The whole walk will take about 90 minutes to the viewpoint and back, and for a long stretch consists of rocky terrain, so suitable hiking boots or robust shoes should be worn.

11 Quenza

Road map C5. 220. Town Hall, Sainte-Lucie village (04 95 71 48 99).

This village at the foot of the ascent leading to the Col de Bavella is surrounded by a thick oak and chestnut forest. Quenza has two churches. **St-Georges**,

The façade of the Chapelle de Ste-Marie, just outside Quenza

in the village, has a pulpit carved in the form of a Moor's Head supported by sea monsters. The second church, the Romanesque **Chapelle de Ste-Marie**, was founded around the year 1000 and stands on the road to Aullène.

12 Levie

Road map C5. 750. Town Hall, Rue Sorba (04 95 78 00 00); Town Hall, Sainte-Lucie village (04 95 71 48 99). **w** levie-altarocca.com

The area around Levie, a short distance from the Aiguilles de Bavella, is one of the most interesting prehistoric zones in Corsica, with many important sites unearthed by digs.

Levie also houses one of the main archaeological museums in Corsica. The **Musée Départemental d'Alta Rocca** contains information on the flora, fauna and geology of the island and also boasts the famous *Dame de Bonifacio*, the skeleton of an old woman who was buried in 6570 BC. It is the most ancient relic of the island's past. The museum features a fascinating display of cardial ware (named after the decorative patterns carved with the use of the sharp edges of the *Cardium* cockle shell; *see p42*), skeletons of small mammals and an ancestor of the cow. The explanations and descriptions given by the museum staff are very enlightening and

The ancestor of the cow at the Musée Départemental d'Alta Rocca

offer a better understanding of the evolution of prehistoric civilization on the island.

🏛 Musée Départemental d'Alta Rocca

Quartier Pratu. **Tel** 04 95 78 00 78/75.
Open May–Sep: daily; Oct–Apr: Tue–Sat. **Closed** public hols. 🅿 ♿

Environs

About 8 km (5 miles) from Levie, across the deep Fiumicicoli river valley, is **Carbini**. It was in this small village that, around the end of the Middle Ages, the religious sect of the Giovannali was founded (1352) and thrived. Inspired by St John the Baptist and founded by Giovanni Martini, a Franciscan monk from Marseille, this cult found fertile ground in Carbini and then spread throughout the island. The meeting place of the followers was the Pisan Romanesque church of St-Jean-Baptiste, which was built in the 14th century. The church is flanked by a structure – still visible – thought to correspond to the foundations of an earlier church dedicated to San Quilico and destroyed during the tragic repression of the Giovannali. As a result of the 1362 crusade ordered by Pope Urban V against the "satanic heretics", the members of this sect were burned at the stake at the foot of the Monte Kyrie Eleison, the name of which (Greek for "Lord, have mercy") has a particularly poignant ring in this context.

🔟 Cucuruzzu and Capula

Road map C5. 🚹 Town Hall, Ste-Lucie village (04 95 71 48 99); Levie Town Hall, Rue Sorba (04 95 78 00 00). **Open** Apr–Oct: daily. By appt with town hall during the other months.
🅿 📷 ♿ 🆆 levie-altarocca.com

The visit to the archaeological site of Cucuruzzu and the medieval castle of Capula is organized as a pleasant walk in the oak and chestnut forest on the plateau.

Right by the ticket office, where audio-guides are handed out, is the start of a mule track. The ruins of Cucuruzzu appear after a 15-minute walk. This *casteddu (see p43)*, with its wall, fireplaces and inner stairway leading to the upper levels, dates from the second millennium BC. Digs carried out in the 1960s brought to light an entire citadel covering a surface area of 1,200 sq m (12,900 sq ft). Some of the enormous blocks that make up the citadel's walls weigh more than one tonne.

Once back on the trail, a short walk leads to the Chapelle San Lorenzo, which was built using stone blocks from an earlier church, the ruins of which can also be seen here.

A short distance above these are the ruins of the medieval castle of Capula, a Roman fortification that was destroyed in 1259 by Giudice della Rocca, who had been made count of Corsica by the Pisans. This site

The bell tower at Carbini

of Capula had already been inhabited in prehistoric times, as confirmed by the nearby menhir-statue of an armed prehistoric warrior (Capula I), which was unearthed during the course of archaeological digs.

🔟 Ste-Lucie de Tallano

Road map C5. 🏔 460. 🚹 Town Hall, Sainte-Lucie village (04 95 71 48 99). 🆆 zonza-saintelucie.com

On the road descending west from the Alta Rocca plateau towards the Golfe de Valinco is the village of Ste-Lucie de Tallano, famous for its **Couvent St-François**, a monastery founded in 1492 by the local lord, Rinuccio della Rocca. St-François is being restored, call the tourist office for more information.

On the village square is the church of **Ste-Lucie**, which contains a beautiful Catalan-style altarpiece with Christ, St Peter and St Paul in the middle, and three small figures of saints below them. The altarpiece is attributed to the Master of Castelsardo, an artist from the late 15th to the early 16th centuries who probably came from the large Franciscan monastery of Castelsardo, in Sardinia. The church of Ste-Lucie also boasts a *Crucifixion*, which some art historians have attributed to the same artist.

📌 Couvent St-François & Église Ste-Lucie

Open daily (call the tourist office for opening hours).

The charming hamlet of Ste-Lucie de Tallano

The austere grey houses of Sartène perched on the rocks

⑮ Sartène

Road map C5. ⛰ 3,500. 🚌
ℹ Cours Soeur Amélie (04 95 77 15 40). 📷 Catenacciu Procession (Good Friday). 🌐 lacorsedesorigines.com

Prosper Merimée, who in the mid-1800s was the Inspector of Antiquities in Corsica, described Sartène as "the most Corsican of Corsican towns". Located in the middle of an area rich in prehistoric ruins, this town with a history of vendettas lies halfway up the hill in the valley of the Rizzanese river.

The old town has a maze of narrow streets lined with dark-coloured houses as well as many aristocratic mansions. The alleyways are often surmounted by arches and vaults.

On Good Friday evening, the Baroque church of **Ste-Marie**, in Place de la Libération, is the starting point for the Catenacciu Procession (see p36). One of the most ancient religious ceremonies in Corsica, it re-enacts the crucifixion walk to the Golgotha. The Catenacciu ("chained one") represents the Great Penitent. After spending two fasting days in isolation, he dons the traditional long red tunic and a hood covering his face while bearing the Cross and heavy chains through the streets. The White Penitent, who represents Simon of Cyrene, helps him carry the large oak cross, while behind them eight black-clad

figures bear the statue of the Dead Christ. A traditional chant, "*Perdonu miu Diu*" (Forgive me, Lord), accompanies the slowly moving procession, which comes to a halt back in front of the church where it started. After the blessing, the ceremony ends.

Sartène is also worth a visit for the **Musée Départemental de Préhistoire Corse et d'Archéologie**, which is similar to the one in Levie (see pp128–9) and features the long, ancient history of the island. The museum is based in a large, modern building. Among the items on display, the cardial ware (see p42) is worth

a look, as are the obsidian arrowheads from Sardinia and the collection of funerary vases dating from the second and first millennia BC.

🏛 **Musée Départemental de Préhistoire Corse et d'Archéologie**
Blvd Jacques Nicolai.
Tel 04 95 77 01 09. **Open** May–Sep: Tue–Sun; Oct–Apr: Mon–Fri. ♿ 🅿

⑯ Roccapina

Road map B6.

About 25 km (16 miles) south of Sartène, on the N196 road towards Bonifacio, a terrace on a hilltop affords a fine panoramic view of the Golfe de Roccapina and the Pointe de Roccapina promontory, with its characteristic pink granite rocks, which were inhabited in prehistoric times. One of these rocks, which is flanked by a massive Genoese tower, looks very much like a colossal crouching lion, hence the name **Le Lion de Roccapina**, or Lion's Rock.

The Golfe de Roccapina at nightfall

Handmade Knives

With their curved blades and handles that fit perfectly in the hand, knives have always been one of the shepherds' most indispensable work tools. Traditionally, the top of the blade also had a sawtoothed section and the handle was made of wood or goat's horn. Called *cursina* in the local language, this type of knife is now protected by a registered trademark and is still handmade by a dozen craftsmen. Their size and the ratio between the blade and handle have always been the same, but the artisans' creativity has led to the use of new materials. Thus, the blades are now made of damask steel and the handles range from white cedar to manta ray skin. Corsican tradition has also produced the *runchetta*, a jackknife, and the *temperinu*, a small, pointed knife. Most famous of all is the *stiletto*, which, along with pistols, was part of the bandits' arsenal in the 19th century and is now sold as a souvenir, with the word "Vendetta" carved on it.

Two *cursine*, typical knives

⑰ Tour of the Megaliths of Cauria

In the region of Sartène alone, after almost two centuries of archaeological research, no fewer than 500 prehistoric sites have been explored. According to the experts, the southern part of Corsica was much more densely populated than the north in prehistoric times. A tour of the barren plateau of Cauria, south of Sartène, allows the chance to visit some of the island's most important sites with megalithic monuments *(see p43)*, which here are in the form of alignments. Although it is not easy to reach Palaggiu, it is worth the effort, because this is one of the most important menhir alignments in the world.

Tips for Drivers

ℹ️ Rt D48, Cours Soeur Amélie, Sartène (04 95 77 15 40 or 04 95 79 13 00). **Length of tour:** from Sartène to Palaggiu, ca 15 km (9 miles); from D48-A turn-off to Stantari, ca 5 km (3 miles). **Duration:** 1 day. **Stopping-off points:** Sartène and Tizzano.

① Palaggiu

With its 258 menhirs, discovered in the late 1800s, Palaggiu is an amazing sight. About 5 km (3 miles) after the Cauria turn-off on the D48 road, on the right is a mule track marked by a metal gate. A 20-minute walk leads to the "stone forest".

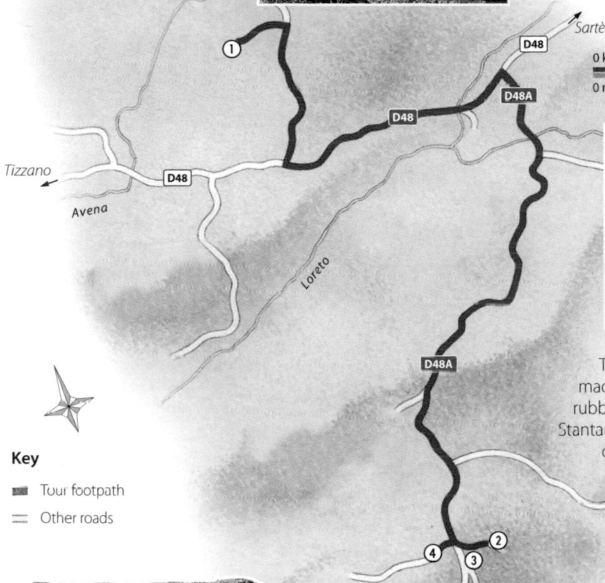

Sartène

D48

0 kilometres   1
0 miles   0.5

D48A

D48

D48

Tizzano

Avena

Loreto

D48A

② Stantari

Tall, pink at sunset and made smooth by animals rubbing against them, the Stantari menhirs have traces of faces and weapons.

Chiusu di a casa

Key

🚶 Tour footpath
= Other roads

④ ③ ②

④ Fontanaccia

Discovered in 1840 by Prosper Merimée, then Inspector of Antiquities in Corsica, this is the island's best-preserved dolmen. It stands about 100 m (320 ft) from the parking area.

③ Renaghju

Here is the most ancient Neolithic settlement in Corsica, with two alignments of menhirs. The most ancient ones date from 4000 BC; around their bases are remains of round fireplaces.

The tranquil bay of Campomoro, with its crystal-clear sea

⑱ Campomoro

Road map B5. 🏔 260. 🛈 Town Hall, Belvedere-Campomoro (04 95 74 20 27). 🌐 **lacorsedesorigines.com** Tour de Campomoro: **Tel** 04 95 76 01 49. **Open** mid-Apr–Sep: Mon–Fri. 🌀

Situated on the south coast of the Golfe de Valinco, the small village of Campomoro is a peaceful place to relax.

A ten-minute walk along a well-marked path dotted with informative signs leads to the door of the **Tour de Campomoro**, built in the 16th century by the Genoese. This fortress, the largest in Corsica, allows visitors to explore the interior of a typical defensive tower and offers magnificent views of the gulf.

Experienced hikers can also explore another splendid coastal path that runs south from Campomoro to Tizzano.

The round Genoese tower at Campomoro

⑲ Propriano

Road map B5. 🏔 3,700. 🚌 🛈 Quai St-Erasme (04 95 76 01 49). 🌐 **lacorsedesorigines.com**

The town of Propriano lies at the innermost point of the Golfe de Valinco, tucked in between the green hills behind it and the transparent blue sea. It is an attractive and popular yacht harbour and seaside resort thanks to the beautiful beaches and coves dotting the gulf.

Because of its strategic position, Propriano was much sought after throughout its history. In ancient times, it developed as a famous port, and as a landing place and trade centre for Etruscans, Greeks, Carthaginians and Romans, especially in the 2nd century BC. In the 1980s, while restructuring work was being carried out on the port, numerous remains from this period were found.

During the Middle Ages, Propriano was governed first by the Pisans and, then, from 1230 onwards, by the Genoese. In 1563, Sampiero Corso *(see p49)* landed here and initiated a period of anti-Genoa revolts. His actions, however, proved to be disastrous for Propriano, because the village was then left at the mercy of pirate raids and virtually destroyed. The same period also saw the demise of the beautiful Santa Giulia di Tavaria abbey, mentioned in chronicles but now in ruins.

In the 19th century, Propriano came to life again, becoming a commercial port for the entire region, a role consolidated in the early 20th century. Now the village is a lively tourist locality. The beautiful beaches and well-developed facilities make it one of the leading resorts on the island.

Environs
About 9 km (6 miles) from Propriano, going northwest on the N196 road, is **Olmeto**, a large hamlet 870 m (2,850 ft) above sea level that dominates the gulf. Just above the village are the ruins of the **Castello della Rocca**, the fortress that Arrigo della Rocca used as a base when he began his rebellion against the Genoese rulers. In 1376–90, he governed the entire island, leaving only Bonifacio and Calvi to the foreign invaders.

The white lighthouse at Propriano looming over the sea

⑳ Porto-Pollo

Road map B5. 🏔 360. 🚌 🛈 Town Hall (04 95 74 02 12); Quai St-Erasme, Propriano (04 95 76 01 49). 🌐 **lacorsedesorigines.com**

At the mouth of the Taravo river, Porto-Pollo is a small seaside resort. During the summer, it is popular with people who are attracted by the tranquillity of the place and its delightful beach along the Golfe de Valinco.

Not far from the village, on top of the Pointe de Porto-Pollo, is the Genoese **Tour de Capriona**.

The sea and sea bed along the promontory are very popular with scuba divers, who love to dive down to the so-called *cathédrales*, rocky pinnacles at a depth of about 10 m (32 ft).

㉑ Filitosa

Road map B5. 🛈 Station
Préhistorique de Filitosa, Sollacaro
(04 95 74 00 91). **Open** Apr–Oct: daily;
Nov–Mar: by appointment. 🖼 ▢
🖼 🖿 filitosa.fr

The most famous prehistoric
site in Corsica is managed
with great care by the
heirs of Charles-Antoine
Cesari, who made the
first discoveries here
in 1946.

Filitosa offers almost
5,000 years of history.
Populated in very
ancient times because
it was both fertile and
easy to defend, the
area was filled with
large constructions
and menhirs from
1800 BC to 1100 BC.
The fortified town dominated
the valley of the small Taravo
river. It was here, among the
stones of one of the structure's
walls, that one of the most
significant alignments of

The front of Filitosa V

anthropomorphic menhirs
(see below) was found.
Details of the faces,
weapons and helmets of
ancient warriors are still
clearly visible on the
surface of these rocks.

Most of the ruins of
Filitosa date from
between the late
second millennium BC
and 700 BC. With the
rise of Christianity,
the menhirs were
considered pagan and
therefore destroyed.
Their remains were
heaped together in
piles, like mere
stones, and had to
wait many centuries
to be rediscovered.

The tour of
Filitosa begins with
a splendid statue (Filitosa V)
standing on the track that leads
to the fortified settlement, also
known as *oppidum*. Here are
the ruins of a village and three
monuments, the middle one

Detail of the central monument

of which is well preserved.
Below, in a small valley, is the
quarry where the stone for
the sculpture was extracted.
Some statues found in the
surroundings have been
placed around the quarry.

Next to the entrance to the
site is a small museum that
illustrates the history of the
site. It displays fragments
of three menhir statues, the
most famous of which is the
Scalsa Murta menhir (1400 BC).
Armour and weapons can be
seen on these menhirs, as
well as holes on the upper
part of the head, probably
where ornamental ox horns
were placed.

The Evolution of the Anthropomorphic Menhirs

Megalithic monuments, used to worship the dead in the Neolithic era (6000–2000 BC),
were found on five Mediterranean islands: Corsica, Sardinia, Malta, Majorca and Minorca.

The Corsican megalithic culture (3500–1000 BC) is divided into three periods
Megalithic I, II and III – which show an evolution in burial practices. The early
subterranean tombs on mounds of earth sealed with long stone slabs were replaced
by outdoor monuments known as dolmens, consisting of horizontal monoliths
representing the souls of the deceased.

In the Megalithic III period, which, in turn, is divided into six stages, the
horizontal monolith becomes a vertical anthropomorphic statue, that is, one
resembling a human.

These statues have different features, depending on the populations that sculpted
them. In the period of invasions, for example, they were armed, but later they became plain
again. Near the end of Megalithic III, the so-called Torréens *(see p41)* settled in Corsica, introducing
tower-like structures. Over time, these towers replaced the anthropomorphic statues.

*The front of
Filitosa IV*

Statues of Stages 5 and 6 of the Megalithic III period. The statues seen below are among the most
famous in Corsica. They were named after the localities in which they were discovered; their numbers
indicate that more than one statue was found on the same site.

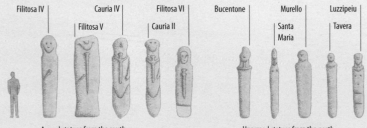

Filitosa IV | Cauria IV | Filitosa VI | Bucentone | Murello | Luzzipeiu
Filitosa V | Cauria II | Santa Maria | Tavera

Armed statues from the south — *Unarmed statues from the north*

CORTE AND THE INTERIOR

The ancient Romans who conquered Corsica in 259 BC were aware of the strategic importance of Corte as the geographical heart of the island. Originally a fortress, the city soon became the symbol of all Corsica and its struggle for independence, the home of the island's parliament, university and national heroes. Corte is also the starting point for excursions into the valleys in the interior.

The colours of the sea, the jagged coastline and the iridescent sea beds are perhaps the best-known features of Corsica. But also deserving of a visit are the mountains inland, which, with Monte Cinto, reach a height of 2,706 m (8,877 ft). Traversed by valleys and paths leading to refuges, in the summer the mountains are ideal for a wide range of hiking excursions.

In the middle of this natural setting made up of rocks, spring waters and forests, lies Corte. The town's fortunate geographic location meant that on several occasions potential conquerors, including the Romans, had to stop short of this region. In the 18th century, Corsica's first National Constitution was drafted here and ever since then Corte has been the symbol of the island, of its culture and yearning for independence. From its Citadelle, which is the home of the Musée de la Corse, there are commanding views of the surrounding territory. To the west are the wildest valleys and tallest peaks; to the east are hills covered with woods, small villages and remains of the past. These hills descend towards the sea of Aléria, the first Roman colony in Corsica. The regions of Bozio, Fiumorbo and Castagniccia (named after its rich chestnut groves) have a series of chapels and churches that bear witness to various artistic styles and that reach in the Romanesque church of La Canonica and the Baroque church of La Porta the apogee of Corsican religious tradition.

Fresco decoration in the small church of San Pantaleo, Castagniccia

◀ The Tavignano river, carving a path through narrow gorges

Exploring Corte and the Interior

Corte is the geographic heart of Corsica, as well as its
cultural centre. The city is skirted by a region of tall,
rugged mountains forming the very backbone of the
island: Monte Rotondo, Monte d'Oro and Monte Renoso
stand southwest of Corte, while Monte Cinto and Capo
Tafonato are northwest of the city. To the northeast,
descending towards the coast, are the hilly regions of
Bozio and Castagniccia, where, from the period of
Genoese domination (late 12th century) onwards,
the less harsh terrain favoured the birth of many
small villages. The area surrounding Corte is also
known for its gastronomy, which includes game,
wild boar and traditional cheeses.

Key

— Major road

=== Minor road

-- Hiking trail

— Scenic route

+-+ Railway

△ Summit

⊁ Mountain pass

ST-FRANÇOIS DE CACCIA ❻

Moltifa

VALLÉE DE L'ASCO

Asco

D147

❶❾

Asco

Haut-Asco

Forêt de
Carozzica

Monte Cinto
△ 2706m

Punta Minuta
2556m

SCALA DI
SANTA REGINA ㉑

Golo

Capo Tafonato
2340m

Albertacce

㉒ CALACUCCIA

GR20

D84

㉓ CASAMACCIOLI

COL DE
VERGHIO ㉕

❶⓪

FORÊT DE
㉔ VALDU NIELLU

GORGES DU TAVIGNAN

Porto

Lac de Nino

Capo Chiostro △
2295m

GORGES DE
RESTONIC

❸

△ Monte Rot
2622m

Monte d'Oro
△ 2389m

CASCADE DES ANGLAIS

COL DE VIZZAVONA

Gravona

Bocog

N193

Monte Ren
23

Ajaccio

Prunel

Basteli

Soveria, a village in the vicinity of Corte, with a view of the
magnificent mountains in the background

Getting Around

Corte lies on the N193 road, which, coming from Ajaccio,
crosses the Col de Vizzavona in the inland valleys. North
of Corte, at Ponte Leccia, the N193 divides, going either
northeast in the direction of Bastia (N193) or north to
L'Île Rousse and Calvi (N1197 and N197). Other roads
branch off from this main artery, traversing the splendid
side valleys both west, towards the mountains, and east,
towards Bozio and Castagniccia. An enjoyable way to
travel to Corte from Bastia or Ajaccio is to take the small
train – jokingly called the TGV, or Train of Great Vibrations –
which stops at almost all the stations along the way.

For additional map symbols *see back flap*

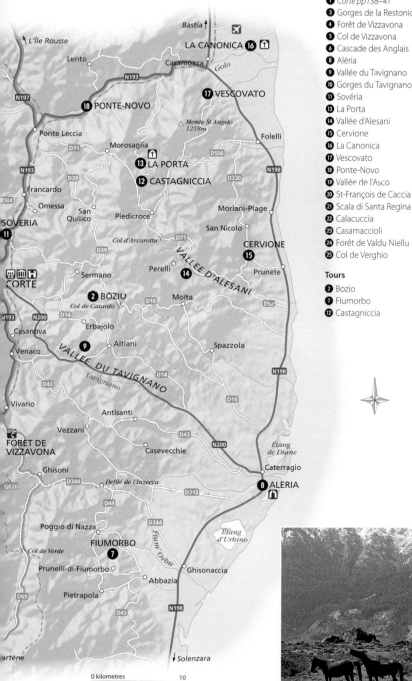

Horses in high pastures near Calacuccia, in the valley of the Verghio

❶ Corte

Located in the heart of Corsica, Corte was fortified in 1419 by the viceroy of Aragón, Vincentello d'Istria. Later, it was ruled intermittently by the Genoese and the French. In 1735 it became the cradle of Corsican patriotism when the constitution for an independent state was drafted here. In 1755, when Corsica was liberated by Pascal Paoli, Corte became its capital. Ten years later, Paoli founded the island's first university here.

Corte still maintains a proud spirit of nationalism. It is part of the city's charm and can be discovered through a walk in the old town and a tour of the Citadelle. The latter, the symbol of the military power of past ages, is now home to the Musée de la Corse, one of the leading centres of Corsican culture. A hike to the Belvedere overlooking the Gorges du Tavignano and the Gorges de la Restonica reveals the natural beauty of the area.

The nave in the 15th-century Église de l'Annonciation

Place Gaffori and the monument to the hero of the taking of Corte

🏛 Place Paoli

At the foot of the upper city (*haute ville*) is a large and lively square named after Pascal Paoli (*see p51*). Laid out in the late 19th century by Victor Huguenin, the centre of the square features a large monument to the renowned patriot and hero of Corsican independence.

🏛 Place Gaffori

West of Place Paoli are the ramps of Rue Scoliscia, which lead to the heart of the city and Place Gaffori. In the middle of this square is the statue commemorating General Jean-Pierre Gaffori. On the pedestal are two bas-reliefs depicting the feats of this Corsican hero and those of his brave wife Faustina (*see p50*). Also on the square are the Église de l'Annonciation and the house where Gaffori was born.

⬆ Église de l'Annonciation

Place Gaffori. **Open** call the tourist office for details.
Founded around the mid-15th century, this church is one of the oldest buildings in Corte. However, the façade as it stands today dates from the 18th century. Commissioned by Alexandre Sauli, who later became bishop of Aléria, it has five pilasters with Corinthian capitals. The tall, slender bell tower that dominates the entire quarter is Baroque. Inside the church is a series of Baroque statues and an altar made of the local grey marble.

A short, steep descent along Rue Feracci leads to a pretty Baroque mansion known as Maison Palazzi.

⬆ Chapelle Ste-Croix

Rampe Ste-Croix. **Open** Mon–Sat.
Past the Maison Palazzi is the austere façade of the 17th-century church of Ste-Croix. The pillarless nave has a barrel vault and an aisle paved in grey marble. By the altar is a colourful Baroque retable and a large medallion with a relief of the *Madonna of the Apocalypse*.

This church is also the home of the Ste-Croix Confraternity, which has always played a leading role in the religious life of the city.

A short descent along a ramp in front of the church

Jean-Pierre Gaffori

The hero of the Corsican independence movement along with Pascal Paoli, Jean-Pierre Gaffori was born in 1704 in Corte and studied medicine. In 1745, during the armed revolt against the Genoese occupation, he was elected as one of the triumvirate of the "Protectors of the Nation". One of his exploits was the taking of Corte in 1746. According to local lore, during the battle against the Genoese troops, Gaffori realized that his enemies were using one of his sons as a shield. He was uncertain about what to do, but his courageous wife Faustina urged the Corsican patriots to continue attacking, allegedly shouting: "Don't think about my son, think about your country!" Made a general, Gaffori managed to conquer most of the island but was assassinated in an ambush organized by his brother, who was in the service of the Genoese. In the square named after him is his statue, and on the façade of his house, opposite the Église de l'Annonciation, there are still marks of the shots fired by the Genoese during the 1746 siege of Corte.

Statue of Jean-Pierre Gaffori

Fontaine des Quatre-Canons

leads to the square and the Fontaine des Quatre-Canons.

Fontaine des Quatre-Canons

Place des Quatre-Canons.
Commissioned by Louis XVI, this fountain ("of the four cannons") was completed in 1778. Its purpose was to channel water from the Orta torrent to the city to furnish the local garrison with a sorely needed supply of water.

From the square, ramps go up to the massive walls of the Citadelle (*see pp140–41*).

Place du Poilu

In front of the entrance to the bastions of the Citadelle is Place du Poilu, with the house where General Arrighi di Casanova, one of Napoleon Bonaparte's generals, was born. It was here that Napoleon's father lived and that his brother Joseph, who was to become king of Spain, was born in 1768.

The 17th-century **Palais National**, once the residence of the Genoese governors and then of Pascal Paoli, is where Corsican independence was declared. For 14 years (1755–69, *see pp50–51*), this palace was the home of the new Corsican parliament. It now houses the University Institute of Corsican Studies, a separate branch of the University of Corte, which is based in the Citadelle.

Plaque on the house where Joseph Bonaparte was born

Belvedere

Before visiting the Citadelle, it is worth making time for a walk along the uphill road that skirts its walls. This road leads to the platform of the Belvedere, which offers a magnificent view of the castle, the Nid d'Aigle ("eagle's nest") tower and, below this, the city and the confluence of the Tavignano and Restonica rivers.

From the Belvedere, a steep path leads to the banks of the Tavignano river. The reward for making this trek is an impressive panoramic view over the rocky cliffs of the Citadelle.

Corte Town Centre

1. Place Paoli
2. Place Gaffori
3. Église de l'Annonciation
4. Chapelle Ste-Croix
5. Fontaine des Quatre-Canons
6. Place du Poilu
7. Belvedere
8. *Citadelle pp140–41*
9. *Musée de la Corse p141*

0 metres 200
0 yards 200

Corte: the Citadelle

Aleady fortified before the Genoese conquest in the 13th century, the Citadelle was transformed into a true fortress in 1419. After many years of foreign rule, the Citadelle became the symbol of the islanders' struggle for independence, especially when Pascal Paoli established Corsica's first university here. When the French took control of Corsica in 1769, the Citadelle became a military zone. Today, it houses the tourist office, a museum, an art institute and many historic archives, located on the lower level. On the upper level is the castle, with the Nid d'Aigle, the tallest tower, overlooking the Restonica and Tavignano valleys. Restoration projects have included the preservation of battlements perched high on the western part of the Citadelle.

★ Castle
Built in 1419 on the southern tip of the rocky spur by Vincentello d'Istria, the castle is the oldest part of the Citadelle.

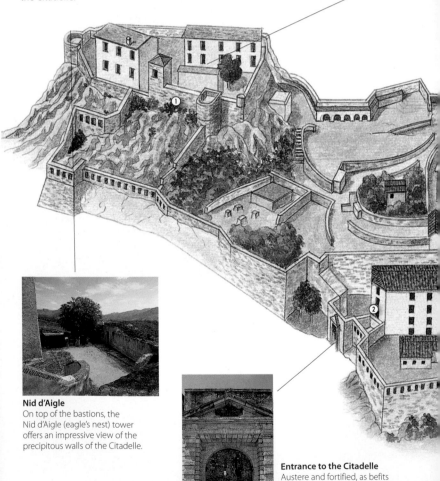

Nid d'Aigle
On top of the bastions, the Nid d'Aigle (eagle's nest) tower offers an impressive view of the precipitous walls of the Citadelle.

Entrance to the Citadelle
Austere and fortified, as befits a military structure, the entrance portal to the Citadelle is a simple arch surmounted by a tympanum.

Panorama of the Citadelle
Perched on a huge rock, the Citadelle can be seen from Corte and the surrounding area. Many people consider it one of the symbols of Corsica.

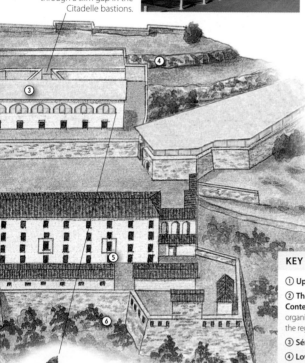

Entrance to Musée de la Corse
Entrance to the museum is through a slim gap in the Citadelle bastions.

Exploring the Musée de la Corse

This museum houses a fine anthropological collection, the core of which consists of the objects gathered from the 1950s onwards by abbot Louis Doazan. On display are various relics of the island's past, from the costumes of the confraternities of Corte, Bonifacio and other towns, to farmers' work tools. An interesting feature are the booths where visitors can listen to the traditional religious and secular music of the region. The first floor hosts temporary exhibits, and the museum also organizes concerts of traditional Corsican music here. The Nid d'Aigle tower and its spectacular views can be reached by a short walk after exiting through the first-floor doors.

KEY

① **Upper level**

② **The Fond Régional d'Art Contemporain** is an institute that organizes shows of modern art of the region.

③ **Sérurier barracks**

④ **Lower level**

⑤ **Padoue barracks**

⑥ **The bastions** are in keeping with late 18th-century military architecture. The large casemates and terracing accommodated pieces of artillery that made the Citadelle virtually impregnable.

★ **Musée de la Corse**
The exhibition rooms are in the former Sérurier barracks, once used by the Foreign Legion.

❷ A Tour of Bozio

The hilly regions of Bozio and Castagniccia (see pp150–51), respectively east and northeast of the town of Corte, have many surprises in store for art lovers. Do not expect grandiose basilicas or majestic bell towers, however. The art in these areas consists of a series of chapels – sometimes in a tiny hamlet, sometimes in open countryside – that require a degree of patience to find, and just as much patience to track down the person with the keys (who is always quite courteous). The Bozio tourist office organizes tours of the chapels with frescoes in the area, many of which benefited from restoration work during 2005 to 2010. The regions east of Corte are worth exploring for their natural landscape, which features hills, gorges and winding valleys. The constant curves and hairpin turns make the average speed on these roads extremely low. However, they do offer beautiful views.

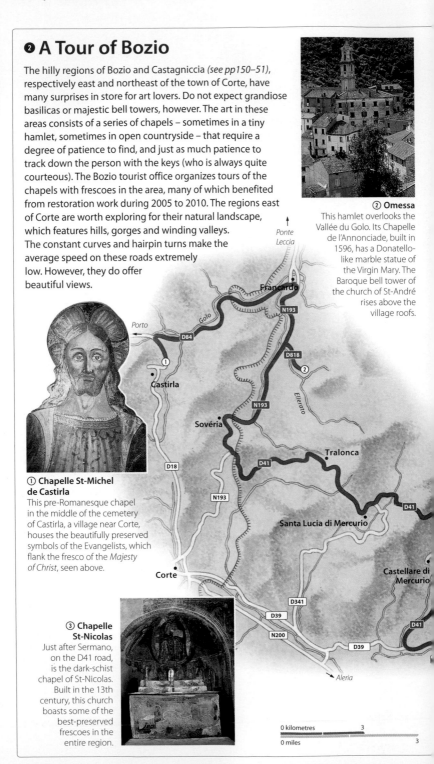

② **Omessa**
This hamlet overlooks the Vallée du Golo. Its Chapelle de l'Annonciade, built in 1596, has a Donatello-like marble statue of the Virgin Mary. The Baroque bell tower of the church of St-André rises above the village roofs.

① **Chapelle St-Michel de Castirla**
This pre-Romanesque chapel in the middle of the cemetery of Castirla, a village near Corte, houses the beautifully preserved symbols of the Evangelists, which flank the fresco of the Majesty of Christ, seen above.

③ **Chapelle St-Nicolas**
Just after Sermano, on the D41 road, is the dark-schist chapel of St-Nicolas. Built in the 13th century, this church boasts some of the best-preserved frescoes in the entire region.

0 kilometres 3
0 miles 3

④ Chapelle Ste-Marie
Near Favalello, on a curve along the road, is this tiny chapel, which is usually open on Wednesdays. Its noteworthy frescoes reflect the faith of the Corsican artists who lived five centuries ago.

D441

Bustanicu/Sant' Andrea Di Bozio

mano

alello ④

ey

Tour route

Other roads

❸ Gorges de la Restonica

Road map C3. 🚌 Bus across the length of the valley (Jul–Aug); at these times the last stretch of the D623 might be closed to private cars due to congestion. ℹ️ Station Touristique de l'Intérieur, La Citadelle, Corte (04 95 46 26 70). Tuani Camping **Tel** 04 95 46 11 65. **Open** mid-Apr–mid-Sep. 🌐 campingtuani.com

The narrow valley that descends from the seven lakes of Monte Rotondo *(see p28)* towards Corte lies between steep slopes, creating a series of awesome gorges. Despite the terrible fires that, in 2000, damaged the centuries-old forest covering its slopes, this fascinating valley is still very popular among hikers who, from spring onwards, look for relief from the heat along the pebbled shores of the torrent.

After leaving Corte, the Restonica road (D623) goes past the small Hotel Dominique Colonna and up the hills. For certain stretches, the gorge becomes deep and seems to be hewn out of the rock. After about 14 km (9 miles) are the Bergeries de Grottelle, which lie 1,375 m (4,511 ft) above sea level. These typical stone-hut complexes house shepherds and sheep in the summer. This is where the motorable road ends and there are some kiosks open in spring and summer. From the Bergeries de Grottelle, a steep path goes over a rocky crest. Here, the hardest stretches have metal ladders; should it rain,

The Restonica, flowing quickly down through the rocks

be careful of the slippery rocks. After about an hour's walk is the first of the small lakes in this area, the Lac de Mélo, at an altitude of 1,711 m (5,613 ft). From the shore of the lake, the views encompass the surrounding mountains and the Vallée de la Restonica.

Further along the path, at 1,930 m (6,331 ft), is the Lac du Capitellu, a glacial lake surrounded by steep cliffs.

At an altitude of about 2,000 m (6,500 ft), where the forest ends, the landscape is open and impressive: to the left is the 2,622-m (8,602-ft) high Monte Rotondo, and to the right the crest of Capo Chiostro, which reaches 2,295 m (7,529 ft).

The two sides of the valley have many paths leading to lakes and *bergeries*. In summer, it is possible to stay at the Tuani camp site, renowned for its delicious pizzas, midway along the D623.

A Vanessa butterfly, typical of this zone

A breathtaking view of the Gorges de la Restonica

Fortress perched on a rock above the ancient town of Corte ▶

Panoramic view of the large Forêt de Vizzavona

❹ Forêt de Vizzavona

Road map C4. 🚉 Vizzavona. 🚌
ℹ️ Station Touristique de l'Intérieur, La Citadelle, Corte (04 95 46 26 70).

Of all the forests in the large green heart of the island, the Forêt de Vizzavona is one of the most famous and popular. This partly depends on the fact that the area is traversed by the GR20 long-distance path *(see p29)*, and in spring and summer, groups of hikers disembark at the small railway station of Vizzavona, 3 km (2 miles) away.

The forest is the home of hazelnut and chestnut trees as well as Corsican pines and other conifers. Ask at the tourist office about local environmental events.

The Forêt de Vizzavona is also crossed by the N193 road linking Ajaccio and Bastia and by the railway line inaugurated in 1894.

❺ Col de Vizzavona

Road map C4. 🚉 Vizzavona. 🚌
ℹ️ Station Touristique de l'Intérieur, La Citadelle, Corte (04 95 46 26 70).

The road linking Bastia and Ajaccio (the N193, one of the main roads on the island) crosses Corsica's inland mountain ranges at the pass of Col de Vizzavona. This mountain, at an altitude of 1,161 m (3,809 ft), marks

the border between Haute-Corse and Corse-du-Sud *(see p53)*. The pass has tables and benches for a stopoff and picnic and is populated by wild pigs that are not disturbed by visitors.

From Col de Vizzavona, which is often quite windy, there is a fine view of the impressive silhouette of the 2,389-m (7,838-ft) high Monte d'Oro. An easy, uphill path leading north off the N193 road to Bastia stretches for about 400 m (1,300 ft) to the ruins of a Genoese fortification. Many other footpaths cross this area, including the GR20 long-distance path *(see pp26–31)*.

Fresh hazelnuts

❻ Cascade des Anglais

Road map C4. 🚉 Vizzavona. 🚌
ℹ️ Station Touristique de l'Intérieur, La Citadelle, Corte (04 95 46 26 70).

One of the most popular walks in this area is the hike along the GR20 long-distance path *(see pp26–31)*, which goes from the road near the hamlet of La Foce to the Cascade des Anglais ("waterfall of the English"), a beauty spot much admired by early English visitors to this area. This trip, which is on an easy and well-marked path, takes less than two hours up and back, and follows the course of the Agnone torrent.

Beyond the Cascade des Anglais, which stands 1,100 m (3,600 ft) above sea level, the water has carved a series of deep potholes that are ideal for a swim.

In fair weather, and with adequate equipment, it is possible to continue up to the head of the valley towards the summit of Monte d'Oro. However, this is a strenuous hike of around 7–8 hours from Vizzavona and is only recommended for fit and experienced hill walkers.

The summit of Monte d'Oro overlooks all the main Corsican peaks and from there it is even possible to see the Italian coast.

The Genoese Bridges

The architectural works that the Genoese bequeathed to the island of Corsica comprise not only buildings, squares, citadels and watchtowers *(see pp33 and 97)*, but also a great many bridges. Over the centuries, these have facilitated communications with the interior, which is traversed by numerous watercourses that more often than not are quite swift. Many of these bridges, which were built from 1284 onwards, are intact and still in use today. They are made of dry-stone, have a single arch and are never more than 20 m (65 ft) long. The bridges are usually supported by two piers that are often reinforced with corner brackets on the upper part; there may be circular openings on the sides of the arch to let the water pass through in case of a flood. Originally quite simple, the bridges began to be decorated only after the Renaissance.

The Genoese bridge in the Vallée de l'Asco

❼ Tour of the Fiumorbo

This area is named after the Fium'Orbu ("blind river" in Corsican). The river starts from the slopes of Monte Renoso and winds its way down through the deep Strette and Inzecca gorges to the east coast, a short distance south of the archaeological site of Aléria. This wild region was one of the last in Corsica to agree to abide by French law, and tales of the battles between the French army and the locals have become legendary. The small villages have not changed much in the last two centuries and are not famous tourist attractions, but a tour of the rugged scenery and isolated hamlets is certainly worthwhile.

Tips for Drivers

ℹ️ RN 198, Ghisonaccia (04 95 56 12 38).
Length of tour: 90 km (56 miles).
Duration: one or two days, depending on the stops.
Stopping-off points: in the villages; Auberge Vecchia Mina (04 95 57 63 42).
🔲 corsica-costaserena.com

⑤ Auberge Vecchia Mina
On the Route de Ghisonaccia, about 5 km (3 miles) from Ghisoni, is this charming hotel. To its left is a path that descends towards Ponte a Mela, a lovely Genoese bridge.

④ Defilé de l'Inzecca
The D344 road, going from the coast to the village of Ghisoni, crosses the narrow gorge known as Defilé de l'Inzecca, followed by Lac de Sampolo and the Defilé des Strette.

Corte ↑

D344   ④   D344A

Fium'Orbu   D344
Fium'Orbo

D44
Lugo di Nazza

② Pietrapola
Near the village of Pietrapola are the hot springs that were frequented by the ancient Romans who lived in Aléria. They are still in use today.

Poggio di Nazza

Poggio

D244

Aleria ↗

③ Prunelli-di-Fiumorbo
The main village in this region is dominated by an austere fortified church. From here, there is a great view of the region and the coast.

Acciani   ③   D345   N190

D44   **Abbazia**
D45   D145   **Agnatello**
D45   **Abatesco**   ②   ①   D45

↓ Solenzara

0 kilometres   3
0 miles   2

Key
▬ Tour route
═ Other roads

① Serra-di-Fiumorbo
Overlooking the Abatesco river valley, parallel to the Vallée du Fium'Orbu, the village of Serra-di-Fiumorbo offers a fine view towards the coast, the ancient site of Aléria and the small Étang de Palo.

❽ Aléria

Road map D4. 🚗 2,230. ℹ️ 80 Avenue St-Alexandre Sauli (04 95 57 01 51). 🌐 oriente-corsica.com

The history of the ancient settlement of Aléria, on the marshy east coast of Corsica, began when Greek colonists set up a commercial outpost here around the mid-6th century BC. The outpost, then known as Alalia, served as a strategic base for trade with the populations on the nearby Italian and southern French coasts. For the Greeks, Corsica was also a vital source of raw materials, from timber to lead and copper from the mines inland.

After a period of Carthaginian domination, in 259 BC Alalia was invaded by the Roman troops of consul Lucius Cornelius Scipio. The Romans renamed the settlement Aléria and initiated the conquest of the island, which lasted for more than a century. Aléria was the capital of Corsica in the Imperial Age, and Augustus, Hadrian and Diocletian beautified it with large public works. In the 5th century AD,

Courtyard of Fort Matra, home of the Musée Jérôme Carcopino

the increase of malaria and invasion by the Vandals led to the abandonment of the city.

Visits to the archaeological site begin at a Genoese fort, Fort Matra. Built in 1484, it is now the home of the **Musée d'Archéologie Jérôme Carcopino**, named after the great scholar of Corsican origin. The items on display in this archaeological museum illustrate the historic continuity of Aléria

and the great number of trade relations it had with the entire Mediterranean region. Greek, Phoenician, Roman, Apulian and Etruscan vases and ceramics were found on the hill where the city rose up. Among the most interesting works are two rhytons (wine vessels) that were made in Attica, Greece, one in the shape of a mule's head, the other representing a dog.

Outside the museum are the ruins of the Roman city. To the left of the Forum is a large temple flanked by two porticoes and, to the right, the Praetorium – the official residence of the governor of the island – and the Capitol. Everything gives the impression of an efficient city with all the typical Roman amenities. In addition, tombs and traces of past civilizations dating as far back as the 6th century BC have been found throughout the area.

🏛️ **Musée d'Archéologie Jérôme Carcopino & site of Aléria**
Fort Matra. **Tel** 04 95 57 00 92.
Open daily. **Closed** Nov–Mar: Sun; public hols. 🎫

The Ruins of Aléria

① Forum
② Temple
③ *Domus cum Domus* (townhouse)
④ *Domus cum Impluvium* (water storage)
⑤ Shops
⑥ South portico
⑦ North portico
⑧ *Thermae* (warm baths)
⑨ *Balneum* (baths)
⑩ *Calidarium* (steam rooms)
⑪ Chambers
⑫ Industrial edifices
⑬ Pools
⑭ *Praetorium* (governor's residence)
⑮ Capitol
⑯ North arch
⑰ South arch
⑱ *Decumanus* (street)
⑲ Bastions

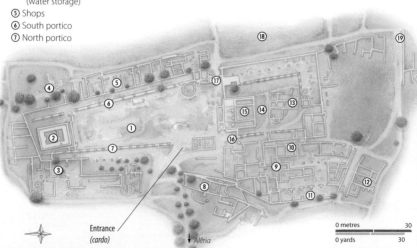

Entrance (cardo)

↑ Aléria

0 metres 30
0 yards 30

The Genoese bridge of Altiani, decorated with a series of small blind arches

❾ Vallée du Tavignano

Road map C3. 🛈 Station Touristique de l'Intérieur, La Citadelle, Corte (04 95 46 26 70).

The Vallée du Tavignano is traversed by one of the oldest roads on the island, the N200, connecting Aléria and Corte.

Travelling from Aléria along the course of the Tavignano river, which begins at Lac de Nino, in the middle of Corsica, there are many narrow gorges.

On the north side of the valley, the narrow D14 road leads to villages typical of the region, perched halfway up the hills in panoramic positions. One of these, **Piedicorte di Gaggio**, offers a fine view towards the coast and has an ancient Roman architrave in the wall of the parish-church bell tower.

A Genoese bridge still stands at **Altiani**, as promised by its engineers, who guaranteed the bridge would remain standing in all circumstances "save a deluge". The village of **Erbajolo**, towering over the canyon

The village of Piedicorte, in the Vallée du Tavignano

carved by the Tavignano river, offers a breathtaking view of the profiles of Monte Renoso and Monte d'Oro. On the belvedere square is a plaque indicating interesting natural and historic attractions.

❿ Gorges du Tavignano

Road map C3. 🛈 Station Touristique de l'Intérieur, La Citadelle, Corte (04 95 46 26 70).

While, east of Corte, the lower course of the Tavignano river extends to Aléria and the sea, its upper course consists of a narrow valley. Here are fascinating gorges that can be reached only by walking along easy paths paved for much of their length in original medieval cobbles and steeped in nature.

One of these paths starts off from below Corte's Citadelle and leads to the Arche de Corte (also known as Arche de Padule), a rocky crest surrounded by *bergeries* lying at an altitude of 1,500 m (4,921 ft). The path passes through chestnut groves in the hilly zone and then, above 1,000 m (3,300 ft), through conifer woods. Strenuous rather than difficult, it entails

Niche with statue, Santa Mariona

a walk of over five hours each way. Looking back from the gorges, the impressive rock of the Citadelle can be seen, still seeming to have control over the entire region.

⓫ Sovéria

Road map C3. 🚗 120. 🚍 Sovéria. 🛈 Station Touristique de l'Intérieur, La Citadelle, Corte (04 95 46 26 70).

Not far from Corte is the pretty village of Sovéria, located high over the Vallée du Golo, a stone's throw away from the Vallée de l'Asco and the regions of Bozio and Castagniccia. Sovéria is appreciated for the harmonious architecture of its houses.

In antiquity, the countryside around Sovéria was given over to vineyards and winemaking. The landscape has changed, however, and today the soft hills are covered with oak and chestnut groves; the area is renowned for its production of excellent nougat.

Along the D18 road, just outside Corte, is the 10th-century Romanesque church of **Santa Mariona**. The only remaining original parts of this church are the twin apses made up of grey stone from the local schist mountains.

⑫ A Tour of Castagniccia

With its rolling green hills, the region east of Corte offers quite a different landscape from Corsica's mountainous interior. Named after its numerous chestnut *(castagna)* groves, Castagniccia was one of the first areas on the island to be inhabited. The highlights of a journey through this region include small villages, between 12th- and 16th-century Baroque chapels with impressive frescoes, many of which were restored between 2005 and 2010, and the complex 17th- and 18th-century architecture of the churches of La Porta and Piedicroce. Castagniccia also played a significant role in the history of Corsica – Morosaglia was the birthplace of independence hero Pascal Paoli, and the region became the centre of a thriving arms industry during the Corsican revolution.

① San Tommaso di Pastoreccia
This chapel has survived excessive restoration that, in the 1930s, destroyed half of its original structure. In the apse, above the hieratic image of *Christ Pantocrator*, is an *Annunciation*; on the walls are the remains of a *Last Judgment*.

② Morosaglia
Corsicans attach special importance to this village where Pascal Paoli, the national hero during the period of independence *(see pp50–51)*, was born. His ashes are interred here. A short walk from Paoli's house-museum is the small church of Santa Reparata, decorated with sculptures that reveal its Romanesque origin (Pisan).

③ San Pantaleo
The small church of San Pantaleo is on the D639 road going down from Morosaglia in the direction of the village of Saliceto. It is worth a visit for the splendid apse that was frescoed in the 15th century.

④ San Quilico
On the D639 road is the Pisan chapel of San Quilico, the lovely tympanum of which is sculpted with Adam and Eve being tempted by the serpent, and with a bas-relief of a man fighting a dragon with his bare hands.

Ponte Leccia

Corte

N193
D15-B
D71
D71
Quercitello
D639
Saliceto
Nocar
D39

Key

▬ Tour route

═ Other roads

0 kilometres 5

0 miles 3

⑤ La Porta
A masterpiece of Corsican Baroque architecture, the church of St-Jean-Baptiste towers over the village of La Porta with its tall bell tower, to the left of the façade.

⑥ Piedicroce
At Piedicroce, the Baroque church of Sts-Pierre-et-Paul dominates a soft landscape of rolling green hills. Built between 1684 and 1696, its light-coloured façade is decorated with white pilasters and friezes. Inside are frescoes and Rococo decorations.

D506

⑦ Couvent d'Orezza
An assembly met in this large monastery in the outskirts of Piedicroce in 1751 and conferred military and executive power on Jean-Pierre Gaffori (*see p138*). The monastery was reduced to ruins during World War II.

⓭ La Porta

Road map D3. **⛰** 215. **i** Mairie (04 95 39 21 48). St-Jean-Baptiste: **Open** daily.

Situated in a fertile area covered in woods, the village of La Porta ("the door") owes its name and prosperity to its location – in the past, this village was the only access route to the region of Castagniccia.

Today, La Porta is famous because of the beautiful church of **St-Jean-Baptiste**, which, together with its imposing bell tower, stands out among the slate roofs of the village. It is considered to be the most complete work of Baroque architecture in Corsica. Construction of the church began in 1648 and continued for nearly half a century under the Italian architect Domenico Baina. The façade was completed in 1707, although it had later alterations. It has been restored to its original ochre colour, which, combined with the vertical white pilasters, gives quite a spectacular impression.

The lower part of the façade is rather austere, with tall pilasters forming a strict pattern. This is broken up by the upper level's elaborate Baroque elements with hints of Rococo, in the shape of pilaster strips, swirly volutes and cartouches.

Pulpit, St-Jean-Baptiste

The Baroque influence is also predominant around the entrance, which is surmounted by friezes. The excesses of the Italian Baroque style have been avoided through this juxtaposition of the plain base with detailing on the higher parts, while the overall harmony of the building has been maintained. The 45-m (147-ft) bell tower next to it shares the same pattern of design: simpler at the base and growing more elaborate for each of its five storeys.

The interior has a single nave flanked by side chapels separated from one another by columns with Corinthian capitals. The walls and ceiling are decorated with late 19th-century stucco work and trompe l'oeil by the artist Girolamo da Porta. Above the entrance is a magnificent monumental organ used in concerts. Other interesting works here include the high altar, made of white Carrara marble, with the altarpiece framed by two small columns, and the pulpit.

The interior contains many fine works of art. Among these are a *Decapitation of St John the Baptist* to the right of the choir, and two 17th-century wooden sculptures representing Christ and the Virgin Mary.

The village of La Porta, dominated by the Baroque bell tower

⑭ Vallée d'Alesani

Road map D3. ⛰ 140. ℹ Tourist office, Piedicroce-Castagniccia (04 95 35 82 54 or 04 95 33 38 21).

This area consists of a group of hamlets scattered on the upper course of the Alesani river. The region is known for the circumstances linked to the rise and fall of Theodor von Neuhof, the first and only king of Corsica (see p50), who was crowned in the **Couvent St-François** in 1736 at Piazzali. The monastery was founded in 1236, but the current Baroque building dates to 1716. One of the side chapels has the *Virgin of the Cherry* (1450), an oil painting on a wooden panel attributed to Sano di Pietro, an artist from Siena.

The neighboring village of Perelli was also the home of the legendary Grosso-Minuto.

The bell tower of Ste-Marie-et-St-Erasme at Cervione

⑮ Cervione

Road map D3. ⛰ 1,700. ℹ Tourist office, Piedicroce-Castagniccia (04 95 35 82 54 or 04 95 33 38 21).

At the foot of Monte Castello and in the easternmost part of Castagniccia, Cervione is surrounded by vineyards, olive orchards and chestnut groves. After the destruction of Aléria, Cervione became a bishopric and, for that occasion, the cathedral of St-Erasme was built. In 1714, the original church was replaced by a new complex, **Ste-Marie-et-**

Grosso-Minuto's Witticisms

A Corsican donkey

A famous figure in Castagniccia folklore, Grosso-Minuto's real name was Pietro Giovanni Ficoni. He was a poor travelling vendor born in Perelli-d'Alesani in 1715. Because of his frail body, he was nicknamed Minuto (tiny), to which Grosso (fat) was added when he became fat in his old age. Ficoni, who was at Pascal Paoli's side for many years, was famous for his sarcastic witticisms, one of the best-known of which concerned a donkey. A woman heard Minuto's donkey bray and asked him if the animal was in love. His reply was: "You're mistaken, Madame, it probably smelled a female donkey."

St-Erasme, the present-day cathedral. The Bishop's Palace and the seminary – now the home of a small ethnographic museum – were also built in this same period. Cervione is the starting point of the panoramic D330 road, also called **Corniche de la Castagniccia**. About 2 km (1 mile) from the town, along this route, is the 9th-century Chapelle Ste-Christine, with twin apses and some frescoes.

⑯ La Canonica

Road map D2. ℹ Tourist office, Rond Point de Mariana, RN 193, Lucciana (04 95 38 43 40). **Open** summer: daily; winter: Mon–Fri. Ask for the key at Lucciana Town Hall. 🌐 **lucciana-mariana.com**

During the period of the Roman conquest (c.259 BC), various colonies were founded in Corsica. While the main colonial city was Aléria (see p148), another one, Mariana, lay nearer to present-day Bastia. It was named after the Roman general Marius, who in 100 BC founded a colony for the veterans of his army near the waters of the Étang de Biguglia. Mariana, where Augustus had a

Detail of a frieze, La Canonica

port built on the Golo river, was the base for the conquest of nearby Cap Corse and for the reclamation and cultivation of the entire plain surrounding the city. Destroyed by the Vandals in the 5th century AD, as was Aléria, Mariana was dealt its final blow by the malaria epidemics that struck the inhabitants of the coastal plains in medieval times.

The Pisans built one of their cathedrals nearby, La Canonica, which was consecrated in 1119 by the archbishop of Pisa. He resided in the nearby bishop's palace, of which only traces of the foundations remain. Known by its original name, even though it was dedicated to Santa Maria Assunta, this church was abandoned for reasons of health and security two centuries later, when the bishop moved to the hills of nearby Vescovato. This church is considered the prototype of all the Pisan churches in Corsica.

The austere Romanesque church La Canonica

The nave is divided into three sections and ends in a semi-circular apse; its elegance is created by the colours of the stone (from the Cap Corse quarries) and by few architectural decorative elements. Above the main portal are friezes representing griffons, a lamb, a wolf and a deer being chased by a dog. The series of holes on the outer walls of the church have sometimes been said to have originally contained multicoloured stone inlays, but they are in fact damage caused by scaffolding.

The famous Ponte-Novo, site of a battle between Corsicans and French

⑰ Vescovato

Road map D2. 🏠 2,500. 🛈 Mairie (Town Hall), Place Luce de Casabianca (04 95 36 70 19).

On a mountainside at the northern end of the Castagniccia region, the town of Vescovato was founded by refugees who had abandoned the city of Mariana, which had proved too vulnerable to invasions and malaria.

For centuries, Vescovato was the capital of the small hilly region of Casinca, which lies between the Golo river and the Vallée du Fium'Alto and which, thanks to its fertile soil, for a long period had the largest population on the island. Formerly called Belfiorito, it was later renamed Vescovato ("bishopric") because it was the bishop's seat from 1269 to 1570, when it was replaced by Bastia. To make the best of a visit here,

The fountain in the square of Vescovato

it is advisable to park at the only tree-lined square and walk through the alleys. In the middle of the village is the Baroque church of **San Martino**, with a 16th-century tabernacle sculpted by the Italian Antonello Gagini. Next to the church, a vaulted passageway leads to the main square, which has a handsome fountain guarded by an eagle. There are three other churches in town, reminders that this was once a bishopric: the church of the Capuchin monastery, the chapel of the Ste-Croix Confraternity and the Romanesque Chapelle San Michele.

The coast east of Vescovato is lined by increasingly popular sandy beaches and tourist resorts.

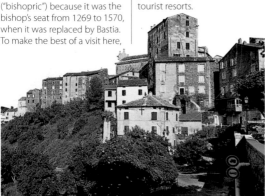

View of Vescovato, formerly a bishopric

⑱ Ponte-Novo

Road map D2. Along the N193 road, 8 km (5 miles) northeast of Ponte Leccia. 🛈 Station Touristique de l'Intérieur, La Citadelle, Corte (04 95 46 26 70).

This locality was named after a bridge built by the Genoese, but its fame throughout the island is due to the battle fought on the banks of the Golo river between the French troops commanded by Count de Vaux and the Corsican patriots led by Pascal Paoli *(see pp50–51)*.

On 8 May 1769, the invading French troops, who had been defeated the year before at Borgo, were trying to find an entry point to the interior of the island, which was under the control of the independence fighters. The 2,000 Corsican patriots were driven back by the French and retreated along the bridge, where they were quickly overcome. After this defeat, Paoli was forced to abandon the struggle against the French and, in June 1769, left the island for England. Thus ended the Corsicans' dream of independence and freedom.

Today, the original bridge is in ruins because of bombardments during World War II. A bridge was built over the river, but the battle is commemorated by a monument and a plaque, accompanied by flags with a Moor's head, the symbol of the Corsican nation *(see p51)*. A visit here offers a great insight into the spirit of the Corsicans.

Cirque de Trimbolocciu, in the Haut-Asco region

⑲ Vallée de l'Asco

Road map C2–C3. **ℹ** Station Touristique de l'Intérieur, La Citadelle, Corte (04 95 46 26 70).

The long, diagonal Vallée de l'Asco – which runs for 30 km (18 miles) southwest of Ponte Leccia – is one of the most isolated areas in Corsica. The road that traverses it follows the winding course of the river Asco up to Corsica's most striking range of mountains, dominated by the dark profile of **Monte Cinto**, the highest peak on the island at 2,706 m (8,878 ft). Along the road is the spectacular **Cirque de Trimbolocciu**, near Monte Cinto, at the head of the Vallée de l'Asco.

In an open area of the valley is the village of **Asco**, which in the 16th century was one of the centres of the Corsican resistance against the Genoese troops. An unsurfaced road full of hairpin bends drops down from Asco towards the banks of the river and then to a marvellous Genoese bridge with the typical arched span.

As the valley rises, the vegetation changes, and the shrubs give way to the pines and larches of the **Forêt de Carozzica**. After this forest, the road ends in the small ski resort at **Haut-Asco**. At an altitude of 1,450 m (4,757 ft), this resort is one of the favourite starting points for hikers on their way towards Monte Cinto (eight hours up and back) or for those

who follow the GR20 long-distance path *(see p26)*, which crosses the Haut-Asco area, passes near the 2,556-m (8,385-ft) high Punta Minuta and arrives at the Tighjiettu refuge *(see p27)*.

The Genoese bridge crossing the river near Asco

⑳ St-François de Caccia

Road map C2. Castifao. **ℹ** Office de Tourisme de Ponte-Leccia-Morosaglia, Place de la Mairie, Ponte-Leccia (04 95 47 70 97). **W** ponteleccia-morosaglia.com

At the beginning of the Vallée de l'Asco, leaving the D47 road in the direction of Moltifao, a detour of about 4 km (2 miles) leads to the ruins of the monastery of St-François de Caccia, near the village of Castifao.

Founded in the early 16th century and destroyed by the Genoese in 1553, the monastery and its church were reconstructed thanks to the efforts of friar Augustinu da Populasca and then entrusted to a group of Franciscan monks. The church, built in 1569 and rebuilt in 1750,

collapsed in 1782. Here, in 1755, Pascal Paoli *(see p51)* took part in the assembly of Corsican deputies who drew up the island's constitution.

㉑ Scala di Santa Regina

Road map C3. **ℹ** Office de Tourisme, Route de Cuccia, Calacuccia (04 95 47 12 62). **W** office-tourisme-niolu.com

The Vallée du Golo has always been an important communication link between the interior and the west coast of Corsica.

Following the course of the Golo river leads to the highest motorable pass on the island, the Col de Verghio, at 1,464 m (4,803 ft) above sea level. From here, one can descend towards Porto and Ajaccio.

Along the valley, on the right-hand side of the road, is the Scala di Santa Regina gorge, which, according to popular tradition, was created thanks to the intervention of the Virgin Mary at the end of a fierce battle between St Martin and Satan. With the reddish hues of the local granite, this narrow gorge is an impressive sight from the road, stretches of which are often cut from the steep rock.

Parts of a narrow mule track along which commercial traffic travelled in the past are still visible from the paved road on the opposite slope of the valley.

The impressive gorges known as Scala di Santa Regina

Wild horses near Calacuccia

㉒ Calacuccia

Road map C3. 🏔 300. ℹ️ Office de Tourisme, Route de Cuccia (04 95 47 12 62). 🌐 office-tourisme-niolu.com

The main town in the Niolo mountain region and in the pass that leads to the Col de Verghio, Calacuccia stands 1,000 m (3,300 ft) above sea level. It is famous for its superb position on the banks of the lake created by a dam that blocks the flow of the Golo river. Small hotels and restaurants that are quite crowded in summer provide relaxation and magnificent views of Monte Cinto to the northwest (see p27) and Capo Tafonato, which rises up next to Col de Verghio.

From Albertacce, 5 km (3 miles) southwest of Calacuccia, orange waymarks lead from opposite a large white crucifix on the western edge of the village to the **Pont de Muricciolu**, an old Genoese footbridge over-looking natural pools that are popular bathing spots.

On the south bank of the artificial lake is the hamlet of Casamaccioli, and going up towards the 1,592-m- (5,223-ft-) high **Bocca di l'Arinella** pass, an unpaved road offers breathtaking views.

㉓ Casamaccioli

Road map C3. 🏔 100. ℹ️ Office de Tourisme, Route de Cuccia, Calacuccia (04 95 47 12 62). 🎭 Nativity of the Virgin (7–10 Sep). 🌐 office-tourisme-niolu.com

Opposite Calacuccia, across the artificial lake and at an altitude of 850 m (2,800 ft), is Casamaccioli, a hamlet with fewer than 100 permanent inhabitants. Besides offering a marvellous view of the lake, the Monte Cinto massif and the surrounding chestnut forests, this village has an interesting tradition that attracts visitors. In the Nativité parish church, beside a wooden statue of St Roch, there is one of the Virgin Mary, or "La Santa". On 7–10 September, this statue is carried in the Nativity of the Virgin procession (see p38) during the festivities in her honour.

㉔ Forêt de Valdu Niellu

Road map C3. ℹ️ Office de Tourisme, Route de Cuccia, Calacuccia (04 95 47 12 62). 🌐 office-tourisme-niolu.com

Southwest of Casamaccioli, on the left-hand side of the road is this forest, the largest in Corsica. Although severely damaged by fires, this forest covers a surface area of more than 46 sq km (18 sq miles) in a mountain zone at an altitude of about 1,000–1,600 m (3,300 5,250 ft). The forest is dominated by birch and beech trees as well as Laricio pines, trees found only on the island of Elba, in parts of the Italian region of Calabria and here in Corsica. At Valdu Niellu, there are Laricio pines as much as 500 years old.

The forest offers many activities, including hiking paths of several levels of difficulty. There is one that takes an hour, going from the Popaja rangers' house to the heart of the forest and then to the Bergeries de Colga. A harder path goes to the 1,743-m- (5,718-ft-) high glacial Lac de Nino (a walk of 3½ hours), the source of the Tavignano river (see p28). The descent to the Cascades de Radule takes a further 90 minutes.

㉕ Col de Verghio

Road map C3. ℹ️ Office de Tourisme, Route de Cuccia, Calacuccia (04 95 47 12 62). 🌐 office-tourisme-niolu.com

The road towards Porto (D84) passes over the Col de Verghio, the highest point in the island's road network. Just east of the Col de Verghio pass, along this route is the small winter-sports resort of **Verghio**, which is a favourite with hikers in the summer.

Here, it is possible to make the ascent to the small Lac de Nino (see p28), the grassy basin of which is grazing land for small herds of wild horses during the summer.

Beaten by the wind and extremely wild, Col de Verghio is part of the itinerary of the GR20 long-distance path (see p26), which, heading north, passes by the Cascades de Radule and then heads up to the Ciuttulu di i Mori refuge at the foot of the majestic Capo Tafonato mountain and the nearby peak of Paglia Orba.

A humid meadowland area near the Col de Verghio

TRAVELLERS' NEEDS

WHERE TO STAY

From holiday villages along the coast to working farms in the mountains, Corsica offers a wide range of places to stay. The greatest concentration of accommodation is to be found in the gulfs of Ajaccio, Calvi, Porto-Vecchio, Bonifacio and St-Florent. Luxury hotels with a private beach or swimming pool tend to be located near the main seaside resorts. It is also possible to rent flats in residences and holiday homes, most of which are located in the south of the island. The many camp sites, both in the interior and on the coast, offer an affordable alternative. *Gîtes ruraux*, or rural holiday homes, are yet another option. Offered by small, family-run establishments, they enable visitors to become better acquainted with Corsican people and their customs.

Hotel Grading

As in the rest of Europe, hotels in Corsica are graded on a star-rating system. One star is for inns with only the most essential services, while four stars are awarded to first-class hotels that offer high-quality amenities.

The highest rating bracket is reserved for luxury and boutique hotels, such as **La Villa** (see p162) in Calvi, **Best Western Premier Hôtel Dolce Vita** (see p164) in Ajaccio and **Le Genovese** (see p164) in Bonifacio.

Three-star hotels often offer surprisingly good value for money. These include the **Hôtel Holtzer** (see p165) in Porto-Vecchio and **Dolce Notte** (see p163) in St-Florent; a few, such as **Castel Brando** (see p162) in Erbalunga, are located in historic buildings. All the four-star and most of the three-star hotels in resorts along the coastline

The pool at the Hôtel Les Mouettes in Ajaccio *(see p163)*

provide either a swimming pool or, if located on the seaside, private access to a beach.

Pleasant accommodation can also be found in two-star establishments, such as **Hôtel** Le Grillon (see p162) in L'Île Rousse.

Single rooms in hotels are rare, so solo travellers should expect to pay the price for a double room. Any extra bed in the room must also be paid for separately. Hotels are increasingly offering at least one or two family rooms.

Travellers with Disabilities

Few hotels in Corsica are able to offer unrestricted wheelchair access. However, most resorts and hotels, as well as many B&Bs, have at least one or two accessible rooms. Larger hotels have lifts, and hotel staff will go out of their way to assist guests with disabilities.

Information is available at the holiday website of the **Association des Paralysés de France (APF)**. Other sources of information are **Mobility International** and **Tourism for All**, which publish a guide listing specialized tour operators for travellers with disabilities.

Prices

French law requires hotels to post a price list – both outside the premises and in each room. This list shows the maximum prices *TTC*, or *Toutes Taxes Comprises* ("including all taxes"), for each season. The prices shown (or quoted when you book a room) also include service. It is illegal to exceed the listed prices.

In the summer, hotels along the coast often quote a rate that includes obligatory half-board. Not all hotels have their own restaurant, and usually breakfast is not included in

Main entrance to the Hostellerie de l'Abbaye in Calvi *(see p162)*

◄ Patio of a hotel near Propriano, on the southwest coast

the price. The same applies for food or drinks served in your room, beverages taken from the minibar, and telephone calls. Many hotels, however, offer free Wi-Fi, which makes it easy to keep in touch with home and avoid expensive telephone surcharges.

Seasons and Booking

Most hotels in Corsica are run on a seasonal basis, from April to October. High season corresponds with the summer months of July and August, when French schools are on holiday. Should you decide to visit the island's seaside resorts during these months, it is vital to arrange accommodation well in advance since many hotels will get booked up early. Outside of July and August, prices often drop dramatically.

From November to March, finding any accommodation at all, especially in the smaller tourist resorts, may also prove difficult, as many hotels close for the winter season. However, hotels in the main cities tend to stay open all year round.

Most hotels now accept online bookings from their websites. You may be asked either to pay a certain amount of money as a deposit or to supply your credit card details. Be sure to read the terms and conditions on the website.

Beautiful views at the Grand Hôtel Miramar, Propriano *(see p165)*

Holiday Villages and Résidences

Holiday villages and *résidences* (holiday homes) along the coast offer visitors a less formal atmosphere than that found in a hotel. The level of accommodation in these establishments varies – from simple rooms in a bungalow with a restaurant and entertainment to self-catering apartments.

All the holiday villages offer entertainment, one or more pools and a wide range of sports and activities, including windsurfing, tennis, diving and sailing.

Among the best such places are the **Club Med** holiday villages at Cargèse and Sant'Ambroggio, not far from Calvi.

Some villages offer all-inclusive packages, in which everything, even drinks at the bar, is covered in the price. The prices of these packages are quoted on a weekly basis. Other clubs allow you to rent an apartment and leave you free to choose whether you want to make use of the services, activities and entertainment or not.

For information on holiday villages, visit the Club Med website or get in touch with a tour operator. For information on *résidences*, contact the **Agence de Tourisme de la Corse**.

Camping

Staying at a camp site is an inexpensive way to enjoy Corsica. There are about 200 camp sites across the island, most of which are situated between Bonifacio and Porto-Vecchio, along the coast of the Balagne region and in the Golfe d'Ajaccio. Most sites, such as **Arinella Bianca**, **Les Oliviers** and **Le Bodri**, are open from Easter to October, while very few are open all year round.

The standard of services and facilities varies widely. The more rustic camp sites are mere plots of land with bathrooms, some trees for shade and fairly modest facilities. Others have swimming pools, organized activities and a range of amenities, including food stores, pizzerias, laundry rooms and, occasionally, even restaurants. Some rent out mobile homes and bungalows for two to more people, complete with a private bathroom and kitchenette.

For a small fee, some farmers allow tents to be pitched on their land. This type of camping also includes the use of the farm's bathing facilities.

It is forbidden to pitch tents outside camp sites or sleep on the beach. To camp on private land, you must ask the owner's permission.

As with hotels, it is best to book well in advance, especially for long stays.

Gorgeous waterviews from a guestroom at Hôtel Le Pinarello *(see p165)*

Self-Catering and Chambres d'Hôtes

Whether it is a mini-apartment in Bonifacio or a villa with a garden and swimming pool in Balagne, self-catering is an inexpensive solution for a family or a group, and certainly an option worth considering when there are young children in your party. Many establishments, especially those in rural areas, offer a combination of *chambres d'hôtes* (B&B rooms), which are generally en suite, and self-catering accommodation, or *gîtes*, small flats with a kitchenette and private bathroom, usually in converted stables or rooms where wine was once made. The listings of **Gîtes de Corsica** offer more than 1,200 self-catering cottages and 84 B&Bs. The websites of **Clévacances**, **Owners Direct** and **Homelidays** are also good sources for finding holiday homes and apartments in all price ranges.

Fermes auberges are similar to *chambres d'hôtes* but usually include half-board in the price, which can make them good value. Note that all the guests often eat at the same table, which might not suit people who prefer privacy. However, these types of accommodation are ideal for those who want to relax

One of the many mountain refuges offering shelter to hikers

without being tied down to a hotel routine, and for families with children, who will have plenty of space to play in. The price categories quoted in this guide indicate the maximum price for a double room with breakfast, including tax and service. For additional listings, visit the website of **Bienvenue à la Ferme**.

Corsica also offers a great many upmarket villas and apartments for rent, especially in the south, but it is essential to book early, especially for July and August. Local tourist offices provide lists of holiday homes and *chambres d'hôtes*, as do specialized websites such as **Pour les Vacances**.

Refuges and Hostels

Corsica offers 16 mountain refuges and many more *gîtes d'étapes* (shelters). These are located mostly along the GR20 long-distance path *(see pp26–31 and 188)* and all are marked on IGN maps. Both refuges and *gîtes d'étapes* tend to be small, with 20–50 bed spaces, often in a dorm, and with only one communal shower room. *Gîtes d'étapes* also have self-catering facilities. Listings are available at **Gîtes de Corsica** and on the website for the **Agence de Tourisme de la Corse**, Corsica's official tourist board.

Refuges are staffed from June to September. In high season, it may be hard to find a place, since it is not possible to book

A comfortable, family-run farm-holiday establishment in the Corsican interior

in advance, but for those who cannot find a bed there is always an area with facilities for camping. A handful of refuges also have food, such as cheese and charcuterie, and drinks available.

There is only one youth hostel in Corsica, **U Carabellu**. Located along the GR20, just outside Calvi, this hostel provides beds at low prices.

Recommended Hotels

The hotels recommended in this guide have been chosen for the quality of accommodation they offer, for their location in some of Corsica's most desirable areas, and for their value for money.

For easy reference, they have been divided into several types. Luxury hotels, nearly always located by the sea, often feature gourmet restaurants; boutique hotels boast charming design, while historic hotels, housed in old mansions or other historic buildings, are packed full of

character. Country retreats are located in beautiful inland settings, and seaside hotels are nearly always within walking distance of a beach. Traditional hotels are purpose-built establishments in cities or towns, and they often offer the most affordable option in any given area, along with the B&Bs set in charming locations. Apartments have self-catering facilities which allow for a homely stay. Family-friendly

hotels have activities for those with children.

Among the listings on the next few pages, you will find hotels that have been designated as DK Choice entries. This is in recognition of one or more outstanding features, such as exceptional facilities, the beauty of the location or the views, excellent service or any other appealing aspect that sets them apart from the competition.

Comfortable en-suite room in the 18th-century U Palazzu in Pigna *(see p163)*

DIRECTORY

Travellers with Disabilities

Association des Paralysés de France (APF)
40 Ave Noel Francini, 20090, Ajaccio.
Tel 04 95 20 75 33.
Immeuble San Petru Bat. A, Route Imperiale, 20600, Bastia.
Tel 04 95 30 86 01.
w vacances-accessibles. apf.asso.fr

Mobility International
132 E Broadway, Eugene, Oregon, 97401.
Tel (541) 343 1284.
w miusa.org

Tourism for All
7A Pixel Mill, 44 Appleby Road, Kendal, Cumbria LA9 6ES.
Tel (0845) 124 9971.
w tourismforall. org.uk

Holiday Villages and Résidences

Agence de Tourisme de la Corse
17 Blvd du Roi Jérôme, 20181, Ajaccio.
Tel 04 95 51 77 77.
w visit-corsica.com

Club Med Cargèse
Place du Chiuni, 20130.
Tel 04 95 26 90 00.
w clubmed.com

Club Med Sant'Ambroggio
Marine de Sant'Ambroggio, 20260, Lumio.
Tel 04 95 60 84 00.
w clubmed.com

Camping

Arinella Bianca
Ghisonaccia, 20240.
Tel 04 95 56 04 78.
w camping-corse.fr

Le Bodri
Route de Calvi, 20256, Corbara.
Tel 04 95 60 10 86 or 04 95 60 06 47.
w campinglebodri.com

Les Oliviers
Pont de Porto, 20150, Porto (Ota.)
Tel 04 95 26 14 49.
w camping-oliviers-porto.com

Self-Catering and Chambres d'Hôtes

Airbnb
w airbnb.com
w airbnb.fr
w airbnb.uk

Bienvenue à la Ferme
w bienvenue-a-la-ferme.com

Clévacances
w clevacances.com

Gîtes de Corsica
77 Cours Napoléon, BP 10, Ajaccio.
Tel 04 95 10 54 30.
w gites-corsica.com

Homelidays
w homelidays.co.uk
w homelidays.com

Owners Direct
w ownersdirect.co.uk

Pour les Vacances
w pour-les-vacances. com

Refuges and Hostels

Agence de Tourisme de la Corse
See Holiday Villages and Résidences.

U Carabellu
Route de Pietra Maggiore, 20260, Calvi.
Tel 04 93 81 27 63 or 04 95 65 14 16.
w clajsud.fr

Tourist Offices

Ajaccio
3 Blvd du Roi Jérôme, 20000.
Tel 04 95 51 53 03.
w ajaccio-tourisme.com

Bastia
Place Saint Nicolas, 20200.
Tel 04 95 54 20 40.
w bastia-tourisme.com

Where to Stay

Bastia and the North

ALGAJOLA:
Hôtel Beau Rivage €€
Seaside   Map C2
29 Rue A Marina, 20220
Tel *04 95 60 73 99 or 04 95 60 70 67*
W hotel-beau-rivage.com
Peaceful, clean rooms and a terrace on the sandy beach. Friendly, family-orientated hotel.

ARGENTELLA:
Auberge Ferayola €
Country Retreat   Map B2
Argentella, 20260
Tel *04 95 65 25 25*
W ferayola.com
Located in the Corsican Regional Natural Park, this hotel offers tranquil rooms and cottages close to the beach.

BASTIA: Hôtel Le Central €€
Traditional   Map D2
3 Rue Miot, 20200
Tel *04 95 31 71 12*
W centralhotel.fr
A charming hotel with pleasant rooms and a great location in the old town, next to the port.

BASTIA: Hôtel Ostella €€
Traditional   Map D2
*Avenue Sampiero Corso,
Sortie Sud, 20600*
Tel *04 95 30 97 70*
W hotel-ostella.com
Sunny rooms, suites with private Jacuzzis, and a *hammam*. Good efficient service.

BASTIA: Hôtel Pietracap €€
Boutique   Map D2
20 Route San Martino, San Martino di Lota, 20200
Tel *04 95 31 64 63*
W pietracap.com
A comfortable hotel, swathed in bougainvillea, in a seaside park, just outside of Bastia.

BASTIA: Les Voyageurs €€
Historic   Map D2
9 Avenue Maréchal Sébastiani, 20200
Tel *04 95 34 90 80*
W hotel-lesvoyageurs.com
Bright and uncluttered rooms with a traditional decor. Hearty breakfast buffet.

CALENZANA: A Flatta €€
Country Retreat   Map C2
Calenzana, 20214
Tel *04 95 62 80 38*
W aflatta.com
A rural mountain hideaway with lovely views and sounds of the nearby river. Excellent restaurant.

CALVI: U Carabellu €
Family Friendly   Map B2
Route de Pietra, Maggiore
Tel *04 95 65 14 16*
W clajsud.fr
Close to the Citadelle, with views of the bay, this hostel has low-cost rooms for families and individuals.

CALVI: Hôtel Le Magnolia €€
Historic   Map B2
Rue Alsace Lorraine, 20260
Tel *04 95 65 19 16*
W hotel-le-magnolia.com
Charming rooms in a romantic, historic mansion with a century-old magnolia tree in the garden.

**CALVI: Château Hôtel
La Signoria** €€€
Luxury   Map B2
Route de la Forêt de Bonifato, 20260
Tel *04 95 65 93 00*
W hotel-la-signoria.com
Beautiful rooms, lush gardens, a gourmet restaurant and a private beach. Excellent service.

CALVI: Hostellerie de l'Abbaye €€€
Traditional   Map B2
Montée de l'Abbaye, BP 18, 20260
Tel *04 95 65 04 27*
W hostellerie-abbaye.com
Pretty, ivy-covered hotel set in an old abbey. Close to the town centre and the beaches.

CALVI: The Manor €€€
Boutique   Map B2
Chemin Saint-Antoine, 20260
Tel *04 95 62 72 42*
W manor-corsica.com
Elegant rooms in a restored stone house with vast gardens, a pool and lovely views.

CALVI: La Villa €€€
Luxury   Map B2
Chemin Notre Dame de la Serra, 20260
Tel *04 95 65 10 10*
W hotel-lavilla.com

Price Guide

Prices are based on one night's stay in high season for a standard double room, inclusive of service charges and taxes.

€	up to €100
€€	€100 to €200
€€€	over €200

An opulent hotel with a stunning infinity pool, tennis court and spa. Monthly classical music concerts take place at the restaurant.

DK Choice

ERBALUNGA:
Castel Brando €€
Historic   Map D2
Erbalunga, 20222
Tel *04 95 30 10 30*
W castelbrando.com
Set in a 19th-century house, Castel Brando is located in a park of ancient olive trees and exotic palms. The rooms are spacious and elegant, and there are two pools and a breakfast patio. Superb staff.

L'ÎLE ROUSSE:
Hôtel Le Grillon €
Traditional   Map C2
10 Avenue Paul Doumer, 20220
Tel *04 95 60 00 49*
W hotelgrillon.com
Excellent, fairly central choice with simple, clean rooms, conveniently close to the beach. Excellent value.

**L'ÎLE ROUSSE: Best Western
Hôtel Santa Maria** €€
Seaside   Map C2
Route du Port, 20220
Tel *04 95 63 05 05*
W hotelsantamaria.com
A charming hotel with its own beach. All rooms have mountain and sea views.

Loungers set out next to the spa pool at La Villa, Calvi

L'ÎLE ROUSSE:
Perla Rossa €€€
Boutique Map C2
30 Rue Notre Dame, 20220
Tel *04 95 48 45 30*
w hotelperlarossa.com
Chic luxury retreat in a 19th-
century palazzo hidden away
on a street close to the beach.

MACINAGGIO:
U Libecciu €€
Family Friendly Map D1
Route de la Plage, 20248
Tel *04 95 35 43 22*
w u-libecciu.com
An excellent base for exploring
Corsica's northernmost areas.
Spacious rooms, swimming pool
and friendly staff.

MONTICELLO:
A Piattatella €€€
Boutique Map C2
Chemin Saint François, 20220
Tel *04 95 60 07 00*
w hotel-corse-apiattatella.com
Quiet rooms with magnificent
decor and valley views. There is
a great spa and a heated pool.
Excellent restaurant.

NONZA: Casa Lisa €
B&B Map D1
Paule Patrizi Olmeta, 20217
Tel *04 95 37 83 52*
w casalisa.fr
Authentic Corsican village
house with simple rooms and
great sea views. It is very remote
and accessible only on foot.

PATRIMONIO: Auberge
U Lustincone €
Country Retreat Map D2
Route du Cap, 20253
Tel *04 95 37 15 28*
w u-lustincone.com
Set in Patrimonio vineyard
country, this hotel has lovely
mountain and sea views.
Pleasant swimming pool and a
great restaurant.

PIGNA: U Palazzu €€
Historic Map C2
Pigna, 20220
Tel *04 95 47 32 78*
w hotel-corse-palazzu.com
An elegantly furnished hotel
in an 18th-century palace. The
restaurant is excellent.

SAINT-FLORENT:
Dolce Notte €€
Seaside Map D2
Plage de l'Ospedale,
Route de Bastia, 20217
Tel *04 95 37 06 65*
w hotel-dolce-notte.com
Pleasant rooms, some with large
private terraces and fantastic
views of the bay.

Spacious rooms overlooking the sea in Les Mouettes, Ajaccio

SAINT-FLORENT:
Hôtel de l'Europe €€
Seaside Map D2
Quai du Port de Plaisance,
Place des Portes, 20217
Tel *04 95 35 32 91*
w hotel-europe2.com
Family-run place overlooking the
harbour. Pleasantly-decorated
rooms and a great restaurant.

SAINT-FLORENT:
Demeure Loredana €€€
Luxury Map D2
Cisterminu Suttanu, 20217
Tel *04 95 37 22 22*
w demeureloredana.com
A stately hotel with fabulous
views. Stunning infinity pool and
heated indoor pool.

Ajaccio and the West Coast

AJACCIO: Hôtel Kallisté €
Historic Map B4
51 Cours Napoléon, 20000
Tel *04 95 51 34 45*
w hotel-kalliste-ajaccio.com

Immaculate bathroom with views at
the the historic U Palazzu, Pigna

Surprisingly quiet hotel in a
busy area. Rooms have vaulted
ceilings and rustic decor.

AJACCIO: Hôtel Marengo €
Traditional Map B4
2 Rue Marengo, 20000
Tel *04 95 21 43 66*
w hotel-marengo.com
Located in a city town house,
hidden in a cul-de-sac. Enjoy the
secluded feel of this hotel close
to the beach.

AJACCIO: Hôtel Fesch €€
Traditional Map B4
7 Rue Cardinal Fesch, 20000
Tel *04 95 51 62 62*
w hotel-fesch.com
This long-established hotel on
a quiet street is a good base for
visiting historic sites and a daily
pedestrian market nearby.

AJACCIO: Hôtel Napoléon €€
Traditional Map B4
4 Rue Lorenzo Vero, 20181
Tel *04 95 51 54 00*
w hotel-napoleon-ajaccio.fr
The best rooms in this centrally
located city hotel face a neighbouring garden. Helpful staff.

AJACCIO:
Hôtel San Carlu Citadelle €€
Traditional Map B4
8 Blvd Danielle Casanova, 20000
Tel *04 95 21 13 84*
w hotel-sancarlu.com
Rooms are on the modest side
but have fantastic views of the
sea and the Citadelle. Family
rooms and apartments are
also available.

AJACCIO: Les Mouettes €€
Boutique Map B4
9 Cours Lucien Bonaparte, 20000
Tel *04 95 50 40 40*
w hotellesmouettes.fr
Riviera-style rooms in a lovely
19th-century seaside mansion
with its own private beach.

For more information on types of hotels *see page 161*

Beautiful scenery surrounding Hôtel Les Roches Rouges, Piana

AJACCIO: Best Western Hôtel Dolce Vita €€€
Seaside   Map B4
Route des Îles Sanguinaires, 20000
Tel *04 95 52 42 42*
[W] hotel-dolcevita.com
Enjoy cocktails on the lovely terrace overlooking the rocky shoreline. Spacious rooms.

DK Choice

**AJACCIO:
Hôtel Palazzu u Domu** €€€
Boutique   Map B4
17 Rue Bonaparte, 20000
Tel *04 95 50 00 20*
[W] palazzu-domu.com
Formerly the ancestral mansion of the Duke Pozzo di Borgo, this hotel defines elegance and luxury. Each well-equipped room is furnished in muted, natural tones that complement the stone exterior. There is also a lovely private courtyard.

AJACCIO: Stella di Mare €€€
Seaside   Map B4
Route des Sanguinaires, 20000
Tel *04 95 52 01 07*
[W] hotel-stelladimare.com
Amazing sunset views from the sea-water pool and terraced bar.

CARGÈSE: Le Continental €
Traditional   Map B3
Route de Piana, 20130
Tel *04 95 26 42 24*
[W] lecontinentalhotel.fr
Welcoming establishment with great sea views. Basic rooms, friendly staff and a fine restaurant.

**CARGÈSE:
Hôtel Résidence Hélios** €
Apartments   Map B4
Menasina, 20130
Tel *04 95 26 41 24 or 06 85 23 24 52*
[W] locations-corse-cargese.com
Self-catered apartments with private terraces. Ideal for family holidays.

**CARGÈSE:
ClubMed Holiday Resort** €€€
Family Friendly   Map B4
Plage du Chiuni, 20130
Tel *04 95 26 90 00*
[W] locations-corse-cargese.com
Bungalow living on a mountain-side overlooking the Ajaccio gulf. Activity and sports clubs for kids.

GALÉRIA: L'Auberge €
B&B   Map B3
Centre du village, 20245
Tel *04 95 62 00 15*
[W] hotel-restaurant-auberge.com
Tiny family-run hotel set amid gardens. Ideal for exploring Sandola Nature Reserve.

PIANA: Les Roches Rouges €€
Historic   Map B3
Route de Porto, 20115
Tel *04 95 27 81 81*
[W] lesrochesrouges.com
A charming 100-year-old listed hotel with panoramic views of the Golfe de Porto.

PIANA: Capo Rosso €€€
Boutique   Map B3
Route de Porto, Calvi 20115
Tel *04 95 27 82 40*
[W] caporosso.com
Elegant rooms with either balconies or terraces. Excellent seafood restaurant.

PORTICCIO: Le Maquis €€€
Luxury   Map B3
BP 94, 20166
Tel *04 95 25 05 55*
[W] lemaquis.com
One of the oldest luxury hotels in Corsica, with a stunning location on its own private, protected cove. An excellent hotel restaurant.

PORTO: Bella Vista Hôtel €
Traditional   Map B3
Route de Calvi, 20150
Tel *04 95 26 11 08*
[W] hotel-corse.com
Bright rooms with beautiful views of the Golfe de Porto. Welcoming and helpful staff.

PORTO: Les Flots Bleus €€
Boutique   Map B3
Marina de Porto Ota, 20150
Tel *04 95 26 11 26*
[W] hotel-lesflotsbleus.com
Bright and modern rooms over-looking the Genoese tower and beach. Good value for money.

PORTO: Hôtel Le Colombo €€
Country Retreat   Map B3
Route de Calvi, 20150
Tel *04 95 26 10 14*
[W] hotel-colombo-porto.com
Offers hearty breakfasts and beautiful views over Porto.

SERRIERA: Eden Park €€
Boutique   Map B3
Golfe de Porto, 20147
Tel *04 95 26 10 60*
[W] hotel-edenpark-corse.com
Set in a luxurious park, amenities include a restaurant, tranquil pool, spa and tennis court.

SERRIERA: Hôtel Stella Marina €€
Seaside   Map B3
Plage de Bussaglia, 20147
Tel *04 95 26 11 18*
[W] hotel-stella-marina.com
Close to the beach, this is a good base from which to explore the Calanques. Rented boats available.

Bonifacio and the South

BONIFACIO: Best Western Hôtel du Roy d'Aragon €€
Seaside   Map C6
13 Quai Jerome Comparetti, Port de Plaisance, 20169
Tel *04 95 73 03 99*
[W] royaragon.com
Basic but relatively spacious rooms. Superb location in the port.

BONIFACIO: Hôtel du Golfe €€
Seaside   Map C6
Lieu-dit Santa Manza, 20169
Tel *04 95 73 05 91*   **Closed** *Winter*
[W] hoteldugolfe-bonifacio.com
A quiet hotel by the Gulf of Santa Manza's sandy beaches. Comfy rooms and a good restaurant.

BONIFACIO: Hôtel Santa Teresa €€
Boutique   Map C6
Quartier Saint-François, 20690
Tel *04 95 73 11 32*
[W] hotel-santateresa.com
Built in 1897 as a garrison, this hotel is spectacularly set on a cliff with views to Sardinia.

BONIFACIO: Le Genovese €€€
Boutique   Map C6
Haute Ville, Place de l'Europe, 20169
Tel *04 95 73 12 34*
[W] hotel-genovese.com

Fantastic location close to the marina and old town. Very well-appointed rooms. Great staff.

BONIFACIO: Hôtel A Cheda €€€
Luxury   **Map** C6
Cavallo Morto – BP 3, 20169
Tel 04 95 73 03 82
Ⓦ acheda-hotel.com
A quiet hotel enveloped in lush greenery. Lovely kitchen garden where fresh food is sourced.

LECCI (PORTO-VECCHIO): Grand Hôtel de Cala Rossa €€€
Luxury   **Map** D5
Route de Cala-Rossa, 20137
Tel 04 95 71 61 51 or 04 95 71 78 78
Ⓦ cala-rossa.com
A charming hotel in a lovely beach setting. Indulgent spa and pool.

> ## DK Choice
>
> **PINARELLO (SAINTE-LUCIE DE PORTO VECCHIO): Hôtel Le Pinarello** €€€
> Luxury   **Map** D5
> *Plage de Pinarello, 20144*
> **Tel** 04 95 71 44 39
> Ⓦ lepinarello.com
> Overlooking a beautiful beach with fine white sands, this hotel is ideal for a seaside break. Rent kayaks, jetskis or motor-boats, take sailing lessons or just relax in the spa and wellness centre.

PORTO-VECCHIO: Hôtel Holtzer €€
Boutique   **Map** B5
12 Rue Jean Jaurès, 20137
Tel 04 95 70 05 93
Ⓦ hotel-holzer.com
A simple and chic hotel near the old town. Good value for money.

PORTO-VECCHIO: Hôtel Ranch Campo €€
Country Retreat   **Map** C6
Route de Palombaggia, 20137
Tel 04 95 70 13 27
Ⓦ ranchcampo.com
Hotel rooms and self-catering villas are available at this working ranch.

PORTO-VECCHIO: Hôtel San Giovanni €€
Family Friendly   **Map** C6
Route d'Arca, 20137
Tel 04 95 70 22 25
Ⓦ hotel-san-giovanni.com
Family-run place set in charming flowering woodland. Excellent restaurant.

PORTO-VECCHIO: Kilina €€
Family Friendly   **Map** C6
Route de Cala Rossa, 20137
Tel 04 95 71 60 43
Ⓦ kilina.fr
Simple rooms, two large pools and a summer kids club, this is the perfect choice for families.

PORTO-VECCHIO: Private Hôtel E Casette €€€
Boutique   **Map** C6
Route de Palombaggia, 20137
Tel 04 95 70 13 66
Ⓦ private-hotel-corsica.com
Rooms have private Jacuzzis and terraces. Stunning sunset views over Porto-Vecchio and a spa.

PROPRIANO: Le Bellevue €
Traditional   **Map** B5
13 Avenue Napoleon, 20110
Tel 04 95 76 01 86   **Closed** *Winter*
Ⓦ hotel-bellevue-propriano.com
The best rooms here have sea-facing balconies. Excellent location on the marina.

PROPRIANO: Grand Hôtel Miramar €€€
Luxury   **Map** B5
6 Route de la Corniche, 20110
Tel 04 95 76 06 13   **Closed** *Winter*
Ⓦ miramarboutiquehotel.com
Secluded deluxe rooms, all with great sea views. Chic decor with white-washed walls.

QUENZA: Auberge Sole e Monti €€
Traditional   **Map** C5
Quenza, 20122
Tel 04 95 78 62 53
Ⓦ solemonti.com
This place is perfectly located for hikers and has a great restaurant.

A breakfast table overlooking the beach at Hôtel Le Pinarello, Pinarello

SERRA DI FERRO: Hôtel Les Eucalyptus €€
Traditional   **Map** B5
Porto-Pollo, 20140
Tel 04 95 74 01 52
Ⓦ hoteleucalyptus.com
Close to Filitosa and the sea, this is a great location for history buffs and sun-soakers alike.

TIZZANO: Hôtel du Golfe €€
Seaside   **Map** B6
Quenza, 20122
Tel 06 87 65 80 81
Ⓦ solemonti.com
Family-run hotel located in a small fishing village outside Sartene. Rooms with balconies.

Corte and the Interior

CALACUCCIA: L'Acqua Viva €
Country Retreat   **Map** C3
Lieu-dit Scarduccicole, 20224
Tel 04 95 48 06 90 or 04 95 48 00 08
Ⓦ acquaviva-fr.com
An ideal base for exploring Corsica's interior. Simple, cheerful rooms and camp sites on the lake.

> ## DK Choice
>
> **CORTE: Hôtel Dominique Colonna** €€
> Country Retreat   **Map** C3
> *Vallée de la Restonica, BP 83, 20250*
> **Tel** 04 95 45 25 65   **Closed** *Winter*
> Ⓦ dominique-colonna.com
> A comfy, modern hotel beautifully situated on the riverbanks in the Vallée de la Restonica, with balconies over the water. Do not miss dinner at the Auberge de la Restonica next door.

CORTE: Hôtel du Nord €€
Traditional   **Map** C3
22 Cours Paoli 20250
Tel 04 95 46 00 68
Ⓦ hoteldunord-corte.com
The oldest hotel in Corte is centrally located and dog-friendly.

Classy room with views at the Dominique Colonna, Corte

For more information on types of hotels *see page 161*

WHERE TO EAT AND DRINK

The natural beauty of the island of Corsica is complemented by the pleasures of its rich cuisine, which brings together flavours of the land and the sea. An apéritif at sunset in front of the small harbour in Ajaccio, fresh grilled fish on a small beach in Cap Corse, cannelloni stuffed with *brocciu* cheese at a *ferme auberge* or the elegant refinement of a fine-dining restaurant in a large hotel – Corsica offers no shortage of options when it comes to eating and

drinking. The food here is generally good and not overpriced. Cafés and bistros are ideal for a quick snack and, for those on a budget, there are several pizzerias, especially in the seaside resorts. Tourism is slower-paced inland, which is the ideal place to find a traditional meal at a country inn or *ferme auberge*. Here, good regional food is often accompanied by interesting conversations with the locals or traditional music.

The restaurant at Hôtel Le Maquis in Porticcio *(see p164)*

Types of Restaurants

Corsica has a wide variety of dining establishments. The most exclusive are the gourmet restaurants, located mainly in fashionable resorts along the coast.

Not surprisingly, fish and seafood restaurants are particularly popular along the coast, offering fish soup, grilled shrimp, lobsters, seafood stews, sardines with fresh *brocciu* cheese, and other specialities.

The most common restaurants, though, both inland and on the coast, are those that specialize in traditional Corsican cuisine. Although meat dishes tend to dominate the menu here (charcuterie, lamb, veal, goat kid and boar are especially popular), you can generally also find a seafood or vegetarian option. Fresh, local ingredients are usually the main focus of contemporary Corsican restaurants, where inventive

chefs take great pride in using them in creative ways.

Cities and resorts also have bistros, brasseries and wine bars, which are ideal for a simple meal, a slice of quiche or a plate of cheese or cold cuts. Because Corsica is very popular with Italian visitors, the island also boasts many excellent Italian restaurants and pizzerias.

Fermes Auberges

Try to visit a *ferme auberge* (farm inn) at least once during your stay. You will find genuine Corsican dishes made with products from the farm itself, such as cheese, vegetables and charcuterie.

Bars and Cafés

Many bars and cafés have tables outdoors. These become particularly crowded during the apéritif hour, when people

gather at their local bar or café to have a glass of *pastis*, Cap Corse or Corsican beer, accompanied by olives. Cafés open early and also serve breakfast, and in many pastry shops there are small tables where you can enjoy croissants, biscuits, pastries, cakes and tarts.

Breakfast

In Corsica, the *petit déjeuner* (breakfast) is an important ritual. The day begins with coffee (*café au lait* or *café crème*), accompanied by fresh bread and brioche, eaten with honey or preserves. There are also croissants and *pains au chocolat*. The large hotels often serve continental breakfasts with meat and cheese, while on the farms, breakfast consists of fresh home produce, including honey, milk and assorted preserves.

Interior of La Rascasse restaurant, Saint-Florent

The Glacier du Port restaurant, Solenzara

Prices and Paying

In addition to the à la carte menu, almost all restaurants in Corsica have fixed-price menus or a shorter fixed-priced *formule*, usually served only at lunchtime. These menus offer regional or fish and seafood specialities and sometimes give you the opportunity to try typical dishes that would otherwise be hard to find. Many offer an inexpensive *menu corse*, featuring traditional dishes.

In general, a complete meal in an average-level restaurant with a half-bottle of wine costs about €30, while in bistros and simple restaurants it is €15–€20. If you do not want to spend much, try the pizzerias – a meal here rarely costs more than €10–€12.

Restaurants usually accept the most commonly used credit cards in Europe; however, *fermes auberges* and smaller places in less frequented areas prefer cash.

Opening Hours and Reservations

Opening hours in Corsica are similar to those in mainland France. Lunch is usually served from 12:30 to 2:30pm and dinner from 7:30 to 10pm. However, in summer, tourist resorts in many places close later, while bistros and snack bars tend to stay open throughout the day. The villages inland usually have shorter opening hours. Most establishments close once a week and for their holidays, which usually coincide with the low season.

In the summer, especially in the evening, it is always advisable to book a table in advance, as restaurants can get quite crowded.

Vegetarian Food and Wheelchair Access

Vegetarians will not have too hard a time ordering a meat- or fish-free meal in Corsica. Good options include omelettes, cannelloni with *brocciu*, pasta and pizza.

Wheelchair access and facilities for the disabled may be hard to find, especially in the old historic centres and villages, although many places have now conformed to the new regulations.

Dress and Smoking

There is no need to dress elegantly in restaurants, unless they are exclusive, but avoid going to the opposite extreme: bathing costumes should stay on the beach.

Corsica adheres to strict government regulations that prohibit smoking inside restaurants and cafés. However, smoking is generally permitted at outdoor tables.

Recommended Restaurants

The restaurants listed in this guide are among the best in Corsica. They have been carefully selected for their reliably good food, location, service, value, or a combination of these. The listings cover a vast variety of eateries, from simple pizzerias and cafés to top gourmet restaurants. Whether you are looking for authentic goat kid stew, traditional Corsican charcuterie, or a Michelin-starred dining experience, the following pages offer lots of choice.

Any restaurants highlighted as DK Choice have been chosen for one or more exceptional features: the quality of the food, the atmosphere, a beautiful setting or stunning views.

The elegant dining room of La Caravelle *(see p177)*, in Bonifacio

The Flavours of Corsica

Corsican cuisine reflects centuries of outside influences, while still proudly maintaining its own identity. The Greeks and Phoenicians introduced olives and vines; chestnuts arrived with the Genoese in the 16th century; clementines were first planted in the 20th. All now play a key role in local dishes, along with semi-wild pigs, game, seafood and herbs. Climate, terrain, coastline and history all contribute to the wonderful produce found here, and its island status means that many Corsican specialities are unique and seldom found beyond its shores. In particular, Corsicans are rightly proud of their superb charcuterie *(see p101)* and cheeses.

Clementines

Donkey saucisson on sale in Bastia's colourful market

Meat and Seafood

Goat kid is a favourite meat in Corsica, while pigs are raised for fresh meat and charcuterie. There is also abundant game, including wild boar, rabbit, hare, pigeon and partridge. The semi-wild black pigs that roam the uplands often end up in a distinctive range of hams and sausages that has more in common with Italian than French charcuterie. *Prisuttu* is

a cured ham that is hung to dry for one to two years; *salsiccia* and *salamu* are air-dried sausages made of minced pork. Marbled red *coppa* is made from pork shoulder, and the dark red, peppery *lonzu* from cured pork fillet. Both are lightly smoked. The most unusual product is *figatelli*, a dark, U-shaped, smoked liver sausage which can be grilled or dried and eaten cold.

Corsican seafood includes mullet, bass, swordfish, monkfish, sardines and anchovies, as well as lobster, squid, sea urchins and crabs. Oysters and mussels are cultivated in the Etang de Diane on the eastern side of the island.

Cheeses

A cheese you're sure to come across in one form or another

Mussels   Lobster   Prawns (shrimp)   Sea bass   Monkfish   Squid   Clams

Selection of seafood found in the clear waters off the Corsican coast

Corsican Dishes and Specialities

Numerous pasta dishes testify to Corsica's Italian past: macaroni with *stufatu* stew; ravioli or cannelloni stuffed with Brocciu; or wild boar lasagne. Fresh fish is often simply grilled over charcoal but there is also a *bouillabaisse*-style fish soup called *aziminu*. Sea urchins *(oursins)* scooped out with a spoon or bread are a winter treat. Wild boar and kid are stewed or roasted with herbs and garlic; suckling pig is roasted with herbs; lamb, rabbit or veal may be cooked with olives and tomato.
Vegetable gratins feature, and bean dishes encompass thick soups, a *cassoulet*-style stew, and broad (fava) beans with bacon *(fèves au lard)*. The best-known dessert is *fiadone*; others feature figs or clementines; fritters *(fritelli)* are made from chestnut flour.

Olives and their oil

Soupe corse simmers white beans, onions, cabbage and other vegetables. Ham and pasta are added at the end.

Cheese stall in Ajaccio's open-air market

on the island is *Brocciu* or *Brucciu*, a mild, white, fresh cheese similar to Italian Ricotta or the Brousse of Provence. It is made from whey and usually eaten fresh – within 48 hours – sprinkled with sugar or in many cooked dishes, although it can be left to mature into a hard, dry ball. The island's other cheeses mostly get their names, including Niolo, Venaco, Sartène and Bastelicaccia, from the area where they were first made; others are simply called by the generic name of Tome or Tomme. They vary from mild semi-soft cheeses with washed rinds to hard, pressed cheeses which gain in strength as they age and may be matured until they are hard and crumbly. Newer varieties include Brin d'Amour, which is rolled in herbs, and Bleu de Corse, a Roquefort-like blue ewes' milk cheese.

Fruit and Vegetables

Corsica grows all types of citrus fruit, including kumquats. Clementines are one of the island's main crops, most of the harvest being exported to the mainland. The Corsican

Chestnuts ripening on the tree in the Corsican sunshine

clementine is small and firm with a sharp, tangy flavour and a thin, tightly-fitting skin. You'll also find exotic species such as Barbary figs and the *arbousier* or strawberry tree. Vegetables include aubergines (eggplants), courgettes (zucchini), beans, chard, tomatoes and peppers. Some of the olive trees in the south of the island are over 1,000 years old. The chestnut tree was dubbed *l'arbre à pain* (the bread tree) because it gave islanders a form of flour to supplement that from the limited cereals on the island. Today, chestnuts are found in many recipes, and they are still ground into flour.

On the Menu

Canistrelli Chestnut cookies

Civet de sanglier aux châtaignes Wild boar stewed in red wine with chestnuts

Courgettes farcies Courgettes (zucchini) stuffed with meat, cheese and vegetables and then baked

Pulenda Type of polenta, made with chestnut flour

Ragoût de cabri Kid stewed in red wine with onions

Stufatu Pork, beef, lamb and ham cooked in red wine and served with pasta

Tianu d'agneau aux olives Neck of lamb stewed with herbs and olives

Cabri roti, roast kid, is a celebratory feast, studded with rosemary and garlic, crisp outside and succulent within.

Rouget aux anchois is red mullet fillets with a piquant anchovy stuffing, fried until crisp and golden.

Fiadone is a baked cheesecake made from *Brocciu* along with eggs, sugar and lemon zest.

What to Drink in Corsica

Corsican wines date back to the period when the ancient Greeks and Romans colonized the island, as revealed by the amphoras of wine found in galleys that sank off the east coast. Full-bodied, fruity and strong, Corsican wines are made from three local grapes, Sciaccarellu, Niellucciu and Vermentinu, which, over the years, have been combined with others from the Continent that have flourished on the island. The wines are made in nine zones that have the AOC *(Appellation d'Origine Controlée)* designation, which is a guarantee of superior quality and authenticity. In addition, Corsica produces various liqueurs and brandies that are made from maquis plants such as myrtle and strawberry tree and that reflect the strong flavours of the island. There are also local mineral water springs and aromatized beers.

The tables of the Café Napoléon, in Place St-Nicolas, Bastia

Liqueurs and Aperitifs

As an apéritif, Corsicans drink pastis, an aniseed liqueur that in the summer is enjoyed with ice. Other liqueurs are made from myrtle, strawberry tree and citrus fruits like tangerines, oranges and citrons. Castagniccia also produces a chestnut liqueur.

Cap Corse is a real institution. Its inimitable bitter and acidulous taste derives from quinine. This Corsican apéritif can be purchased at the Maison Mattei *(see p67)*, the historic house founded in Bastia in 1872.

Tangerines

Citrons

Citron liqueur

Water and Beer

Cool mineral water flows from springs in the mountains and is then bottled and sold throughout the island. Beer is also produced on the island. Corsican beer is known for its strong aromas.

Zilia mineral water

Orezza mineral water

St-Georges mineral water

Four brands of beer are produced in Corsica. Pietra Bionda is a premium full-bodied lager; Pietra is amber-coloured and includes chestnuts among its ingredients; Serena is pale and light; and Colomba is a Belgian/German-style wheat beer with a strong taste thanks to the addition of myrtle.

The best-known sparkling *(pétillante)* mineral water is Orezza, from the Castagniccia area, which is bottled and distributed throughout Corsica and even to fine restaurants in Paris. Other mineral water comes from the Zilia springs, in the Balagne area, and from St-Georges, near Ajaccio.

Wine

Corsican wines usually bear the name of the AOC zone in which they are made on their labels. These zones are: Ajaccio, Calvi, Coteaux du Cap Corse, Figari, Patrimonio, Porto-Vecchio and Sartène. Two other AOCs are called Muscat du Cap Corse and Vins de Corse. Wines also bear the name of the winemaker, preceded by the words Clos or Domaine, to guarantee the fact that they are made in the winery or estate on the label.

An AOC Cap Corse wine label

Among the best
Corsican white wines, there is a good, fruity Malvasia made from grapes grown on the terraced vineyards of Cap Corse. The AOC Patrimonio is famous for its Niellucciu, a dry wine made from a local grape. Other first-rate white wines are those from AOC Muscat du Cap Corse.

AOC Coteaux
du Cap Corse

AOC Vins
de Corse

Rosé is a common wine and the Porto-Vecchio, Patrimonio and Vins de Corse AOCs are among the best. The basic grapes used are the local Niellucciu and Sciaccarellu, which are mixed with many other grapes to produce a tasty wine with a fine bouquet that is ideal for summer consumption.

AOC
Patrimonio

AOC Vins
de Corse

Recommended AOC Wineries

The best wines can be purchased directly from the wineries.

AOC Ajaccio
A Cantina, Les Marines, Porticcio. **Tel** 04 95 25 08 90.
Clos Capitoro, Piscatiatella, Porticcio. **Tel** 04 95 53 21 05. **W** clos-capitoro.com

AOC Calvi
Clos Culombu, Chemin San Petru Lumio, Calvi.
Tel 04 95 60 70 68. **W** closculombu.fr

AOC Figari
Clos Canarelli. **Tel** 04 95 71 07 55.
Cave Poggiale, Figari **Tel** 04 95 71 07 04.
Domaine de Tanella, Figari. **Tel** 04 95 70 46 23.
W domaine-tanella.com

AOC Muscat du Cap Corse
Clos Nicrosi, Rogliano/Macinaggio. **Tel** 04 95 35 64 79 or 04 95 35 63 60. **W** closnicrosi.fr
Domaine de Pietri, Morsiglia. **Tel** 04 95 35 30 69.

AOC Patrimonio
Domaine Gentile, St-Florent. **Tel** 04 95 37 01 54.
W domaine-gentile.com

AOC Porto-Vecchio
Domaine de Torraccia, Lecci, Porto-Vecchio
Tel 04 95 71 43 50. **W** domaine-de-torraccia.com

AOC Sartène
Domaine San Micheli, Sartène. **Tel** 04 95 77 06 38.
W domainesanmicheli.com

AOC Vins de Corse
Le Clos d'Órléa, Route de Tallone, Aléria. **Tel** 04 95 57 13 60. **W** closdorlea.com

Red wines, which are full-bodied and have a good bouquet, are mostly made from local grapes. The best reds in Corsica belong to the AOC Patrimonio, thanks to the mild climate and the soil, which is particularly suitable for grape cultivation. Connoisseurs will also enjoy reds from AOC Ajaccio, made from Sciaccarellu grapes, which are every bit as good as Beaujolais. Also worth a try are the reds from Coteaux du Cap Corse, Figari, Porto-Vecchio and Sartène AOCs, the last of which is particularly robust.

AOC
Patrimonio

Dessert wines are mostly made in the Cap Corse and Patrimonio areas, and among the best are the white muscat and red aleatico. A rare white dessert wine from Cap Corse is Rappu, which can be purchased only from the wineries that produce it. Rappu makes a perfect accompaniment for all dry desserts.

The label of a wine originating from the AOC Muscat du Cap Corse

Where to Eat and Drink

Bastia and the North

ALGAJOLA: La Vieille Cave €
Traditional Corsican **Map** C2
9 Piazza à l'Olmo, 20220
Tel *04 95 60 70 09* **Closed** *Mid-Oct–mid-Mar*
A popular spot with a flower-filled terrace. The house speciality, *pierrade*, allows diners to grill their own meat or fish on a hot stone at the table.

ALGAJOLA: U Castellu €
Traditional Corsican **Map** C2
10 Place du Château, 20220
Tel *04 95 60 78 75* **Closed** *Oct–Mar*
Seafood couscous, stewed boar and good-value set menus are served on a terrace nestled below Algajola's castle walls.

BASTIA: Col Tempo €
Bistro **Map** D2
7 Place du Marché, 20200
Tel *04 95 58 14 22* **Closed** *Mon*
Located in the heart of the old port, behind a simple façade, original and gastronomic cuisine is served. Generous portions and efficient staff.

BASTIA: Le Cosi €
Bistro **Map** D2
Quai des Martyrs de la Libération, 20200
Tel *04 95 36 60 20*
Friendly eatery with something for everyone, from burgers and salads to pasta dishes and seafood dinners. Good for families.

BASTIA: L'Agua €€
Seafood **Map** D2
Rue de la Marine, Vieux Port, 20200
Tel *04 95 38 43 71*
Located on the Vieux Port, this excellent seafood restaurant is popular with both well-heeled locals along with visitors in the know.

BASTIA: L'Ardoise €€
Contemporary Corsican **Map** D2
4 Place Hôtel de Ville, 20200
Tel *04 95 35 17 11*
A charming and intimate restaurant offering classic food and specialities such as fondue and stone-wok delicacies. Children's meals are also available.

BASTIA: Chez Vincent €€
Pizzeria **Map** D2
12 Rue St-Michel, 20200
Tel *04 95 31 62 50* **Closed** *Sun; Jan, 2 weeks in Nov*
Situated in the Citadelle, Chez Vincent serves first-rate pizzas, seafood and Mediterranean dishes. Book ahead for a table on the panoramic terrace.

BASTIA: La Fabrica €€
Bistro **Map** D2
1 Blvd du General Giraud, 20200
Tel *04 95 58 32 95* **Closed** *Sun*
Busy and delightful Corsican establishment. Quality meats and fresh produce form the menu.

BASTIA: Grazie Mille €€
Italian **Map** D2
1 Place du Marché, 20200
Tel *04 95 32 38 22* **Closed** *Wed lunch; Tue*
The city's best Italian restaurant is particularly renowned for its pasta dishes, seafood and truffles (in winter). Desserts include a decadent tiramisu. Good value.

BASTIA: Le Guasco €€
Contemporary Corsican **Map** D2
6 Rue Dragon, 20200
Tel *04 95 31 44 70* **Closed** *Mon & Sun*
An intimate place with tables on a quiet square in the heart of

Price Guide
Prices are based on a three-course meal per person, with half a bottle of house wine and service charges.

€	under €30
€€	€30 to 45
€€€	over €45

the Citadelle. The menu changes daily and chefs use only the freshest local produce.

BASTIA: La Table de la Corniche €€
Contemporary Corsican **Map** D2
Castagneto, San Martino di Lota, 20200
Tel *04 95 31 40 98* **Closed** *Mon*
A charming hotel-restaurant in the mountains, with a view over Bastia from the garden terrace and refined cooking based on local and seasonal produce.

BASTIA: Chez Huguette €€€
Seafood **Map** D2
Rue de la Marine, Vieux Port, 20200
Tel *04 95 31 37 60 or 06 23 82 81 69*
Closed *2 weeks at Christmas*
A favourite on the Vieux Port since 1969. Lots of choice, including oysters, grilled fish, spaghetti *à la pescatore* and bouillabaisse. Meat dishes, too, and an excellent wine cellar.

BASTIA: La Table du Marché St-Jean €€€
Seafood **Map** D2
Place du Marché, 20200
Tel *04 95 31 64 25* **Closed** *Sun*
There is always a "fish of the day" on the menu at this local favourite, as well as seafood platters and risottos. In good weather, you can eat on the pretty market square. Good-value lunch menus.

CALENZANA: A Stazzona €
Traditional Corsican **Map** C2
17 Rue du Fond, 20214
Tel *04 95 36 47 12* **Closed** *Dec*
Enjoy generous portions of delicious, traditional dishes such as stewed boar, swordfish, duck breast and fresh seafood on an intimate terrace shaded by orange trees.

CALVI: Le Brunch €
Pizzeria **Map** B2
16 Rue Clemenceau, 20260
Tel *04 95 58 83 29* **Closed** *Nov–Easter*
An informal, fun place known for *nicci* (chestnut flour crêpes). The menu also includes big burgers, pizzas, tortillas and banoffee pie. Drinks and tapas are served in the early evening.

The bistrot Le Cosi, located on Bastia's waterfront

CALVI: Via Marine €
Italian **Map** B2
20 Rue Clemenceau, 20260
Tel *04 95 65 06 30 or 06 14 84 70 57*
Closed *Sep–May*
Good, inexpensive seafood,
pizzas, burgers and a range of
tasty Corsican dishes. Portions are
generous, and the cooking is of a
high standard. Ideal for families.

CALVI: A Funtana €€
Contemporary Corsican **Map** B2
Place Marchal, 20260
Tel *04 95 65 09 52 or 04 95 35 60 24*
Closed *Jan–Feb*
This hip restaurant/wine bar
serves stylish food to match an
impressive wine list. The reasonably
priced menu includes unusual,
delicious pizzas. Wines are served
by the glass as well.

CALVI: Le Bout du Monde €€
Seafood **Map** B2
Plage de Calvi, 20260
Tel *04 95 65 15 41* **Closed** *Nov–Mar*
Enjoy seafood platters,
langoustine ravioli and scallops
in orange butter at this friendly
beach eatery with charming
views across to the Citadelle.

CALVI: La Licorne €€
Seafood **Map** B2
Plage de Calvi, 20260
Tel *04 95 65 08 62* **Closed** *Nov–Mar*
A laid-back spot right on the
beach, with a view of Calvi. Hire
a lounger, sip tasty cocktails and
enjoy good seafood and desserts.

CALVI: L'Abri Cotier €€€
Contemporary Corsican **Map** B2
10 Rue Joffre, Port de Plaisance, 20260
Tel *04 95 46 00 04* **Closed** *Mon
lunch; Nov–Apr*
The cosmopolitan Mediterranean
menu includes grilled veal and
Corsican charcuterie. There is also
a good selection of champagnes
and wines.

CANARI: Au Bon Clocher €€
Traditional Corsican **Map** D1
Hameau Pieve, 20217
Tel *04 95 37 80 15*
A friendly hotel restaurant,
good for fresh cheese beignets,
pasta dishes, fish cooked *en
croute du sel*, seafood in puff
pastry, grilled steaks and home-
made desserts.

CENTURI: Le Vieux Moulin €€
Seafood **Map** D1
Centuri-Port, 20238
Tel *04 95 35 60 15* **Closed** *Nov–Mar*
A 19th-century palace-turned-
hotel with a well-deserved
reputation for seafood, especially
the rock lobster. Pretty views
over the fishing port.

The waterfront Le Pirate restaurant, Erbalunga (Brando)

**ERBALUNGA (BRANDO):
A Piazzetta** €
Contemporary Corsican **Map** D1/
D2
Place du Village, 20222
Tel *04 95 33 28 69* **Closed** *Tue;
Jan & Feb*
Popular venue for good-value
seafood, pasta dishes, pizzas and
salads, as well as Mediterranean
fare with a creative touch. In fine
weather, eat on the village square.

**ERBALUNGA (BRANDO):
Le Pirate** €€€
Fine Dining **Map** D1/D2
Port de Plaisance, 20222
Tel *04 95 33 24 20* **Closed** *Mon
& Tue in low season; Jan & Feb*
A rare Michelin-starred restaurant
on Cap Corse, Le Pirate has a
romantic setting on the waterfront.
The fare – local organic lamb,
veal, rock lobster – is sophisticated,
and the presentation beautiful.
Exceptional list of Corsican wines.

L'ÎLE ROUSSE: L'Île d'Or €
Brasserie **Map** C2
Rue d'Agilla, Place Paoli, 20220
Tel *04 95 60 12 05*
Enjoy alfresco dining on a terrace
overlooking the town's main
square. There is a wide range of
meats, seafood, pizzas and salads
on the menu. Family friendly.

L'ÎLE ROUSSE: Les Quatre Becs €
Traditional Corsican **Map** C2
6 Rue Napoléon, 20220
Tel *04 95 60 44 52* **Closed** *Nov–Mar*
A popular brasserie offering
simple regional specialities and
popular brasserie favourites.

L'ÎLE ROUSSE: A Siesta €€
Seafood **Map** C2
*Blvd Charles Marie Savelli,
Promenade à Marinella, 20220*
Tel *04 95 60 28 74* **Closed** *Nov–
mid-Mar*
A trendy eatery with tables on
the beach. The best dishes

include seafood ravioli,
carpaccio of tuna, shellfish
tempura and lobster. For
dessert, order the Tarte
Isula Rossa.

**L'ÎLE ROUSSE:
Loria Beach** €€
Contemporary Corsican **Map** C2
Plage de Caruchetta, 20220
Tel *04 95 62 03 06* **Closed** *Mid-
Sep–Apr*
A beach restaurant in a lovely
setting, with unusual cuisine
that lends an Oriental touch to
Corsican cooking. There is also a
sushi bar and a cocktail bar.
Romantic sunsets.

DK Choice

**L'ÎLE ROUSSE:
U Spuntinu** €€
Traditional Corsican **Map** C2
1 Rue Napoléon, 20220
Tel *04 95 60 00 05* **Closed** *Mid-
Dec–mid-Feb*
This unassuming restaurant
in L'Île Rousse's pretty historic
centre offers a delightful
taste of the island's culinary
heritage. Savour rich baked
pasta, roast meats,
vegetable tarts, beignets,
local *brocciu* cheese,
charcuterie, herbs from the
maquis and produce from
the restaurant's own garden.

**L'ÎLE ROUSSE:
Pasquale-Paoli** €€€
Fine Dining **Map** C2
2 Place Paoli, 20220
Tel *04 95 47 67 70* **Closed** *Sun
& Mon; Jan–Mar*
Michelin-starred dining on a
covered terrace. Only the
finest local seasonal
ingredients are used to
prepare the dishes, and the
traditional Corsican menu
changes frequently.

For more information on types of restaurants *see page 166*

LUMIO: L'Oggi €€€
Fine Dining Map C2
Le Village, Route de Calvi, 20260
Tel *04 95 60 61 71* **Closed** *Mon; Nov–Apr*
Michelin-starred dining at the Hotel Chez Charles, one of the island's top hotels. L'Oggi offers exquisite traditional Corsican cuisine with international influences. The weekday lunch menus are reasonably priced.

MACINAGGIO: U Lampione €
Contemporary Corsican Map D1
Le Port, 20248
Tel *04 95 35 45 55* **Closed** *Oct–Mar*
An unpretentious restaurant with a pleasant terrace on the port. Dishes include a wide range of fresh fish (depending on the day's catch) and crisp pizzas. Great selection for vegetarians.

MACINAGGIO:
Osteria di u Portu €€
Seafood Map D1
Marina, Route du Port, 20248
Tel *04 95 35 40 49* **Closed** *15 Jan–15 Feb*
This no-frills, family-run seafood restaurant serves tasty mixed grills and delicious *salades composées*. Fish is priced by weight, so enquire about the size before you order. The set menus are great value for money.

MURATO: La Ferme Auberge
Campo di Monte €€
Traditional Corsican Map D2
Lieu-dit Peru, off the D305, 20239
Tel *04 95 37 64 39* **Closed** *Mon–Wed; late Sep–May*
This charming stone farmhouse up in the hills offers a five-course set menu – there are no alternatives. Enjoy generous portions of hearty regional food accompanied by carafes of good wine.

Harbourside dining at La Rascasse restaurant, Saint-Florent

NONZA: La Sassa €€
Contemporary Corsican Map D1
Tour de Nonza, 20217
Tel *04 95 38 55 26* **Closed** *Oct–15 Apr*
A sophisticated café offering light lunches, and grills and tapas in the evening. It has an amazing setting on a terrace atop a crag, high over the sea. There's usually live music on summer nights.

OLETTA: Auberge A Magina €€
Traditional Corsican Map D2
Le Village, 20232
Tel *04 95 39 01 01* **Closed** *Mid-Oct–Mar*
Formal but friendly place with breathtaking sunset views over the Gulf of Saint-Florent. The creative menu features traditional Corsican dishes with a twist. Great choice of wine and deliciously decadent desserts.

OLMI CAPPELLA:
Auberge de la Tornadia €€
Traditional Corsican Map C2
Route de la Forêt de Tartagine, Pioggiola, 20259
Tel *04 95 61 90 93* **Closed** *Mid-Nov–mid-Mar*
Excellent authentic regional fare makes this hard-to-find restaurant worth the effort. Tables are laid out under chestnut trees, with a great view of the surrounding mountains.

PATRIMONIO:
A Pergola Chez Roger €
Traditional Corsican Map D2
Le Village, 20253
Tel *04 95 37 16 16*
Located in northern Corsica's wine capital, this modest, pleasant restaurant specializes in savoury crêpes, pizzas and traditional Corsican cuisine. Very helpful owner.

PIGNA: A Casarella €
Bistro Map C2
Pigna, Rue Barcelone, 20220
Tel *04 95 61 78 08* **Closed** *Nov–Mar*
A sophisticated but informal café with sea views. The menu is lined with tapas, salads, platters of cheese and charcuterie, as well as organic juices, wines and cocktails.

PIGNA: A Mandria di Pigna €€
Contemporary Corsican Map C2
Entree du Village, Pigna, 20220
Tel *04 95 32 71 24 or 06 17 53 23 41*
Closed *Mon (Apr–Jun, Sep); Nov–Mar*
This stylish restaurant offers delicious *salades composées* and pasta dishes at lunch, and hearty grilled and roast meats in the evening. Don't miss the fantastic home-made desserts.

SAINT-FLORENT: L'Arriere Cour €
Contemporary Corsican Map D2
Place Doria, 20217
Tel *04 95 35 33 62* **Closed** *Tue; Jan & Feb*
Delicious food and a relaxed ambience in a charming courtyard. Dishes include crêpes, cheese beignets, Moroccan tajines and Corsican cuisine. The home-made bread is especially good.

SAINT-FLORENT:
Le Petit Caporal €€
Brasserie Map D2
Port de Plaisance, 20217
Tel *04 95 37 20 26* **Closed** *11 Nov–Dec*
This restaurant has been serving excellent pizzas, pasta dishes and *moules-frites* for over a century. Also on the menu are succulent steaks, seafood risottos and grilled fish.

SAINT-FLORENT: L'Auberge
du Pêcheur €€€
Seafood Map D2
Route de Bastia, 20217
Tel *04 95 36 30 42* **Closed** *mid-Oct–May*
Located in a semi-tropical courtyard behind a fish shop, this local gem is run by a real fisherman and serves sophisticated seafood dishes. By reservation only.

SAINT-FLORENT:
La Rascasse €€€
Fine Dining Map D2
Quai d'Honneur, Port de Plaisance, 20217
Tel *04 95 37 06 09* **Closed** *Oct–Apr*
Enjoy inventive cooking with an emphasis on seafood – grilled lobster, langoustes, bouillabaisse – while gazing at the yachts moored in the harbour.

SALECCIA: U Santu Petru €
Traditional Corsican Map C2
Saleccia Plage, lieu-dit Casta, 20217
Tel *04 95 37 04 60* **Closed** *Nov–Apr*
A simple and welcoming oasis in the Désert des Agriates, with beignets and brochettes, salads and grilled meats. Lovely views during the day; candlelight and sometimes live music at night.

SANT'ANTONINO: I Scalini €€
Contemporary Corsican Map C2
Sant'Antonino, 20220
Tel *04 95 47 12 92* **Closed** *Oct–Apr*
Reservations are essential at this chic café with a spectacular panoramic view from the terrace. The menu offers tasty Corsican dishes, salads and pasta, and great local wine. Fantastic service.

Ajaccio and the West Coast

AJACCIO: Auberge du Cheval Blanc €
Pizzeria   Map B4
18 Rue Bonaparte, 20000
Tel *04 95 21 17 98*
A no-frills, inexpensive place offering simple Mediterranean cuisine, including consistently good pizzas, chops and salads. Popular with the city's younger set.

AJACCIO: Chez Paulo €
Pizzeria   Map B4
7 Rue du Roi de Rome, 20000
Tel *04 95 51 16 47*
A favourite among Ajaccio's night owls, this laid-back spot is the place to grab a quick pizza, omelette or salad, or a full meal.

AJACCIO: Da Mamma €
Traditional Corsican   Map B4
3 Passage Guingette, 20000
Tel *04 95 21 39 44*   **Closed** *Jan & Feb*
Tucked away in a shaded courtyard in a back alley off Cours Napoléon, Da Mamma serves tasty seafood and grilled meat.

AJACCIO: Restaurant des Halles €
Traditional Corsican   Map B4
4 Rue des Halles, 20000
Tel *04 95 21 42 68*   **Closed** *Sun; Dec*
A local favourite since 1933, des Halles has white tablecloths, crystal glasses and inviting booths. It is especially good for seafood. Music on Fridays and Saturdays. Piano bar on Saturdays.

AJACCIO: Vino del Diablo €
Tapas Bar/Brasserie   Map B4
Port l'Amirauté, 20000
Tel *04 95 22 70 10*   **Closed** *Sun; Jan*
Situated on the waterfront of Ajaccio's port, this trendy live music venue combines a tapas and cocktail bar with a good-value brasserie. Great lunch menus.

AJACCIO: Le 20123 €€
Traditional Corsican   Map B4
2 Rue du Roi de Rome, 20000
Tel *04 95 21 50 05*   **Closed** *Mid-Jan– mid-Feb*
The daily set menu of traditional fare can be washed down with local wines at this eatery. Booking is essential in summer.

AJACCIO: Le Bistrot d'Emile €€
Bistro   Map D2
6 Rue de l'Assomption, 20000
Tel *04 95 51 00 81*
The tasting menu includes modern Corsican cuisine and inventive desserts. The wine bar menu is organised around local vineyards.

Chequered floors at Le Grand Café Napoléon in Ajaccio

AJACCIO: Le Grand Café Napoléon €€
Brasserie   Map B4
10 Cours Napoléon, 20000
Tel *04 95 21 42 54*   **Closed** *Sun*
Ajaccio's oldest café has an air of faded grandeur, but it is still great for an elegant lunch or an apéritif. French-brasserie fare.

AJACCIO: Le Neptune €€
Seafood   Map B4
Route des Sanguinaires, 20000
Tel *04 95 52 00 11*
This is an informal place at lunchtime, serving fresh seafood platters, sandwiches and salads. It takes on a classier feel in the evening, and offers more elaborate fish and meat dishes, followed by rich desserts.

DK Choice

AJACCIO: Palm Beach €€€
Fine Dining   Map B4
Route des Sanguinaires, 20000
Tel *04 95 52 01 03*   **Closed** *Sun eve; Mon*
Ajaccio's top, Michelin-starred restaurant offers impeccably prepared dishes such as lobster and fennel lasagne, *ris de veau* (sweetbread) with nori and baby clams, and sublime desserts. An evening meal here doesn't come cheap, but the lunch menu is less pricey. There is also a separate beach restaurant, where you can dine with your toes in the sand.

BASTELICA: Chez Paul €
Traditional Corsican   Map C4
Stazzona, 20119
Tel *04 95 28 71 59*
In a village high above the Gorges de Prunelli, Chez Paul offers authentic Corsican fare – try the veal sauté with Soisson beans. The charcuterie and local cheeses are also recommended.

BASTELICACCIA: Auberge du Prunelli €€
Traditional Corsican   Map B4
Pisciatello, 20129
Tel *04 95 20 02 75*   **Closed** *Tue*
A perennial local favourite renowned for dishes such as snails, courgette blossoms, sea anemone beignets and roast goat kid. There's a garden terrace and a cosy feel in winter.

CARGÈSE: Bel'Mare €
Mediterranean   Map B3
Route d'Ajaccio, 20130
Tel *04 95 26 40 13*   **Closed** *Nov–Feb*
Enjoy spectacular sea views from the terrace as well as a wide choice of pizzas, seafood platters, delicious pasta dishes, steaks and salads.

CARGÈSE: A Volta €€
Contemporary Corsican   Map B3
Place de l'Eglise Latine, 20130
Tel *04 95 26 11 96*
As well as scrumptious ice creams, A Volta serves sophisticated *salades composées*, seafood and meat dishes with unique savoury sorbets. Try the beef tartare with red pepper or mustard sorbet.

Rustic setting at Ajaccio's Le 20123, known for traditional Corsican cuisine

For more information on types of restaurants *see page 166*

CUTTOLI-CORTICHIATTO:
A Casetta €€
Contemporary Corsican   Map C4
Plaine de Cuttoli, lieu-dit Canteghe Canale, 20167
Tel *04 95 25 66 59*   **Closed** *Mon*
Traditional fare is given a modern slant at this rustic eatery – try the duck with orange-infused caramelized porcini mushrooms. The charcuterie is also first-rate.

GUAGNO-LES-BAINS:
L'Auberge des Deux Sorru €€
Traditional Corsican   Map C3
Poggiolo, 20125
Tel *04 95 28 35 14*   **Closed** *mid-Oct–Mar*
Located in a tiny mountain spa, this restaurant has great views and wholesome home cooking. Highlights include millefeuille pastry with *brocciu*, duck breast with honey, and chestnut flan.

OTA: Chez Félix €
Traditional Corsican   Map B3
Capo Sottano, 20150
Tel *04 95 70 68 49 or 06 80 87 71 28*
Closed *Nov–Feb*
Enjoy flavoursome Corsican dishes based on Félix Ceccaldi's family recipes, handed down over generations. Good desserts and lovely views from the terrace.

PIANA: La Voute €
Seafood   Map B3
Centre Village, Piana, 20115
Tel *04 95 27 80 46*
Unpretentious and friendly, La Voute serves fresh, tasty seafood and delicious home-made desserts. One of the best eateries in the area.

PIANA: Les Roches Rouges €€
Fine Dining   Map B3
Golfe de Porto, Piana, 20115
Tel *04 95 27 81 81*   **Closed** *Nov–Mar*
The inventive cuisine here has an emphasis on seafood. Frescoes decorate the charming Art Deco dining room, and there are lovely views, especially at sunset.

Beautiful courtyard setting at the lovely Le Maquis, Porto

Wicker chairs in the Art Deco dining room at Les Roches Rouges, Piana

PORTICCIO: Le Piano
Chez Toinou €€
Contemporary Corsican   Map B4
Les Candilelli, 20166
Tel *04 95 92 66 81*   **Closed** *Tue lunch; Mon*
A lively, friendly place offering creative dishes such as lamb with pickled garlic, and *foie gras* with clementine jelly. The seafood menu is also good. A great range of wines from the region.

PORTO (OTA): Le Mini-Golf €
Pizzeria   Map B3
Porto Marina, 20150
Tel *04 95 26 17 55*   **Closed** *Nov–mid-Apr*
This shaded hideaway is located between the river and the sea. On the menu is a wide choice of pizzas, pasta dishes, grills and salads. An ideal spot for the whole family.

PORTO: Le Maquis €€
Corsican   Map B3
Route de Calvi, 20150
Tel *04 95 26 12 19*   **Closed** *Mon & Tue; mid-Nov–mid-Feb*
Corsican recipes are prepared with local ingredients and artfully re-imagined. Leave room for the sinfully rich desserts. The terrace has views over Porto.

SAGONE: A Stonda €
Contemporary Corsican   Map B4
Route d'Ajaccio, 20118
Tel *04 95 28 01 66*   **Closed** *Mon; Dec–mid-Jan*
This warm, welcoming place serves great thin-crust pizzas, fresh seafood and mixed grills.

SAGONE: L'Ancura €€
Seafood   Map B4
Port de Sagone, 20118
Tel *04 95 28 04 93*   **Closed** *Nov–mid-Mar*
An excellent place to enjoy the freshest catch of the day, as well as grilled meats, such as pork with rosemary. L'Ancura also

boasts a great location, with tables on the terrace right on the waterfront.

SOCCIA: A Merendella €€
Corsican   Map C3
Piazza al Brignone, 20125
Tel *04 95 28 34 91*   **Closed** *Wed (May, Jun, Sep); Oct–Apr; Sep–Jun*
Tucked away in a picturesque mountain village, this local secret serves up a seasonal menu featuring produce from the owner's vegetable garden. Dine outside on the delightful garden terrace.

TIUCCIA: La Gourmandise €€
Traditional Corsican   Map B4
D81, Calcatoggia, 20111
Tel *04 95 72 91 32*
This no-frills restaurant serves superb food, including home-made charcuterie, mixed seafood grills and roast meats. A gourmet surprise in this tiny village.

Bonifacio and the South

BONIFACIO: Cantina Doria €
Traditional Corsican   Map C6
27 Rue Doria, 20169
Tel *04 95 73 50 49*   **Closed** *Nov–Mar*
Don't be put off by the bustling tourist crowds – this place serves good food. Try *soupe corse*, lasagne with Corsican cheese and *aubergines à la bonifacienne*.

BONIFACIO: The Kissing Pigs €
Bistro   Map C6
15 Quai Banda del Ferro, 20169
Tel *04 95 73 56 09*   **Closed** *Wed & Sun in low season*
Lots of charcuterie, but also creative *salades composées*, omelettes, grills and a good selection of wines. Located on the port, it can get very crowded in the summer months.

BONIFACIO: Ciccio €€
Contemporary Corsican Map C6
6 Rue Saint Jean-Baptiste, 20169
Tel *06 16 98 81 68* **Closed** *Jan–Mar*
This place has a wide choice of
quality dishes, such as sea urchin
ravioli and boar stew. Smallish
portions. Take-away available.

BONIFACIO: Les 4 Vents €€
Seafood Map C6
29 Quai Banda del Ferro, 20169
Tel *04 95 73 07 50* **Closed** *Mon
& Tue out of season; 2 weeks in Nov*
Ignore the kitsch nautical decor –
this is a great spot for delicious
seafood, with a wide choice of
shellfish and seafood pasta dishes.

**BONIFACIO: Stella d'Oro
"Chez Jules"** €€
Traditional Corsican Map C6
7 Rue Doria, 20169
Tel *04 95 73 03 63* **Closed** *Nov–Mar*
Enjoy refined traditional
cooking in this tavern in the old
town, a favourite with French
celebrities. Among the
highlights are seafood ravioli
and lamb brochettes.

**BONIFACIO:
Au Jardin d'A Cheda** €€€
Fine Dining Map C6
Cavallo Morto, BP 3, 20169
Tel *04 95 73 03 82* **Closed** *Oct–
mid-Feb*
The creative menu here
combines the exotic and the
traditional. The emphasis is on
seafood and produce from the
restaurant's own organic garden.

BONIFACIO: La Caravelle €€€
Seafood Map C6
37 Quai Camparetti, 20169
Tel *04 95 73 00 03* **Closed** *Nov–Mar*
Grab a table on the quayside at
this upmarket restaurant, and
tuck into fresh seafood platters,

lobster risotto and langoustines
in basil butter. Superb selection
of French wines.

BONIFACIO: Le Voilier €€€
Fine Dining Map C6
81 Quai Jérôme Comparetti, 20169
Tel *04 95 73 07 06* **Closed** *Wed; Sun
pm (low season); mid-Jan–mid-Feb*
This chic place is renowned for
its seafood but also offers good
tapas and succulent Corsican
cochon noir (pork from black
pigs). In summer, the mozzarella
bar is perfect for a light lunch.

**CAMPOMORO (SARTÈNE):
Hôtel Le Ressac** €€
Contemporary Corsican Map B5
D121, Belvédère, 20110
Tel *04 95 74 22 25 or 06 10 55 13 39*
Closed *Mid-Oct–mid-Apr*
One of the best restaurants on
the Valinco Gulf, this cheerful,
family-run place serves good
wood-fired pizzas, as well as tasty
seafood and Corsican dishes.

LEVIE: A Pignata €€
Traditional Corsican Map C5
Route du Pianu, 20170
Tel *04 95 78 41 90* **Closed** *Nov–Mar
(except 1 wk at Christmas)*
Among the oldest *fermes
auberges* in Corsica, and one of
the most upmarket. The owners
grow everything they need, and
the food is first-rate. Try the *daube
farcie* (stew) or the caramelized
roast lamb. Book in advance.

OLMETO: La Crique €
Italian Map B5
*Route d'Abbartello,
Olmeto Plage, 20113*
Tel *04 95 74 04 57* **Closed** *Mid-
Nov–Mar*
A touristy beach restaurant
offering good-value salads,
pizzas, pasta dishes and

seafood, as well as tropical
desserts and cocktails.
There is also a children's menu.
A great spot for watching the
sun set.

PORTO-POLLO: A Pignata €€
Seafood Map B5
Departmentale 757, 20140
Tel *04 95 24 77 95* **Closed** *Nov–Mar*
Laid-back and casual, this
beach restaurant has lovely
views across the bay. On the
menu are simple catch-of-the-
day dishes, but also Corsican
specialities such as jugged boar
and sautéed veal.

**PORTO-VECCHIO:
Chez Anna** €
Italian Map C6
*16 Rue Docteur Camille de Rocca
Serra, 20137*
Tel *04 95 70 19 97* **Closed** *Oct–Mar*
Modern and minimalist,
Chez Anna is known for its
home-made pasta dishes,
seafood, Corsican specialities
and rich desserts. Try the
gnocchi with mussels.

Relaxed dining, overlooking the beach at La Cantine du Golfe, Porto-Pollo

For more information on types of restaurants *see page 166*

Stone walls and well-stocked bar at
A Cantina di l'Orriu, Porto-Vecchio

PORTO-VECCHIO:
Costa Marina　　　　　　€
Traditional Corsican　　Map C6
Route de Palombaggio, 20137
Tel *04 95 70 36 57* **Closed** *Nov–Mar*
Located above the beautiful
beach of Palombaggio, Costa
Marina serves Corsican dishes,
pasta, wood-oven pizzas, grilled
chops and salads. Cash only.

PORTO-VECCHIO:
A Cantina di l'Orriu　　€€
Wine bar　　　　　Map C6
5 Cours Napoléon, 20137
Tel *04 95 25 95 89* **Closed** *Oct–mid-Mar*
Charcuterie is the star of the
show here, but there is also *foie
gras* and a selection of cheeses.
Extensive wine list.

PORTO-VECCHIO: Le Bistro
Contemporary Corsican　Map C6
4 Quai Paoli, Port de Plaisance, 20137　€€
Tel *04 95 70 22 96* **Closed** *Sun; Feb*
Lively spot on the marina, with a
pretty terrace and friendly staff.
Good for fresh fish and rock
lobster, as well as grilled meats,
beef carpaccio and stewed boar.
Opt for the day's special.

PORTO-VECCHIO:
La Table de Nathalie　€€
Bistro　　　　　　Map C6
4 Rue Jean-Jaurès, 20137
Tel *04 95 71 65 25* **Closed** *Sun; Dec–mid-Mar*
This popular little bistro offers
light and creative dishes. The
blackboard menu changes daily.

PORTO-VECCHIO:
Casadelmar　　　　€€€
Fine Dining　　　　Map C6
Route de Palombaggia, 20137
Tel *04 95 72 34 34* **Closed** *Nov–mid-Apr*
A striking modern pavilion by
the sea is the perfect setting for

sumptuous Michelin-starred
cuisine with an Italian influence.
Reservations essential.

PORTO-VECCHIO:
Grand Hôtel de Cala Rossa　€€€
Fine Dining　　　　Map C5
RN 196, Rte de Cala Rossa, 20137
Tel *04 95 71 61 51* or *04 95 71 78 78*
Closed *Nov–Apr*
This Michelin-starred restaurant
is the perfect place for a special
occasion. The food is created
with the finest seasonal
ingredients, and the desserts
are justifiably famous.

PROPRIANO: Tempi Fa'　€€
Wine bar　　　　　Map B5
7 Avenue Napoléon, 20110
Tel *04 95 76 06 52* **Closed** *Jan–Mar*
Part of a gourmet food shop, this
is a wonderful place to sample
charcuterie, farm cheeses and
fine Corsican wines by the glass.

PROPRIANO: Terra Cotta　€€
Seafood　　　　　Map B5
31 Avenue Napoléon, 20110
Tel *04 95 74 23 80* **Closed** *Sun;
Nov–Mar*
Excellent, informal harbourside
restaurant offering beautifully
prepared fish dishes at affordable
prices. A great value lunch menu.

ROCCAPINA: Auberge Coralli　€€
Contemporary Corsican　Map B6
*Route de Bonifacio,
Roccapina Beach, 20100*
Tel *04 95 77 05 94* **Closed** *Wed (Oct–Apr); Nov–Mar*
Located on a terrace with views
of Lion's Rock. The dishes rely on
local ingredients – lamb, veal and
seafood. Book in advance.

SANTA GIULIA: Les Trois Deux　€
Contemporary Corsican　Map C6
Baie de Santa Giulia, 20137
Tel *06 10 35 50 46* **Closed** *Oct–Mar*
This restaurant enjoys a lovely
setting on the beach south of

The informal Glacier du Port in Solenzara,
popular with families

Porto-Vecchio. The menu offers
delicious grilled meat, seafood
and salads. Book ahead for a
table on the beach.

SARTÈNE:
La Bergerie d'Acciola　　€
Traditional Corsican　Map C5
Route de Bonifacio Orasi, 20100
Tel *04 95 77 14 00* **Closed** *Oct–May*
This country restaurant offers
exceptional home cooking and
stunning views of the sea and
surrounding countryside. Sample
the grilled brochettes followed
by delicious chestnut ice cream.

SARTÈNE: Le Jardin
de l'Echauguette　　€€
Traditional Corsican　Map C5
Place de la Vardiola, 20100
Tel *04 95 77 12 86* or *06 20 40 71 49*
Closed *Oct–mid-Apr*
Tuck into stews, *soupe corse* and
other classic dishes on a shady
terrace that was once a bastion
in Sartène's fortifications. The
assiette du maquis (a platter of local
delicacies) is a great light lunch.

SARTÈNE: U Campanile　€€
Corsican　　　　　Map C3
Place de l'eglise, 20250
Tel *06 25 78 12 49* **Closed** *Nov–Mar*
Simple Corsican cuisine using
local produce. Excellent home-
made desserts and gorgeous
views from the outdoor terrace.

SOLENZARA: Glacier du Port　€
Bistro
Port du Plaisance, 20145
Tel *04 95 57 42 21* **Closed** *Nov–Mar*
A fun, informal to bring the
family for huge ice-cream treats
or a light lunch. It also serves
excellent crêpes, salads, pasta
dishes, seafood and sandwiches.

SOLLACARO:
Le Moulin Farellacci　　€
Traditional Corsican　Map
Hameau de Calvese, 20140
Tel *04 95 74 62 28* **Closed** *mid-Sep–mid-Jun*
The delicious food justifies the
journey to this remote restored
olive oil mill in the mountains.
The menu mainly consists of
authentic Corsican country fare,
but also offers wood-fired pizzas.
Traditional music some evenings.

ZONZA: Auberge du
Col de Bavella　　　€
Traditional Corsican　Map C5
Col de Bavella, 20124
Tel *04 95 72 09 87* **Closed** *mid-Nov–Mar*
This rustic inn at the pass, just
below the extraordinary Aiguilles
de Bavella, is renowned for its
charcuterie, boar stew with

polenta, chestnut tarts and dishes made with fresh *brocciu* cheese. A fantastic place to stop if you are hiking in the area.

ZONZA: La Terrasse €
Traditional Corsican **Map** C5
Le Village, 20124
Tel *04 95 78 67 69 or 04 95 78 66 03*
Closed *Nov–Mar*
Grilled mountain trout, pork with beans, and stewed boar are the specialities at this friendly century-old establishment. Good desserts, too. The terrace, shaded by chestnut trees, offers beautiful mountain views.

Corte and the Interior

CORTE: A Chjusellina €
Contemporary Corsican **Map** C3
Ferme Leonelli, RN 200, lieu-dit Avantu, 20250
Tel *04 95 47 13 83 or 06 22 39 73 12*
Closed *Sun*
Located just outside Corte, this modern farm offers set meals featuring tender pork, veal and lamb – all raised on the farm – along with garden vegetables and chestnut-based desserts. Family friendly, with a special menu for children. Be sure to book ahead.

CORTE: L'Osteria di l'Orta €
Traditional Corsican **Map** C3
Villa Guelfucci, Pont de l'Orta, 20250
Tel *04 95 61 06 41 or 06 81 87 83 20*
Closed *Sat & Sun; Oct–Mar*
Located in a 19th-century farmhouse, this restaurant serves delicious meals made with home-grown produce and meats raised and cured on the property. Great home-made liqueurs, too.

CORTE: La Rivière des Vins €
Traditional Corsican **Map** C3
5 Rampe Sainte-Croix, 20250
Tel *04 95 46 37 04*
A dream come true for carnivores, La Rivière des Vins cooks succulent meats in the fireplace. Dine in the rustic interior or out on the terrace for fantastic views. If you fancy a bit of everything, try the *plateau gourmand*. Music some evenings.

CORTE: U Museu €
Contemporary Corsican **Map** C3
Rampa Ribanelle, 20260
Tel *04 95 61 08 36* **Closed** *Mon (Apr & May); Oct–Mar*
In a lovely setting, just below the Citadelle and the national museum, U Museu has a tree-shaded terrace where diners can enjoy tasty pizzas, pasta dishes and salads, as well as beautifully prepared traditional Corsican specialities.

CORTE: U Valentinu €
Pizzeria **Map** C3
1 Place Paoli, 20250
Tel *04 95 61 19 65* **Closed** *Oct–Apr*
Pizzeria with a Corsican flair. Good ambience to share excellent pizza, pasta and some Corsican specialities. Locally made desserts.

CORTE: Auberge de la Restonica €€
Traditional Corsican **Map** C3
2 km (1 mile) south of Corte, Route de Restonica, 20250
Tel *04 95 46 09 58* **Closed** *Nov–Mar*
An old inn with a gorgeous riverside terrace offering a range of Corsican classics, as well as steaks. Try the duck breast or the sea bass *à la plancha* (grilled on a metal plate). In summer, enjoy pizzas and snacks by the pool.

CORTE: La Trattoria €€
Brasserie **Map** C3
6 Cours Paoli, 20250
Tel *04 95 54 02 48*
There is an excellent atmosphere at this vibrant place with great food and good prices. A fun spot to gather family and friends.

DK Choice

GUITERA-LES-BAINS: Chez Paul Antoine €
Traditional Corsican **Map** C4
Guitera-les-Bains, 20153
Tel *04 95 24 44 40 or 06 84 22 40 47* **Closed** *2 weeks in Oct/Nov*
For a truly authentic taste of Corsican cuisine, head to this delightful family-run place in the mountains. Sample the day's menu under a shady pergola. All dishes are made from fresh local or home-grown produce. Specialities include home-made charcuterie, and wild boar and other meats grilled on a fire scented with herbs from the maquis. Booking is essential.

LA PORTA: L'Ampugnani €
Traditional Corsican **Map** D3
D 515, Castagniccia, 20237
Tel *04 95 39 22 00* **Closed** *Jan*
Gorgeous views over the forests of the Castagniccia. The short menu features Corsican classics. There is also a delicious cheese platter, an express lunch menu and a children's menu.

MORIANI: U Catagnu €
Contemporary Corsican **Map** D3
Moriani Plage, San Nicolao, 20230
Tel *04 95 38 52 24*
This family-friendly restaurant serves a range of tapas, pasta dishes and pizzas, as well as meat and seafood, all in a contemporary dining room.

VIVARIO: Le Chalet €
Traditional Corsican **Map** C3
Col de la Serra, RN 193, 20219
Tel *04 95 47 22 40*
Opt for the daily set menu at this wooden chalet with a bar. There is also a selection of grilled meats, wild boar stew, pasta dishes and big salads. An on-site delicatessen sells home-made jams.

VIZZAVONA: Hôtel-Restaurant du Monte d'Oro €€
Traditional Corsican **Map** C4
Col de Vizzavona, Vivario, 20219
Tel *04 95 47 21 06* **Closed** *Oct–Apr*
This ivy-covered 19th-century restaurant with a garden terrace serves traditional family recipes. The portions are generous. Be sure to book in advance.

Vibrant decor and unique setting at U Museu, below Corte's national museum

For more information on types of restaurants *see page 166*

SHOPPING IN CORSICA

Corsica offers a great variety of locally produced foods – from honey and a wide range of chestnut-based products, to charcuterie, sausages and cheeses prepared by shepherds with maquis herbs. The best places to buy this produce are the lively, colourful food markets in the main towns. It is also interesting to visit the centres of production, including the alpine *bergeries* and the many wineries throughout the northern part of the island. Handicraft production is quite varied and efforts to revive the ancient arts of knife-making, pottery and stoneware, basket-weaving and glass-blowing are proving increasingly popular. There are handicraft centres in the cities, but it is more enjoyable to go directly to the workshops to see how these objects are made. The most active region for handicraft production is Balagne.

Opening Hours

In Corsica, shops operate from Tuesday to Saturday (9am to noon; 3 to 6pm). Food shops are open from 8am to noon and from 2 to 6pm, and also on Sunday morning. In the summer, especially in tourist resorts, opening hours are usually extended, and some shops are also open on Monday.

Credit Cards

Credit cards are accepted almost everywhere, but some shop owners might set a minimum purchase of about €15. Workshops and smaller shops inland tend to prefer cash payment.

Shopping Centres

On the outskirts of Bastia and Ajaccio there are shopping centres and supermarkets. They are usually open from 9am to 8pm, except for Monday morning and Sunday. On sale are clothes, shoes, sports accessories, perfumes, books and food, at reasonable prices. These centres also have restaurants and cafés.

Handicrafts

For quality products, try any of the craftsmen's workshops belonging to the Casa di l'Artigiani, a network of about 50 artisans who guarantee the authenticity of their products. You can also try shops that display the sign Association d'Artisans de Corse or Corsic'Arte. The best option, however, may be to go directly to the workshops, such as those in Balagne *(see pp80–81)*.

Among the best souvenirs are objects made of olive and chestnut wood, straw and wicker baskets, handmade scarves and rugs, Orezza's myrtle-wood pipes, blown-glass objects from Feliceto and wooden music boxes from Pigna. The most famous Corsican handicraft products

One of the many wine producers in the Cap Corse area

are knives, and the leading makers are Jean-Pierre Caggiari and Laurent Bellini of **Atelier du Couteau** in Ajaccio and **Pol Demongeot** in Calvi.

Pottery and stoneware are also widespread, with workshops throughout the island. Of particular interest are the ateliers of **Jacques Quilichini** in Pigna and **Julien Truchon** in Patrimonio.

Among the now-scarce luthiers are Christian Magdeleine at **Luthier en Guitare et Cetere** in Bastia *(see p65)*, who specializes in guitars, and **Casa-Liutaui Ugo Casalonga** in Pigna.

Other interesting shops are **Maison du Corail** in Ajaccio, which sells cut minerals (diorite, porphyry and rhyolite) and coral, and **Atelier Duchesse** in Castello di Rustinu, which produces perfumes, incense and scented candles using Corsican plants and oils. Wildflower essences are also sold in the markets.

A stall with an array of tempting products at an Ajaccio market

Browsing at the Sunday market in Bastia

Markets and Fairs

The lively, colourful markets are a must for visitors to Corsica. The one in Bastia is held in the Place de l'Hôtel-de-Ville every morning (except Monday), with stalls that sell vegetables, fish, Corsican specialities and even clothes. There are also vendors who make crêpes and local snacks. The bric-à-brac market is held in Place St-Nicolas, in front of the outdoor cafés. The daily food market in Ajaccio, in Place Campinchi, features mostly regional products, such as charcuterie and sausages, wines, sweets, cheese, oil and honey.

In Calvi, greengrocers and vendors of typical products sell their wares under the roof of the covered market, which can be reached by going up a stairway from Rue Clemenceau.

In nearby L'Île Rousse, the covered market facing Place Paoli dates from the 19th century and is classified as an historic building.

In the second week of September, a handicraft fair takes place at Porto-Vecchio. On the first weekend of July there is a wine fair at Luri and on the first weekend after 14 July there is an olive fair in Balagne.

Regional Specialities

There are many Corsican gastronomic delights, first of all honey, which boasts six AOC designations. A range of honeys can be found at **Bernardi Bellini** in Vero and **Le Rucher d'Aristée** in Santa Maria Poggio.

Corsica's famous *canistrelli* biscuits are for sale at these recommended shops: **Boulangerie Galeani** and **Mathieu Carlotti** in Ajaccio and **E Fritelle Perrin Christian** in Calenzana.

Local charcuterie and cheeses can be found in all food shops, including **Charcuterie Pantalacci** in Ajaccio, and **U Muntagnolu** and **U Paese** in Bastia.

Local wines *(see p171)* are sold at the **Enoteca** in Ajaccio. For apéritifs try the **Maison Mattei** in Bastia *(see p67)*.

The only surviving artisan who makes lobster nets at Cap Corse

---

DIRECTORY

Shopping Centres

Carrefour
Rond Point du Finosello, Ajaccio. **Tel** 04 95 25 26 27.

Centre Commercial de Géant Casino La Rocade
Mezzavia, Ajaccio.
Tel 04 95 23 63 78.

Centre Commercial de Santa Devota
Ave de Borgo,
Borgo, Bastia.

Centre Commercial de Toga
Quartier Port de Toga, Bastia.

Galerie Géant Casino La Poretta
ZI Poretta, Porto-Vecchio.

Galerie E. Leclerc de l'Hypermarché
Quartier de l'Annonciade
- Vallée du Fango, Bastia.

Géant Casino
RN 193, Furiani, Bastia.

Handicrafts

Atelier du Couteau
2 Rue Bonaparte, Ajaccio.
Tel 04 95 52 05 92. *Knives.*

Atelier Duchesse
RN 193, Ponte Novu,
Castellu di Rustinu.
Perfumes and incense.

Casa-Liutaui Ugo Casalonga
Pigna. **Tel** 06 22 96 24 03.
Stringed instruments and wooden music boxes.

Jacques Quilichini
Pigna. **Tel** 04 95 61 77 25.
Pottery.

Julien Truchon
Patrimonio. **Tel** 04 95 36 22 67. *Pottery, ceramics.*

Luthier en Guitare et Cetere
6 Rue Chanoine
Bonevandi, Bastia. **Tel** 04 95 31 78 99. *Stringed instruments.*

Maison du Corail
1 Rue Fesch, Ajaccio.
Tel 04 95 21 47 94. *Coral.*

Pol Demongeot
Fort Mozello, Calvi.
Tel 04 95 65 32 54. *Knives.*

Verrerie Corse
Lieu dit Chioselle,
Feliceto. **Tel** 04 95 61 73 05. *Blown-glass objects.*

Regional Specialities

Bernardi Bellini
Lieu dit Vignacci,
20172, Vero. **Tel** 04 95 53 40 47. *Honey.*

Boulangerie Galeani
3 Rue Cardinal Fesch,
Ajaccio. **Tel** 04 95 21 39 68. *Cakes, beignets and Corsican pastries.*

Charcuterie Pantalacci
Blvd Pugliesi Conti, Ajaccio.

Confiserie Saint Sylvestre
Soveria, 20250. **Tel** 04 95 47 42 27. *Preserves, sweets and chocolates.*

E Fritelle Perrin
Blvd Francois Mariani,
Immeuble Fabianni,
Calenzana. **Tel** 04 95 62 78 17. *Biscuits.*

Enoteca
Rue Maréchal Ornano,
Ajaccio. *Wines & liqueurs.*

Le Rucher d'Aristée
Santa Maria Poggio.
Tel 04 95 58 70 14. *Honey.*

Maison Mattei
15 Blvd de Gaulle,
Place St-Nicolas, Bastia.
Tel 04 95 32 44 38.
Corsican wines & liqueurs.

Mathieu Carlotti
Place Vincetti, Bastia.
Tel 04 95 31 09 93.
Preserves, chocolate.

U Muntagnolu
15 Rue César Campinchi,
Bastia. **Tel** 04 95 32 78 04.
Charcuterie and cheese.

U Paese
4 Rue Napoléon, Bastia.
Tel 04 95 32 33 18.
Charcuterie and cheese.

What to Buy in Corsica

The flavours and scents of Corsica can be enjoyed in the island's gastronomic delicacies – from honey and sweets, to cheese and charcuterie. The result of an age-old tradition, these products are available in all the large towns, especially in the markets, where they can be purchased directly from the producers. There is also a great variety of typical handicraft products that Corsican artisans have adapted to more modern tastes. The Strada di l'Artigiani in Balagne *(see pp80–81)* is where most of their workshops are located.

Corsican knife-making has evolved from old shepherds' tools to elegant knives with manta ray-skin handles and damask-steel blades. Artisans now produce collector's items.

Handicrafts

Wood, sandstone, animal horns and glass are the basic materials for Corsican handicrafts, and indeed are among the earliest ever used by man. Corsican artisans have given free rein to their creativity, without ever losing sight of local traditions. Their craft perfectly combines past and present, making every object unique for visitors from all over the world.

Coral necklaces and pendants are crafted in keeping with the age-old art of the Ajaccio coral carvers. The fresh creativity of young local artisans has produced fine necklaces, earrings, bracelets and pendants.

The art of glass-blowing has produced vases, sculptures, glasses, jugs and many other objects. A master glass-blower in Feliceto, a village on the Strada di l'Artigiani, in the heart of Balagne, makes these items.

Ceramic ashtray

Enamelled shell

Ceramic wares, such as plates, vases, jugs and tiles, are made with a potter's wheel, fired in the oven and enamelled with typical Mediterranean colours. The stoneware and raku ceramics *(see p80)* are also worth purchasing.

Hand-crafted music boxes are made mostly in Pigna. They are brightly coloured and come in the shapes of donkeys and dancing figures. The musical pieces, such as A Muresca and Ciucciarella, are typical Corsican melodies.

Wooden objects are also a common product of Corsican handicraft. They include pipes made from olive, myrtle and heather wood, musical instruments and small pieces of furniture, often with unusual inlay work.

Perfumes

The fragrant oils extracted from Mediterranean maquis vegetation, including juniper, myrtle, lavender, cistus and mastic, can be found in many essences that bring to mind the land of Corsica. The woods also yield the balsamic essence of pine resins.

The essences of lavender, Corsican pine, myrtle and orange blossoms are used to produce perfumes with the scent of the maquis and Corsican forests.

Lavender, one of the components of perfumes

Gastronomic Delicacies

Like all other regions in the Mediterranean, Corsica produces many gastronomic specialities that visitors can take back home as a reminder of their time on the island. These varied local delicacies will satisfy anyone's palate.

Corsican pâtés, charcuterie and sausages are wonderfully tasty. The best ones hail from Bastelica, Castagniccia and Niolo. Boar pâté is also delicious.

Corsican cheeses include the famous *brocciu*, a sort of ricotta, as well as goat's-milk cheeses and others that are aged and flavoured with maquis herbs.

Liqueurs are among the typical products of the island. Some of the best are the Maison Mattei apéritifs, which are famous throughout the world, and products made from myrtle and other maquis herbs. These liqueurs are distilled by artisans in various regions of Corsica.

Aromatic vinegars made from herbs, apples and honey, and extracts of fruit such as hydromel, which are like the old fashioned sweet syrups, are other typical Corsican products.

Chestnut cake, typical of Castagniccia, is among Corsica's best-known sweets. *Fiadone* is a traditional cake made of *brocciu* cheese scented with orange blossoms. The aromatized nougat is also special.

Citron and honey nougat

Home-made preserves are a speciality. They are made from melon, myrtle, peach, citron, clementine and figs. The fig-with-walnut preserve makes for a superb accompaniment to cheese.

The local honey is another product bearing the flavours and scents of the island. It can be strong and bitter (chestnut), delicate (asphodel) or aromatic (lavender or strawberry tree) and is sold in the markets.

ENTERTAINMENT IN CORSICA

Although Corsica's main attractions are the sea and natural scenery, there is no lack of cultural activity and entertainment, especially in the seaside resorts and the main cities, such as Ajaccio and Bastia. For up-to-date information about concerts, theatre productions and cinemas, consult the local newspaper, *Corse-Matin*. In the summer, in addition to the numerous traditional festivals *(see pp36–9)*, many outdoor nightspots, discos and concerts ensure an entertaining evening. During the day, there are many organized excursions by boat and a wide range of sports and outdoor activities available *(see pp188–93)*, as well attractions related to the sea, such as an aquatic park and thalassotherapy centres.

Excursion boat moored near the bastions of Bonifacio

Excursions by Boat

Like all islands, Corsica offers a wide variety of interesting activities related to the sea. For those who do not have their own boat, there are many companies that hire them out *(see p207)*, with a skipper, or even a crew, if necessary. Also, in the summer months, there are numerous organized excursions or cruises along the coast that will allow you to admire the natural marvels of the island from the sea and stop in a secluded cove for a swim.

Among the best-known and most highly recommendable cruises is the one that takes visitors to the beautiful red cliffs of the Scandola Nature Reserve *(see pp108–9)*. The boats depart from various towns, including Ajaccio, Calvi, Porto, Cargèse, Tiuccia, Porticcio and nearby harbours. Do not fail to take the excursions from Ajaccio to the solitary Îles Sanguinaires *(see p96)*, and those departing from Propriano *(see p132)* to the Golfe de Valinco and the southwest coast.

The tours of the cliffs of Bonifacio and the Îles Lavezzi and Cavallo *(see pp120–21)* start from Bonifacio, which is also the departure point for trips across the Straits of Bonifacio *(see p117)* to the coast of Sardinia.

In the northern part of Corsica, most of the excursions to the beaches of Lodo, Cap Corse and the Désert des Agriates depart from the port of St-Florent.

Diving cruises on motorboats are organized more or less anywhere in Corsica, even for an entire weekend. Further information on diving sites and organizers can be found on page 191.

Travelling on the Petit Train

A typical Corsican attraction consists of the small, fairytale-style trains that take visitors on a leisurely tour of the main towns on the island. These vehicles are called *Petits Trains* because they are reminiscent of the train rides in children's amusement parks.

The *Petits Trains* operate in Ajaccio, Bonifacio, Corte and L'Île Rousse, generally departing from the centre of town – at Corte, for example, from the Citadelle – and following itineraries through the streets to show you the main sights and monuments. *Petits Trains* move quite slowly so that you can take photographs and enjoy the views while comfortably seated on the colourful little carriages.

Scuba Diving and Water Activities

Although popular in many seaside resorts all over Europe, amusement parks featuring aquatic activities are

The delightful *Petit Train* in Corte, at the entrance to the Citadelle

Thalassotherapy with a view at the Hotel Sofitel, near Ajaccio

still uncommon in Corsica. Due to Corsica's location, however, the islanders naturally enjoy all kinds of watersports. The **Corsica Diving Center** provides scuba diving lessons and water activities around the Calvi beaches.

Thalassotherapy

Those who feel that holidays are the perfect opportunity to regenerate the body and relax will not be disappointed by what Corsica has to offer.

Like many other French maritime resorts, the island allows the opportunity to undergo sea-water therapy, also known as "thalassotherapy". This consists of a series of completely natural cures that, through the use of sea water, help the body to eliminate the toxins caused by stress and too much work. As a result of these cures, the body feels considerably reinvigorated.

In Corsica, thalassotherapy is provided by the prestigious **Hotel Sofitel**, near Ajaccio. The packages on offer combine board and treatments from a wide selection available in its Mediterranean-styled spa.

Alternatively, you can go to the first-rate spas scattered in the interior of the island.

Music and Dance

The programme of cultural events, in particular music, is especially full during the summer months, even though there are concerts and performances in the low season as well.

In the last week of June, Calvi resounds with the notes of the Jazz Festival (see p37), one of the best-known musical events in Corsica, which features some of the leading names on the international jazz scene.

In early July, the Estivoce (see p37) in Pigna is dedicated to traditional Corsican polyphonic music, and many choirs and groups offer a glimpse into authentic island culture.

In Ajaccio, the first two weeks of July are given over to the Blues Festival "Nuits du Blues" (see p37), which features music performed by famous international artists and groups.

In Patrimonio, during the third week of July, folk, jazz and gipsy musicians give exciting performances for the Guitar Nights festival (see p37), while from July to September Ajaccio plays host to Les Estivales (see p37), with concerts and dance performances.

One of the most popular festivals among Corsicans themselves, though relatively unknown to foreign visitors, is Les Musicales de Bastia (see p39), which is held in October. This is a festival of folk music, jazz and dance. In late May, several venues in Ajaccio host Île Danse (see p36), a festival exploring the art of dance featuring leading European companies.

Local tourist offices offer information regarding the programmes of these various festivals and sell tickets. You can alternatively log on to www.visit-corsica.com.

Cinema and Theatre

During the summer, in the main seaside resorts there are many outdoor cinemas that show the latest films every evening, including the one at Porto, which is situated in the eucalyptus grove of the Marina. A film marked *VO* in listings is in its original language.

The main cinemas are in Bastia (**Le Studio**) and Ajaccio (**Empire, Ellipse, Bonaparte** and **Laetitia**).

March sees the Bastia Film Festival (see p36), which features international film productions. During the first week of October, the city hosts a British Film Festival; in November, the Mediterranean Cultures Film Festival (see p39) is staged here; and in January, the Italian Film Festival (see p39) organizes screenings of Italian films, retrospectives of Italian actors and directors, and lectures. Ajaccio is another centre for film, with Italian, Spanish and Asian festivals.

In the winter, there is an important theatre and opera season in Bastia.

A show performed in a Bastia theatre during the winter

Nightlife

Discotheques in Corsica are relatively few and far between compared to other European seaside resorts, and they are mostly concentrated in the larger coastal towns.

One of the best-known clubs on the island is **La Via Notte**, on the south edge of Porto-Vecchio. A favourite with teenagers, this club hosts famous international DJs in July and August. Porto-Vecchio also has a disco overlooking the water, **Le Clint**.

Among the most famous clubs in Bastia is **Noche de Cuba**, which attracts older crowds into Cuban music. Also in Bastia are **L'Enigme**, an LGBT-friendly dance spot, and **Le Pulp**, a popular late-night disco. To the west, in St-Florent, is **La Conca d'Oro**, while **La Madrague** is located in Lucciana, south of Bastia.

In Ajaccio, **La Place** is a smart private club where DJs play varied styles of music. A popular spot in Porticcio is **Le Blue Moon**, which has a large terrace; in Bonifacio, **B'52** features the latest sounds and serves colourful cocktails. There is a fairly healthy choice of nightlife in Calvi. **La Camargue** has an

Calvi's promenade, illuminated by the neon signs of the nightspots

outdoor dance floor and a swimming pool, while **Chez Tao** is an historic piano bar in the Citadelle.

If clubbing is not your scene and you would rather drink a cocktail while listening to music, Corsican towns have many bars of every kind. In Bastia, the most popular spots are concentrated around the Vieux Port area and the Port Toga quarter, which in the summer becomes a huge pedestrian precinct with shows and entertainment. Here, the tables of the disco bars and restaurants almost touch the water. Among the most popular places are **Dusty Rose Saloon**,

Le Cézanne Café, **Alba**, **Le Pub O'Connors**, **Café Wha!** and **U Spuntinu**, by the Citadelle, a wine bar with live music and a fine wine list where you can drink by the glass or the bottle while enjoying a salad or canapés.

In Ajaccio, the great variety of nightspots includes **Vino del Diablo**, **Le Son des Guitares** and **Le Temple du Jeu**.

Calvi has **La Camargue**, a discotheque and piano bar, and **Le Bar de la Tour**.

Among the best spots in Porto-Vecchio are **La Canne à Sucre**, ideal for an ice cream or a drink, and **La Taverne du Roi**, a popular venue that often hosts jazz and cabaret singers.

Night-time view of the harbour of Bastia, with the church of St-Jean-Baptiste in the background

DIRECTORY

Excursions by Boat

Bordemer
Foce, Porto-Vecchio.
Tel 06 83 54 37 15.

Centre Nautique Valinco
Plage de Mancinu, Port de Plaisance, BP67, Propriano.
W centre-nautique-valinco.com

Colombo Line
Quai Landry, Port de Plaisance, Calvi.
Tel 04 95 65 32 10.
W colombo-line.com

Croisières Grand Bleu
24 Rue Marbeuf, Cargèse.
Tel 04 95 26 40 24.

Nave Va
Ajaccio. **Tel** 04 95 51 31 31.
Porticcio. **Tel** 04 95 25 94 14. W naveva.com

Porto-Vecchio Croisieres
Port de Plaisance.
Tel 04 95 10 42 29.

Rocca Croisières
6 Rue Fred Scamaroni, Bonifacio.
Tel 04 95 73 13 96.
W rocca-croisieres.com

Thalassa Croisières
Parking du Port, Marina, Bonifacio.
Tel 06 86 34 00 49, 04 95 73 01 17.
W vedettes-thalasses.com

U San Paulu
Macinaggio.
Tel 06 14 78 14 16.
W sanpaulu.com

Petits Trains Companies

Autocars Massimi
Quai Noel Beretti, Bonifacio.
Tel 04 95 73 15 07.
W autocars-massimi.com

Chemin de Fer de la Corse (Le Petit Train)
Col de Fogata, L'Île Rousse (departure: Place Paoli).
Tel 04 95 60 00 50.

Le Petit Train
Ajaccio/Iles Sanguinaires.
Tel 04 95 51 13 69, or 04 95 60 00 50.
W petit-train-ajaccio.com

Petit Train Touristique de Bastia
Tel 04 95 31 61 16 or 06 09 37 00 54.
W le-petit-train-bastiais.com

U Trenu
Corte (departure: municipal car park, behind the train station, or Place Paoli).
Tel 06 09 95 70 36.

Scuba Diving & Thalassotherapy

Corsica Diving Center
Plage de Mare e Sole, Coti Chiavaie, Calvi.
Tel 06 12 17 85 29.
W corsicadivingcenter.com

Hotel Sofitel
Golfe d'Ajaccio, Porticcio.
Tel 04 95 29 40 40.
W sofitel.com

Cinemas

Cinema 7eme Art
Route du Village, Furiani.
Tel 04 95 31 12 94.

Cinematheque de Corse
Espace Jean, Lecci, Porto Vecchio.
Tel 04 20 20 20 01/02.

Centre Cultural
Espace Jean Paul de Rocca Serra, Lecci, Porto-Vecchio. **Tel** 04 95 70 35 02.

Ellipse
Rue des Magnolias, La Rocade, Ajaccio.
W ellipse-cinema.fr

Empire
30 Cours Napoléon, Ajaccio. **Tel** 04 95 21 21 00.

Laetitia
24 Cours Napoléon, Ajaccio.
Tel 04 95 21 07 24.

Le Studio
1 Rue Miséricorde, Bastia.
Tel 04 95 31 12 94.

Theatres

Aghja
6 Chemin de Biancarello, Ajaccio. **Tel** 04 95 20 41 15.
W aghja.com

Theatre Municipal à l'Espace Diamant
Blvd Pascal Rossini, Ajaccio.
Tel 04 95 50 40 80.

Discotheques

B'52
35, Quai Camparetti, Bonifacio.
Tel 06 32 82 18 69.

Le Blue Moon
Centre Commercial, Les Marines, Porticcio.
Tel 06 76 59 53 22.
W bluemooncorsica.fr

La Camargue
RN 197, Calvi.
Tel 04 95 65 08 70.

Chez Tao
Rue St-François, Citadelle, Calvi. **Tel** 04 95 65 00 73.

Le Clint
3 Rue Jerome Leandri, Porto-Vecchio.
Tel 04 95 70 19 19.

La Conca d'Oro
Oletta, St-Florent.
Tel 04 95 39 00 46.

L'Enigme
1 Rue Pino, Bastia.
Tel 04 20 03 57 56.

La Madrague
Route de la Canonica, RD 107, Lucciana.
Tel 04 95 30 02 50.

Noche de Cuba
5 Rue Chanoine Leschi, Bastia.
Tel 04 95 31 02 83.

La Place
Place du Diamant, Ajaccio.
Tel 06 18 86 74 30.

Le Pulp
Port de Toga, Rue Sisco, Bastia.
Tel 06 17 51 04 97 or 06 19 84 22 49.

La Via Notte
Route de Pourra, Porto-Vecchio.
Tel 04 95 72 02 12.

Nightspots

Alba
Quai des Martyres, Rue de la Liberation, Bastia.
Tel 04 95 47 03 38.

Le Bar de la Tour
Quay Landry, Calvi.
Tel 04 95 46 39 74.

Café Wha!
Vieux Port, Bastia.
Tel 04 95 34 25 79.

Canne à Sucre
Quai Paoli, Port de Plaisance, Porto-Vecchio.
Tel 04 95 70 35 25.

Le Cézanne Café
Port de Plaisance, Toga, Bastia.
Tel 04 95 34 16 60.

Club 24
Rue Clemenceau, Calvi.
Tel 04 95 65 08 66.

Dusty Rose Saloon
RN 193, Valrose, Borgo, near Bastia.
Tel 06 27 47 72 95.

Le Pub O'Connors
1 Rue St Erasme, Bastia.
Tel 04 95 32 04 97 or 06 16 34 76 33.

Le Son des Guitares
Rue du Roi de Rome, Ajaccio.
Tel 04 95 51 16 47.

La Taverne du Roi
43 Rue Borgo, Porto-Vecchio.
Tel 04 95 70 41 31.

Le Temple du Jeu
2 Avenue de la Grande Armée, Ajaccio.
Tel 04 95 10 19 39.

U Spuntinu
7 Rue Dragon, La Citadelle, Bastia.
Tel 06 29 80 73 87.

Vino del Diablo
Port d'Amirauté, Ajaccio.
Tel 04 95 22 70 10.

SPORTS AND OUTDOOR ACTIVITIES

Corsica is an ideal destination for sports and outdoor enthusiasts. Along the coast, those who love the sea will find beaches with fine sand and coves among craggy cliffs that can often be reached only by boat, as well as splendid sea floors. For hiking or trekking buffs, there is no end of possibilities, with hills, mountains and trails of varying degrees of difficulty. Even the best cyclists will have their work cut out for them along the steep hairpin turns

of the inland roads that lead to the passes in the central mountain range. Canoeing, kayaking and rafting aficionados will love the swiftly flowing torrents. And horse riding is a fascinating way of visiting the hills of Corsica. In keeping with the French passion for the great outdoors, all sports and other activities in Corsica are organized efficiently and thoroughly. The Directory on page 193 lists a selection of useful addresses.

Hiking

More than 25 years ago, Corsica inaugurated its longest hiking route, the GR20 *(see pp26–31)*, which crosses the entire island along a northwest–southeast axis. Annually, more than 17,000 hikers from all over the world walk through woods, forests and rugged ridges following this long-distance path.

Because the GR20 is now overflowing with hikers, other paths have been created to ease congestion. These are less difficult than the GR20 and are called *Mare e Monti* ("sea and mountains"; *see p31*) if the paths start out from the sea and go inland to the peaks, and *Mare a Mare* ("sea to sea"; *see p31*) if they go from coast to coast via the interior.

Among the latter, there are three main routes from west to east: Cargèse to the beach at Cervione, in Castagniccia; Ajaccio to Ghisonaccia; and Propriano

Hikers on their way through Corsica's wild landscape

to Porto-Vecchio. These paths are usually at a low altitude and tend to run on flatter terrain. They also go through villages where it is possible to buy food and drink, so one can hike with a lighter backpack.

Among the most interesting *Mare e Monti* hikes is the one that goes from Cargèse to Calenzana, in Balagne, via Evisa and Galéria.

Besides these long routes, there are many areas that are of interest to hikers. Among these are the Vallée de l'Asco *(see p154)*, at the foot of Monte Cinto, the Calacuccia zone *(see p155)*, the upper Vallée de la Restonica *(see p143)*, the Col de Vizzavona *(see p146)* and the splendid Col de Bavella area *(see pp126–7)*. There are many useful hiking guide books,

such as *Trekking in Corsica*, by David Abram, published by Trailblazer Guides, which covers all the island's best routes (including the GR20), or Robin G Collomb's *Corsica Mountains*, published by West Co, UK. The *Guide de la Randonnée en Corse* ("Guide to Long Hikes in Corsica"), published by Didier Richard, provides many hiking suggestions, as does *Corse*, a guide published by the Institut Géographique National. The topographical maps produced by the same institute are vitally important for difficult hikes.

Before setting off with your backpack, bear in mind that, although the Corsican mountains in summer seem to be hiker-friendly and sunny, bad weather and storms are quite common at high

Amazing rock formations along a hiking trail

An exciting canoeing experience on a rushing torrent

altitudes and may easily cause sudden sharp drops in temperature. Furthermore, remember that the food- and water-supply stations are not always well-stocked.

Climbing

Although there are no internationally famous rock-climbing areas in Corsica, there are plenty of challenging and attractive cliffs and walls.

There are basically two types of rock here – granite and limestone – and they require different climbing techniques and styles.

Among the climbers' favourite sites are Ponte Leccia and Solenzara, the Nebbio region, with the cliffs of Caporalino and Pietralba, the Col de Bavella (see pp126–7), with routes of varying difficulty, and the longest routes in the Teghje Liscie and Balagne areas.

Rafting

One of the main features of Corsica consists of the watercourses, both large and small, in the valleys of the interior. Rafters love these rivers because of the wild scenery they pass through. Rafting is a very technical sport for experts only, and in Corsica there are agencies and specialized guides that organize the descents down the rivers, from the easiest to the most difficult. The easiest gorges are along the course of the Vecchio, Aïtone and Tavignano rivers. More difficult routes are some stretches of the Taravo and the Vacca (near Bavella) rivers, and the long descents of torrents such as the Negretto (near Ponte Leccia), the Sportellu (Porto) and the Pollschellu (Levie).

Canoeing and Kayaking

Corsica has a lot of rainfall, and in the mountains this becomes rather heavy snowfall, sometimes as much as 2 m (6 ft). Consequently, in spring, when the temperatures rise and the thawing season begins, the island welcomes many canoeists who come from all over Europe, eager to take advantage of the abundance of gushing water, as well as beautiful gorges and mountain scenery.

Corsican rivers tend to be technical and spectacular. The Taravo, Rizzanese and Fium'Orbo rivers offer splendid descents. The most famous and difficult are the Tavignano, Golo and Prunelli rivers, as well as the Liamone.

Horse Riding

Corsica offers many opportunities for horse riding. The most interesting areas for this activity are the green hills of the Castagniccia area, the divide between the Bozio and Corte regions, the Tavignano river as far as the plateaus of Lac de Nino, the Désert des Agriates, the Sartène region, with its many prehistoric sights, and the mountainous region of Cagna.

You can also ride on the sandy shores of the east coast or on the grassy top of the white cliffs of Bonifacio.

Riding on the beach

A departure point for canoe or kayak excursions

Sailing

With its rugged coasts, small rocky islands and the Scandola and Lavezzi marine reserves, Corsica is a favourite with yachting buffs from all over the world. This appeal is compounded by the constant presence of wind.

The voyage from the ports in southern France is rather long (Cap Corse is 119 nautical miles from St-Tropez, 100 from Nice and 83 from Menton), but it sails over a zone famous for frequent sightings of fin whales. The stretch of the sea 45 nautical miles northwest of Calvi is where you are most likely to find these marvellous sea mammals.

Departing from the Italian coast, the crossing to Corsica is shorter and one can make a stopover at the islands of the Tuscan archipelago. Cap Corse is 49 nautical miles from Livorno, while the distance from Bastia to the island of Elba is 40 nautical miles.

The circumnavigation of Corsica is also popular with yachtsmen *(see p206)*. This route passes by various types of coastline: sandy and filled with pools on the eastern sides; craggy and indented at Cap Corse; and varied, with tall rock faces on the west side. The strongest wind is around the Straits of

Sailing lessons at Marina de Meria, Cap Corse

Bonifacio, between Corsica and Sardinia. Be careful when sailing here, because the wind is often violent and there are numerous large ships that navigate this part of the sea.

If you do not have a boat of your own, it is possible to hire one in all the ports and tourist resorts, where there are also agencies that offer boat tours of the coast with the skipper and crew included in the price.

Navigating along the coasts of Corsica, you will come across two very important marine reserves: the Scandola Nature Reserve *(see pp108–9)* and the Réserve de Lavezzi *(see p121)*, which, in turn, is part of the Parc Marin International des Bouches de Bonifacio *(see p117)*, an initiative of the French and

Italian governments that has succeeded in protecting and improving this major stretch of sea, where numerous regattas are held.

The Distance in Nautical Miles between Ports

Bastia–St-Florent	48
St-Florent–Calvi	30
Calvi–Girolata	21
Girolata–Porto	6
Porto–Cargèse	12
Cargèse–Ajaccio	21
Ajaccio–Propriano	22
Propriano–Roccapina	15
Roccapina–Bonifacio	12
Bonifacio–Lavezzi	6
Lavezzi–Porto-Vecchio	18
Porto-Vecchio–Bastia	67

Boats anchored at one of the many fabulous coves on Îles Lavezzi

Windsurfing

The areas and resorts where sailing is common and nautical clubs are based also tend to have facilities for windsurfing. All the tourist towns along the coast offer the possibility to practise this sport, which is an exciting combination of surfing and sailing. There are many small schools that rent windsurfing equipment and offer courses at different levels of ability.

Corsica, like most islands, is blessed with good breezes, especially along the west coast and the cliffs in the south. However, in the south the wind is perhaps too strong and potentially dangerous, so windsurfing in this area should be practised by experts only.

A windsurfer in search of wind at Îles Lavezzi

Diving

The sea floors in Corsica are rich in fauna and natural beauty. There are about 60 clubs on the island that have ideal sites for diving. Among these, the **Station Recherches Sousmarines et Océanographiques**, which is situated at the Pointe Revellata promontory, not far from Calvi, offers courses for beginners and short courses on marine biology. It is also possible to stay here and organize your own dives.

Among the most famous diving sites are the beautiful Mérouville zone, northeast of Îles Lavezzi, and the islet of Sperduto, which is part of the Réserve de Lavezzi. As is the case with all protected areas, diving here is subject to strict

A diver swimming to the surface with the day's catch

regulations and limits, so it is best to make enquiries at the Réserve offices or in one of the diving clubs in the area beforehand.

In southeast Corsica, not far from the Golfe de Porto-Vecchio, the small Îles Cerbicale have interesting diving sites in the Île du Toro area, where there are many shipwrecks.

In southwest Corsica, in the Golfe de Valinco, facing Propriano, the most popular sites are those around the rocks of the so-called cathédrales ("cathedrals"), off the coast of Porto-Pollo, and the Secche di Belvedere. Near the Pointe de la Parata, which, together with the Îles Sanguinaires, closes off the Golfe d'Ajaccio to the north, is a diving site called Tabernacle, while in the southern part of the gulf is the shipwreck of the Meulère.

Further north, in the Golfe de Sagone, are the sandbanks of the Provençale and the wreck of a Canadair aeroplane. In the Golfe de Porto, the Punta Mucchilina sand bar offers a great variety of fauna and flora, as well as the wreck of a coal ship.

Divers in the Calvi area often visit the Pointe Revellata canyon,

at the northernmost confines of the Scandola Nature Reserve (see pp108–9), and the wreck of a Boeing B-17 bomber that lies 28 m (90 ft) below sea level. Further north, in the Golfe de St-Florent, there are the sea floors of Punta Vecchiara and the sand bar of Saleccia, while the Île de Giraglia, at the northern tip of Cap Corse, is famous for a wonderful dive west of the lighthouse.

Cycling

Corsica offers several opportunities for cyclists. Many routes follow paths on the hills through the central mountain range, and they are generally located in very beautiful forest areas.

In spring and summer, there is an abundance of cyclists at the Col de Vizzavona, Col de Verghio, Col de Verde and Col de Bavella. The coastal roads are also lovely, but be aware that they tend to be very windy and congested.

Whatever your choice, bear in mind that the roads are narrow, mostly on hills with steep rises, and have many curves. There are few places for food and drinks along the way. Furthermore, the road surface is not always good, so it is advisable to bring along a spare inner tube and the tools needed for repairs.

Cycling fans normally have their own bicycles, but there are agencies that offer bicycle tours of a week or more. The advantage of these tours is that a van is available to carry your luggage from one stop to another. In case of fatigue, cyclists are taken into the van or to a doctor.

Cycling on a mountain road in central Corsica

Mountain Biking

One of the most ecologically friendly ways to discover the interior of Corsica is by mountain bike. The rises are generally steep and the paths quite rough, so make sure you are well equipped and that you take plenty of water with you.

Among the areas suggested by experts for their beauty are the forests of Ospédale, Bavella and Cagna, and the entire central Alta Rocca zone. Except for the summer months, the paths through the maquis in the Désert des Agriates, in the northern part of the island, are splendid, as are some stretches of the *Mare a Mare* and *Mare e Monti* (*see p31*) paths and the long route from Propriano to Ajaccio.

It is easy to find a bike for hire in the summer.

Golf

The ultimate golf course in Corsica is without a doubt the one at Pointe de Sperone (*see p121*), a short distance from Capo Pertusato. The course lies on the soft hills bordered by maquis facing the Îles Lavezzi and Cavallo. This 18-hole, par-72 golf course is more than 6 km (4 miles) long.

The other golf courses and golf schools on the island are at Ajaccio (school), Bastia (9 holes), Lezza (6 holes) and Reginu (6 holes).

Information concerning the golf courses and the various tournaments held on the island is available on the **Ligue Corse de Golf** website (www.liguecorsedegolf.org).

Winter Sports

The tourists who throng to Corsica in the summer may find it hard to believe, but in winter there is a considerable amount of snow on the mountain peaks of the central range. So, from December to March, four small ski resorts inland offer fine downhill runs and even circular cross-country courses to skiing aficionados.

But the real attraction of Corsica, which does not have many ski-lift facilities, are the routes for alpine cross-country skiing (*ski de randonnée*), for which there are various possibilities in spring as well. First of all, there is the difficult route that follows the central divide and runs more or less along the routes marked out in summer by the GR20 long-distance path.

Snow-capped peaks in the Monte Cinto region

There are also many other possible routes starting off from the locality of Ghisoni (towards Monte Renoso), from the upper Vallée de la Restonica, from Haut-Asco and from the Campotile plateau.

Between Quenza and Zicavo, on the Coscione plateau, there are several courses for those who love adventurous cross-country skiing or long walks with snowshoes. Here, the utmost caution is necessary, since the weather can be treacherous. Be sure to have plenty of supplies with you, because supply stations are few and far between. Spring alpine skiing requires the same precautions adopted on other mountains.

Alpine cross-country skiing

The prestigious golf club on the Pointe de Sperone, near Bonifacio

DIRECTORY

Hiking

Compagnie Régionale des Guides et Accompagnateurs de Montagne de Corse
Route de Cuccia, Calacuccia.
Tel 04 95 48 10 43.

Corse Odyssée
Quenza.
Tel 04 95 78 64 05.
[w] gite-corse-odyssee.com

Corsica Raid Aventure (race)
Tel 06 73 01 84 48.
[w] corsicaraid.com

In Terra Corsa
Lieu-dit Baccario, Rt de Calvi, Ponte Leccia.
Tel 04 95 47 69 48.
[w] interracorsa.fr

Parc Naturel Régional de la Corse
Ajaccio.
Tel 04 95 51 79 10.
[w] parc-corse.org

Climbing and Mountaineering

Alpa Corse René Eymerie
(alpine guides).
Tel 06 27 21 66 60.

Corsica Madness
Zonza. **Tel** 04 95 78 61 76 or 06 13 22 95 06.
[w] corsicamadness.com

In Terra Corsa
Lieu-dit Baccario, Rt de Calvi, Ponte Leccia.
Tel 04 95 47 69 48.
[w] interracorsa.fr

Jean-Paul Quilici
Solenzara.
Tel 04 95 78 64 33 or 06 16 41 18 53.

Les Guides de la Compagnie Corse
Tel 06 24 29 65 03.

Montagnes du Corse
Ajaccio.
Tel 04 95 10 52 83.

Pierre Pietri
Cap Corse.
Tel 04 95 32 62 76 or 06 88 73 48 66.

Vallecime
(alpine guides).
Casamacioli & Sant'Andrea di Bozio.
Tel 04 95 48 69 33 or 06 14 74 44 98.
[w] vallecime.com

Rafting

Corse Aventure
Route de Sartène, Corri Bianchi, Eccica-Suarella.
Tel 04 95 25 91 19.
[w] corse-aventure.com

In Terra Corsa
Lieu-dit Baccario, Rt de Calvi, Ponte Leccia.
Tel 04 95 47 69 48.
[w] interracorsa.fr

Canoeing and Kayaking

Altore
Calvi.
Tel 06 08 72 67 19.
St-Florent.
Tel 06 88 21 49 16.
[w] altore.com
Info@altore.com

Commission Nager en Eau Vive
Bastia, c/o Jean Pierre Vergnon.
Tel 04 95 31 51 12.

Horse Riding

Equiloisirs (FAE)
N200, Corte.
Tel 04 95 61 09 88.

In Terra Corsa
Lieu-dit Baccario, Rt de Calvi, Ponte Leccia.
Tel 04 95 47 69 48.
[w] interracorsa.fr

Sailing and Windsurfing

Calvi Marine
Route de Porto, Calvi.
Tel 04 95 65 01 12.

Calvi Nautique Club
Porte de Plaisance, Calvi.
Tel 04 95 65 10 65.

Centre Nautique des Fauvettes
Porto-Vecchio.
Tel 04 95 70 93 00.
[w] lesfauvettescorse.fr

Centre Nautique des Glénans
Route de Santa Manza, Maison de la Mer, Bonifacio.
Tel 04 95 73 03 85.
[w] glenans.asso.fr

Corsica Voile
Port de Plaisance, Macinaggio.
Tel 04 95 35 48 20.
[w] corsica-voile.com

L'Île Bleue
Bonifacio.
Tel 04 95 34 64 65.

Multi Service Plaisance
Marina Santa Giulia, Porto-Vecchio.
Tel 04 95 70 29 13 or 06 10 83 59 25.

Societé des Loisirs Nautiques de Porticcio
Plage de la Viva, Porticcio.
Tel 06 74 98 06 21.
[w] snip.fr

Soleil Rouge Yachting
Porte Tino Rossi, Ajaccio.
Tel 04 95 21 89 21.
[w] soleilrouge.com

Diving

Fédération Française Études et Sports Sousmarins
Solenzara.
(List of 83 Corsican clubs.)
Tel 06 43 17 81 67.

Station Recherches Sousmarines et Océanographiques
Pointe Revellata, BP 33 Calvi.
Tel 06 86 22 32 61.
[w] stareso.com
stareso@stareso.com

Cycling and Mountain Bikes

Europe Active Velo
Tel 04 95 44 49 67.
[w] velo-corse.com

Garage d'Angeli
4 Quartier Neuf, Calvi.
Tel 04 95 65 02 13.
[w] garagedangeli.com

Rent a Car
Ajaccio.
Tel 04 95 51 61 81 (airport and town).
[w] rent-car-corsica.com

Rout'evasion
10 Avenue Noel Franchini, Ajaccio. **Tel** 04 95 22 72 87. [w] routevasion.com

TTC Moto
25 Rue General de Gaulle, Propriano.
Tel 04 95 76 15 32.
[w] ttcmoto.fr

Golf

Bastia Golf Club
Rt de l'Aeroport, Castellarese, Borgo.
Tel 04 95 38 33 99.
[w] golfborgo.fr

Golf Club Sperone
Domaine de Sperone, Bonifacio.
Tel 04 95 73 17 13.
Fax 04 95 73 17 85.
[w] golfdesperone.com

Ligue Corse de Golf
Rue Marcel Paul, Bastia.
Tel 04 95 32 54 53.
[w] liguecorse degolf.org

Winter Sports

Bergeries de Gite U Fugone Capannelle
Ghisoni.
Tel 06 81 25 60 75.

Val d'Ese Ski
Tel 04 95 10 11 20.
[w] ski-bastelica.com

SURVIVAL
GUIDE

PRACTICAL INFORMATION

In Corsica, tourism is an important industry – and not only in summer, when visitors come to enjoy the sea. Spring and autumn are ideal for tours inland, for hikes in the mountains and visits to the archaeological sites. Travelling within Corsica is easy: the hotels, restaurants and camp sites are of a high quality and visitors can rely on the wide-ranging network of assistance from the Agence de Tourisme de la Corse and the local tourist offices. When planning a trip to Corsica, it is best not to have a heavy schedule, and to avoid long trips, despite the apparently short distances: the roads may be extremely scenic, but they are not very fast because of the numerous bends and the sometimes rough surfaces. Furthermore, each village has surprises in store, be they historic, scenic or gastronomic, and it would be a pity to miss them.

The Corsican coastline in the spring

In the tourist offices, you may find brochures and maps of the area, lists of the local hotels and restaurants, and information on the museums and archaeological sites.

The larger cities, such as Ajaccio and Bastia, also print pamphlets promoting festivals and cultural activities such as music, dance and theatre.

If you want to plan your vacation from home, make enquiries at a French tourist organization, such as the **France Tourism Development Agency**, which has much material on Corsica and can also provide information over the telephone.

When to Go

Corsica offers varied natural scenery and many different environments.

July and August are the best months for seaside holidays, but beware: the resorts will be crowded and it will be very warm.

The best period for hiking and climbing is from May to September, but even October can be quite pleasant if you limit your hikes to the foothills.

In order to enjoy the tranquil beauty of the island to the full, it is advisable not to visit Corsica between mid-July and mid-August. However, if you plan on coming in low season, be sure to organize your stay in advance, as many hotels and restaurants close for the winter months.

Visas and Passports

Corsica is a region of France and follows the same laws and regulations. European Union citizens are not subject to customs controls, but it is a good idea to have your documents handy.

For stays of three months or less, no visa is required for citizens of other European countries and for US, Canada and New Zealand nationals. However, visitors from other parts of the world, including Australia, must have a visa, which can be obtained from a French consulate in the country of departure.

Tourist Information

All the main cities on the island have a tourist office, which may be called either Office de Tourisme or Syndicat d'Initiative. Smaller Corsican towns have centres that provide information on that particular area, including nearby villages. Sometimes the town hall itself (*mairie*) is used as a visitors' centre.

Tickets and Opening Hours

As a general rule, archaeological sites and museums in Corsica charge an admission fee. Most of them, however, have reduced prices for visitors aged under 18 and over 60. In some cases, discounted tickets are available for students with international student cards.

The opening hours of museums and archaeological sites vary: generally speaking, the main museums stay open all day,

Logo of Ota-Porto Tourism

◀ A hiker on the footbridge along the Sentier de Spasimata, in the Balagne region

A road sign indicating an historic monument

while digs are closed one day a week (either Sunday or Monday). If you want to visit churches and chapels, it is best to find out the opening hours from the town halls or tourist offices before embarking on your trip. Likewise, if you are planning to take a special tour to minor localities, it is advisable to contact the relevant tourist offices first.

Bear in mind that opening hours differ in high and low season. Detailed information is provided in the central section of this guide, which has the individual descriptions of the resorts, as well as in this section and the *Travellers' Needs* section *(see pp156–93)*.

Disabled Travellers

In terms of providing for the disabled, Corsica is still a long way behind mainland France. Only a relatively small number of establishments – bars, restaurants, hotels and pensions – supply adequate facilities for wheelchair access. However, things are improving.

International Student Identity Card

The French guidebook *Guide Rousseau H comme Handicapés*, published by La Route Robert, contains detailed lists of the places with wheelchair access and other facilities. **Tourism For All** publishes an English-language brochure with information on all the establishments in France and Corsica in which architectural barriers have been eliminated to allow for easier access for the disabled.

Services for Students

Full-time students who own an **International Student Identity Card** (ISIC) are entitled

to reductions in the price of tickets and for numerous tourist initiatives. The ISIC card is an internationally recognized document that can be purchased from student travel agents or via the ISIC website.

Languages

Although the official language in Corsica is French, the local language has also always been in use there, making the island a bilingual area.

In 1974, Corsican was officially recognized as a regional tongue. After the reopening of the University of Corte in 1981, written Corsican was codified and old literary texts re-evaluated *(see pp34–5)*.

Corsican is more like Italian than French – it is reminiscent of Ligurian dialect spoken with a Sardinian accent. As a result, many Corsicans understand and speak Italian. Road signs are in Corsican and French, although the French is often obscured by nationalist graffiti.

Corsican Time

Corsica is one hour ahead of Greenwich Mean Time (GMT) and summer (daylight saving) time operates from spring to early autumn. Corsica uses a 24-hour clock, so 8pm, for example, is indicated as 20h *(vingt heures)*.

Electrical Adaptors

Electrical current in Corsica is 220v AC. Except for some small villages inland, the central hole of the sockets is generally earthed. It is wise to purchase a suitable adaptor, if necessary, before leaving for Corsica.

Personal Security and Health

Corsica is a tranquil and safe region for travellers. The locals welcome foreign visitors, being well aware that they are a positive factor for the island's life and economy. Generally speaking, personal security is not really a problem, for either men or women. The disorders that sometimes make the news are the work of a handful of extremists of the Corsican independence movement and do not represent a danger for foreign visitors. Health standards on the island are high: as well as the hospitals in the main cities, there are physicians on 24-hour duty and medical facilities in all the resorts, especially those popular with tourists.

Personal Security

On the whole, dangerous or harmful incidents in Corsica rarely take place. Visitors, including lone women travellers, are unlikely to come across any problems of personal security.

Anyone walking along the streets on the island cannot help noticing the large amount of graffiti everywhere calling for Corsican independence from France. In recent decades, some violent incidents have been linked to the independence movement. But even though the extremist fringe of this movement has sometimes made recourse to acts of terrorism, this tension is on the wane, and tourists have never been targeted by these factions. It is, however, a good rule to avoid entering into heated arguments or taking part in public demonstrations while in Corsica, as they might have unpleasant consequences.

Corsican Police

In France, there is a police corps called *Gendarmerie Nationale*, which deals with major crimes and operates mainly outside the large cities, although it might intervene should serious incidents occur.

In the cities, those responsible for maintaining law and order act both as traffic wardens and as policemen, also taking care of minor problems. In case of need, go to the nearest police station *(gendarmerie)*. If you are in a small, isolated village, you can go to the local town hall *(mairie)* during office hours.

Road Hazards

The roads in Corsica are not the best maintained in Europe. The road surface is not always in good condition, the lanes are often narrow and there are a great many bends, especially in the mountainous interior.

When travelling by car *(see p205)*, it is therefore a good idea to bring along a spare tyre and tools for minor repairs or problems. You are also required by law to carry reflective safety jackets for yourself and all passengers, and a warning triangle, for use in case of an accident. In the event of a breakdown, get everyone out of the car before attempting a repair or calling the emergency services.

Fire Hazards

Since a large part of the island is covered with luxuriant forests, Corsica appears as a verdant paradise compared to other islands in the Mediterranean.

In the extensive woods in the interior and in the coastal areas with thick maquis vegetation, fire prevention is of vital importance. In these areas, the wind blows almost constantly, the climate is hot and there is abundant vegetation – all factors that favour outbreaks of fire. Furthermore, because of the many steep ridges, canyons and rough terrain on the island, fires can be hard to control and put out. A case in point is the huge fire in the Vallée de la Restonica, which occurred in the summer of 2000, and, in July 2009, around 6,000 ha (15,000 acres) were ravaged by fire in the area around the village of Aullène in southern Corsica.

Firemen intervene both on the ground and, as soon as possible, with firefighting aeroplanes known as Canadair, and smaller, more manageable helicopters that get their water supply from the artificial lakes inland.

Not only is common sense called for, but European regulations must be obeyed as well. It is strictly forbidden to light fires outdoors, except in rigorously controlled areas. Smokers must never throw lighted cigarette butts on the roads or in the brush. You must also keep an eye out for any fire or smoke and make sure you report it to the fire brigade as soon as possible.

A vehicle used by the fire brigade suitable for rough terrain

A Canadair dumping tons of water on to a brush fire

If you are planning to take a long hike on terrain that is a potential fire risk, it is best to inform the local authorities of this before you start off. This way they will know how many people may be in danger should a fire break out in that area.

Legal Assistance

As with any destination, for your own security take out a travel insurance policy.

In case of particular difficulties or serious incidents that require police intervention, the best thing to do is to contact your consulate (see p197) as soon as possible, since it will be able to provide all the necessary assistance in your language.

Personal Belongings

Although Corsica, like so many other tourist areas, is a peaceful region, travellers should take all the necessary precautions dictated by common sense.

Always take out insurance on your personal belongings, do not leave your luggage unattended and visible in a car, keep handbags within sight and do not travel with a lot of cash.

All cases of theft should be reported at the nearest police station immediately. Should you lose your documents, it is best to ask for help at your country's consulate in France (see p197).

Medical Treatment

When visiting Corsica, citizens of European Union countries who are entitled to medical treatment from their own national health service have the right to the same assistance they would receive in their own country. Before leaving the UK, British tourists must get a European Health Insurance Card (EHIC) from a post office or online; it allows complete medical treatment and reimbursement of most of the expenses (which have to be paid on the spot) on the part of the Caisse Primarie d'Assurance-Maladie.

Non-EU citizens must obtain medical insurance from their own countries prior to departure. The number to call for the emergency service is 15.

Hospitals and Pharmacies

Hospitals in Corsica are well organized and efficient. They are situated in the four main cities and in the largest tourist resorts, where there are also 24-hour duty physicians for foreign visitors. Almost all the towns have pharmacies. They can be recognized by the neon sign in the form of a green cross outside.

If a pharmacy is closed, the address of the nearest open one is always listed outside, as are the opening hours. The larger cities also have a 24-hour pharmacy for emergencies.

Pharmacy sign

DIRECTORY

Emergency Numbers

Police
Tel 17.

Fire Brigade
Tel 18.

Ambulance
Tel 15.

Med Cross
Tel 196 (emergencies at sea).

Night-duty Physician (SOS Medicins Corsica)/24-hour Pharmacies Tel 17 or 3624.

Road Emergencies
Tel 112. AA Europe **Tel** 04 72 17 12 00 or 08 25 09 88 76.

Hospitals

Centre Hospitalier Corte - Tattone
Avenue du 9 Septembre.
Tel 04 95 45 05 00 or 04 95 45 05 04 (emergencies).

Centre Hospitalier Notre Dame de la Miscericorde
27 Avenue Impératrice Eugénie.
Tel 04 95 29 90 90.

Hôpital de Bastia
Route Royale, BP 680.
Tel 04 95 59 11 11.

Hôpital de Bonifacio
Lieu dit Valle. **Tel** 04 95 73 95 73.

Hôpital "Cacciabello"
D48 outside Sartène.
Tel 04 95 77 95 00.

Minor Risks

Take precautions to avoid sunburn, which is as much a risk for those hiking in the mountains as for those holidaying on the coast.

If you suffer from allergies, take along insect repellent.

Sign for a Corsican hospital with the building in the background

Banking and Local Currency

Since 2002, most European tourists in Corsica no longer have to deal with the issue of currency exchange, since France is a member of the European Monetary Union and the currency in circulation within the Union is the euro. For visitors from other countries, however, exchanging currency is an easy and rapid procedure, both in banks and at the reception desks of hotels and pensions. The exchange rate of the euro and other non-European Union currencies is established daily and the rates can be found in all newspapers.

A cash dispenser (ATM) outside a bank

Banks

Banks in Corsica have the same opening hours as those in the south of France (8.30am to noon; 1:30 to 4:30pm) and are closed on Saturday and Sunday. Over public holidays, they are often closed from Friday noon to Tuesday morning.

Most European visitors no longer need to exchange currency, since the euro became the common currency of many EU countries in January 2002.

Although documents are not normally necessary when exchanging currency, your identification card or passport may sometimes be requested.

The main foreign currencies can be exchanged in banks, as can traveller's cheques, the rates of which are slightly different (they tend to be less advantageous). Banks also offer other services for foreign visitors; relevant information is provided on the spot.

For security reasons, many banks have double electronically operated doors. You must first push the button outside to open the door leading off the street. Once you are in the area between the two doors, you must wait for the green light to come on (which it does when the outside door is closed) and then the inside door opens automatically.

Cash Dispensers (ATMs)

Cash dispensers (ATMs) can be found in and outside of almost all the banks in Corsica and they operate around the clock. Cash withdrawals can be made by means of bank cash-dispenser cards or credit cards, such as Visa, MasterCard, Diners Club and American Express.

As is necessary across the globe, be aware of your surroundings and make sure that no one sees your personal identity number (PIN) when you withdraw cash from an ATM.

Credit Cards

Even if the amount is small, payment with credit or debit cards in all kinds of shop and in hotels and restaurants is quite widespread and normal in Corsica. However, be aware that small shops and eateries inland might prefer cash. It is worth checking upon entry.

The most widely accepted cards in Corsica are Visa and MasterCard. Note you may find it difficult at times to use American Express and Diners Club credit cards.

An alternative to credit cards is Visa TravelMoney, which works as a pre-paid ATM card. This service can be arranged with Visa or Travelex before your departure, creating an account that will hold your pre-determined holiday funds. The Visa TravelMoney card can then be used to withdraw cash from any Visa ATM by means of a PIN number. When the funds in the holiday account are exhausted, the card can be thrown away.

DIRECTORY

Banks

Banque Populaire
6 Ave Antoine Serafini, Ajaccio.
Tel 04 95 24 63 00;
15 Blvd du General de Gaulle,
Bastia. **Tel** 08 20 82 00 01.

Crédit Agricole
Centre Commercial de Montesoro,
Bastia. **Tel** 04 95 33 83 71.

Travelex
w travelex.fr

Lost Credit Cards

American Express
Tel 0800 832 820.

Visa/MasterCard
Tel 0800 901 179/0800 901 387.

Bureaux de Change

Airports and the largest tourist resorts have exchange offices where the exchange rates are quite close to the official ones. Before you exchange your money, check the official rate that day and the commissions charged for every single currency- exchange operation.

Many hotels also have currency- exchange services for their clients. Again, it is best to know what the rates and commissions are beforehand, since these operations are usually expensive. There is no limit to the amount of money you may take into France, but if you bring more than €10,000 into the UK, you need to declare it on arrival.

One of the very few bureaux de change in Corsica

Local Currency

The euro (€) is the common currency of the European Union. It went into general circulation on 1 January 2002, initially for twelve participating countries. France was one of those twelve countries taking the Euro in 2002, with francs phased out by March 2002. EU members using the Euro as sole official currency are known as the Eurozone. Several EU members have opted out of joining this common currency. Euro notes are identical throughout the Eurozone countries, each one including designs of fictional architectural structures. The coins, however, have one side identical (the value side) and one side with an image unique to each country. Both notes and coins are exchangeable in each participating country.

Bank Notes

Euro bank notes have seven denominations. The €5 note (grey in colour) is the smallest, followed by the €10 note (pink), €20 note (blue), €50 note (orange), €100 note (green), €200 note (yellow) and €500 note (purple). All notes show the stars of the European Union.

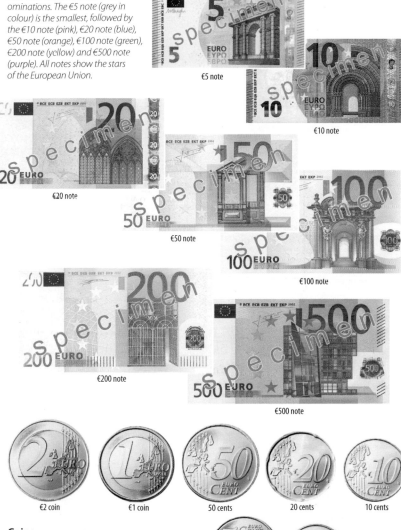

€5 note

€10 note

€20 note

€50 note

€100 note

€200 note

€500 note

€2 coin

€1 coin

50 cents

20 cents

10 cents

Coins

The euro has eight coin denominations: €1 and €2; 50 cents, 20 cents, 10 cents, 5 cents, 2 cents and 1 cent. The €2 and €1 coins are both silver and gold in colour. The 50-, 20- and 10-cent coins are gold. The 5-, 2- and 1-cent coins are bronze.

5 cents

2 cents

1 cent

Communications

The French national telephone company is *France Telecom*, rebranded as *Orange*, while the postal service is called *La Poste*. Post offices can be found throughout Corsica. Internet access is less widespread, even though all the public offices and tourist bureaus have email and there are various information websites for visitors on the island. There are also four networks for mobile phones. It is easy to negotiate dates and minutes with the mobile network provider; call before travelling for more information. In the summer, some foreign newspapers can be found in the main towns, but they usually arrive a day after publication.

Two examples of telephone cards used in France and Corsica

Postal Service

The French postal service is efficient and punctual. In the post office *(bureau de poste)*, it is possible to purchase stamps *(timbres)*, either singly or in sheets *(carnets)* with ten stamps, and to post letters and parcels in various ways (priority, special delivery and so on). Here, you can also consult telephone directories *(annuaires)*, purchase pre-paid telephone cards *(télécartes)*, receive or send money by means of postal money orders *(mandats)*, and cash postal giros. The main post office of every city or town also offers *poste restante*, or a post-office box service. In addition, French post offices feature a variety of financial services.

The main post offices are open from 8am to 7pm, sometimes with an hour's break for lunch. In smaller towns, and everywhere on Saturday, they are open only in the morning.

There are eight different postal rates for international post. The least expensive is for items destined for European Union countries, which is the same as the domestic rate. The most expensive is for items sent to Asia and Australia. Sending bulky parcels is usually rather expensive.

Corsican postboxes are yellow, with the blue logo of

Corsican postbox

La Poste on them, and in larger towns and cities they may have up to three different slots: for local post; post for another *département*; and international post.

The Départements

The administrative system in France dates back to the time of the French Revolution, when the nation was divided into administrative units with equal authority and value. These were the 96 *départements* that are still operative; they are grouped into *régions* and subdivided into 35,000 local *communes*.

Corsica is a region with two *départements*: 2A Corse-du-Sud and 2B Haute-Corse, which correspond more or less to the old separation into the *Delà des monts* and *Deça des monts* areas *(see p44)*.

Addresses in France always have a five-digit postcode. The first two digits correspond to the *département*, the third indicates the city, and the last two are for the quarters or minor localities.

Public Telephones

Though rapidly disappearing due to the increased use of mobile phones, most public telephones in Corsica are touch-tone and function with pre-paid

telephone cards, which come in various denominations, measured in units *(unités)*. For local calls, a *unité* lasts about six minutes; this time progressively decreases as the distance increases (for example, for a call to Australia a unit lasts four seconds).

Bars and restaurants have a different type of phone, coin- or token-operated, while post offices have booths where you pay after the call.

The international-calls service is called *pays direct*. With this system, you call the operator and then pay either with your credit card or by making a collect call.

Phoning in Corsica

All phone numbers in France have ten digits and they include the former area codes. The first two figures indicate the four zones into which France is divided – in Corsica these digits are 04, which stand for the southeast zone. The next two figures, which, in the case of Corsica, are 95, indicate the *région*. For police emergencies, dial 17; for local directory enquiries, dial 118 followed by 000, 008 or 218. Be aware that you will be charged for this service.

International Calls

If you want to make an international call, you must dial 00 and then the international number for the country you're phoning (44 in the case of the UK), followed by the area code and the number you want to reach. Other country codes are 1 for Canada and the USA, 353 for Ireland, 61 for Australia and 64 for New Zealand.

Logo of the French postal and telecommunications service

To call Corsica from abroad, dial 0033 followed by the number of the person or business you want to contact, leaving out the initial 0.

If you want the operator for information on international numbers, you should dial 3200.

Visitors standing by a public telephone booth on a Corsican street

Mobile Phones

Corsica has four companies that manage mobile-phone services: *Orange*, *Bouygues*, *Free* and *SFR*. Mobile phones from all European countries work perfectly well along the coast of the island, but less so in the interior, where both coverage and reception can be patchy.

It is also worth bearing in mind that, should you make a call from Corsica to a foreign country, added to the cost of the call is the price of the international portion. Likewise, when you receive a call, the price of the international part of the call is charged to the mobile phone that was called. For more detailed information on the fees charged by the various mobile-phone companies and the best rates available, contact your mobile-phone company in your own country. For long

phone calls, it is usually cheaper to use one of the many telephone booths throughout the island.

Radio and TV

As well as the national television networks, Corsica has local TV and radio stations, some of which broadcast in Corsican.

Due to the proximity to Sardinia and Tuscany, many private homes and hotels in Corsica also receive the main Italian TV channels.

Hotels tend to offer the leading European and American satellite channels, such as Sky News, BBC World and CNN.

The France Arte channel shows foreign films in their original language every night.

Newspapers

As in the other regions in France, there are two kinds of newspapers in Corsica: those distributed on a nationwide scale, such as *Le Monde*, *Le Figaro* and *Libération*, and the local, regional ones, such as *Corse-Matin*. Local papers provide useful information regarding cultural events, cinema, theatre and sports, but they do not leave much space for foreign news.

In the summer, in the main cities it is easy to find foreign newspapers, which usually arrive one day late.

The daily newspaper *Corse-Matin*, with its weekly insert

TRAVEL INFORMATION

Corsica has excellent connections with the rest of Europe and there are regularly scheduled flights linking the airports in Ajaccio, Bastia, Figari Sud Corse (near Bonifacio) and Calvi with others in Provence and southern France, as well as Paris. There are also several charter flights in the high season. Another popular means of transport to the island from both southern France and Italy is the ferry. To get around the island,

there are few alternatives to a car. The only railway line connects Bastia to Ajaccio and Calvi. There is a network of public buses, but they do not go to all the inland resorts and you may have to wait a long time for connections. When driving, bear in mind that the roads are often winding and panoramic, and the average speed limit is rather low; be very careful when the traffic is heavy, especially if the weather is bad.

Arriving by Air

In the summer, Corsica is well served by charter flights departing from Gatwick (Calvi, Ajaccio, Figari and Bastia), Heathrow (Ajaccio), Stansted and Manchester (Figari, Bastia and Calvi), Birmingham (Bastia) and Edinburgh (Calvi). **Charter Flights** offers flights at good prices, as well as package holidays.

Direct scheduled flights to Corsica from London and Manchester are offered by **easyJet**. The flight time is about 2 hours from London and 2 hours 30 minutes from Manchester. **British Airways**, **Air France** and **Air Corsica** also have flights to Corsica, but via Paris, Marseille or Nice.

US visitors often travel via France, which is served by Air France, **United Airlines** and **Delta** among others. From France, Corsica can be reached with a regional carrier (such as **Nouvelles Frontières/Corse Air International**).

Air Fares

Generally speaking, air fares to Corsica are fairly expensive during the summer season. However, for those willing to shop around, there are also good-value last-minute deals to be had, as well as various combinations, with a minimum and maximum number of days, that allow you to stay in Corsica without spending too much. Price comparison websites can help you find the best deal for your needs. In the low season, the offers are cheaper.

One of the large car ferries serving Corsica

Package Holidays

There are several package-tour operators dealing with Corsica. A package holiday includes at the very least air fare and accommodation; some also include food, car rental and activities.

One of the most reputable package-tour operators is **Club Med**. Renowned for the high level of service and excellent facilities, Club Med has a holiday village *(see p159)* near Cargèse. Childcare and all activities are included in the price.

Package tours are also handled by **Simpson Travel** and **Corsican Places**, both of which offer hotel rooms and a variety of self-catering accommodation.

Arriving by Ferry

Ferries are a popular means of transportation for visitors travelling to Corsica from France or Italy. Because of the large number of visitors, if you plan to go to the island by car in

the summer, it is best to book well ahead, especially if you are towing a caravan or travelling in a camper.

In the summer, there are fast car ferries that save you a lot of time in the crossing, but they cost more than the normal ferries.

The port of Bastia has many routes, with links to Marseille, Nice, Toulon, Genoa and Savona, La Spezia, Livorno, and Piombino. Ajaccio is accessed via ferries departing from southern France and from Genoa, and there is also a line that goes from Ajaccio to Porto Torres, in Sardinia. Bonifacio can be reached by ferry only from Sardinia. The **Societé Nationale Maritime Corse Mediterranée** (SNCM) and **Compagnie Méridionale de Navigation** (CMN) are the French shipping lines. If you leave from Italy or France, **Corsica Ferries** offers several links with the island, including departures from

On the train from Ajaccio to Bastia

Civitavecchia (only in summer) and Livorno and Savona (all year round), as well as Toulon and Nice. **Moby Lines** connects Bastia and Piombino (July and August), Livorno and Genoa for about the same price.

In the summer, there is also a frequent ferry service from France and Italy to Calvi, L'Île Rousse and Porto-Vecchio.

Ferry Fares

The highest fare for two people and a car 4–5 m (13–16 ft) long on the Livorno–Bastia ferry is about €260 return, but there are special rates and discount tickets (up to a minimum of €105).

Travelling by Train

Investment in a modern autorail system in Corsica aims to improve journey times and passenger comfort. The Bastia–Corte–Ajaccio railway affords magnificent views and has five trains per day in each direction.

One of the most frequented train stations is Vizzavona, which many visitors use as a departure point for the GR20 long-distance hiking path (see pp26–31). To get to Calvi by train from Ajaccio (and vice versa), change trains at Ponte Leccia.

Information about timetables can be found at main railway stations, and at **www.train-corse.com**, **www.ter-sncf.com** and **www.cf-corse.fr**, where information on service upgrades can also be found.

Travelling by Bus

The bus line that offers service in the area around Corte is the

Société des Autocars Cortenais. The central-north area of Corsica is covered by **Autocars Santini**. Ajaccio, Sartène and Bonifacio are served by bus lines such as **Eurocorse**, while **Société des Autobus Bastiais** covers the area around Bastia.

Because of the seasonal variation in the schedules, it is always a good idea to make enquiries at the local tourist offices before setting off on a bus journey.

Travelling by Car

A regular driver's licence is the only document required to travel by car in Corsica. Naturally, the great number of minor roads is an invitation to explore the lesser-known areas on the island; these require a much lower speed and particular attention and caution. When planning a tour or excursion, you should base it on an average speed of 40–50 km/h (25–30 mph). There may be animals on the road or, in summer, large caravans and campers that go slowly on hairpin turns, so you must reduce your speed.

You can travel faster only on the Routes Nationales (Bastia–Calvi, Bastia–Corte–Ajaccio, Bastia–Porto-Vecchio and Ajaccio–Bonifacio). There are

more petrol stations along the coast than inland, and in the tourist resorts near the sea it is easy to find automatic petrol pumps that will accept bank notes or credit cards.

Car Rental

The offices of the main car-rental companies are in airports and port passenger terminals. These include **Avis**, **Hertz**, **Europcar** and **Budget Rent a Car**, as well as local companies such as **Ada**, which offers very different rates according to the season. By paying a small surcharge, you can pick up your car in one place and return it in another.

Travelling by Motorcycle

Corsica is a paradise for motorcyclists. The roads are difficult but rewarding, and the dry summers are favourable for this means of transportation. Motorcycles are also advantageous in avoiding traffic jams, especially along the coast.

As is the case with cars, you must be extremely careful, especially on the mountain roads.

Motorcycles can be hired from most main cities in Corsica (Ajaccio, Porto-Vecchio, Bastia, Calvi, Porto and Propriano). You will also find centres that hire motorcycles and offer assistance for those arriving with their own bikes.

Travelling by camper in Corsica – a simple way to enjoy the scenery

Travelling by Boat

Boats of all kinds can be found in Corsican waters during the summer months. You can use your boat to travel from one resort to another within Corsica or for making the crossing from a port in Italy or France *(see p190)*. Obviously, this voyage should be made only by expert navigators whose boats are able to withstand the hazards of the open sea. Even the shortest crossing, from Sardinia in the Straits of Bonifacio *(see p117)*, is not without its pitfalls due to the strong winds that often blow in this part of the sea.

Sailing remains undoubtedly one of the best ways to explore the coasts of Corsica. Even a simple dinghy or a small sailboat, rented or brought along with your car in a ferry, are ideal for leaving in the morning and returning in the evening after a fine day's boating.

Boat Hire

There are many possibilities for hiring boats in Corsica. The boat-hire companies have all types of craft to offer

The harbour at Cargèse, one of the stages on a tour of the coast

their clients, and they also provide assistance and maintenance. The rates can be by the hour or by the day, and there are even weekly rates for those who are interested in making long trips. In such cases, the agencies offer boats with a skipper or even a crew.

Naturally, the price varies according to the type of boat you hire, the duration of the trip and whether a skipper or crew are provided. The period of rental is also a factor, the highest rates being in July and August.

Circumnavigating the Island

A classic choice of trip for experienced yachtsmen is a tour around the island. This is a fascinating adventure because the coast of Corsica is spectacular and has many secluded coves that cannot be reached by car or even on foot.

The chart below lists the ports on the island and their facilities. Although temporary berths are added in summer, ports are likely to be crowded, so phone beforehand or arrive in the early afternoon.

Ports	Information	Boat Berths		Fuel Station	Maintenance and Repair
		Total	Temporary		
Ajaccio, Ornano	04 95 22 31 98	830	50	●	●
Ajaccio, Tino Rossi	04 95 51 22 72	300	150	●	●
Bastia, Port de Toga	04 95 34 90 70	357	50	●	●
Bastia, Vieux Port	04 95 31 31 10	350	40	●	●
Bonifacio	04 95 73 10 07	330	120	●	●
Calvi	04 95 65 10 60	550	100	●	●
Campoloro	04 95 38 07 61	464	50	●	●
Cargèse	04 95 26 47 24	235	25	●	●
Lumio	04 95 60 70 88	250	0	●	●
Macinaggio	04 95 35 42 57	585	200	●	●
Pianottoli Caldarello	04 95 71 83 57	160	80	●	●
Porto-Vecchio	04 95 70 17 93	350	150	●	●
Propriano	04 95 76 10 40	430	30	●	●
St-Florent	04 95 37 00 79	750	150	●	●
Solenzara	04 95 57 46 42	450	100	●	●

DIRECTORY

Airports

Ajaccio
Campo dell'Oro. **Tel** 04 95 23 56 56. **W** 2a.cci.fr/aeroports

Bastia
Poretta. **Tel** 04 95 54 54 54. **W** bastia.aeroport.fr

Calvi
Ste-Catherine.
Tel 04 95 65 88 88.
W calvi.aeroport.fr

Figari-Sud-Corse
Tel 04 95 71 10 10.
W 2a.cci.fr/aeroports

Airlines

Air Corsica
Marseille, Nice, Lyon.
Tel 08 25 35 35 35.
W aircorsica.com

Air France
Tel 3654 or 09 70 80 88 16 (France). **Tel** 0871 663 3777 (UK). **W** airfrance.com

British Airways
Tel 0844 493 0787 (UK).
W britishairways.com

Delta Air Lines
Tel 0811 640 005 (France).
Tel 0845 600 0950 (UK).
W delta.com

easyJet
Tel 08 26 10 33 20
(France). **Tel** 08 71 24 43 66 (UK). **W** easyjet.com

Nouvelles Frontières/Corsair International
Paris, Marseille, Bordeaux, Strasbourg, Lyon, Lille, Nice, Toulouse, Brussels, Bastia. **Tel** 08 25 00 07 47. **W** nouvelles-frontieres.fr

United Airlines
Tel 01 71 23 03 35
(France). **Tel** 0845 607 6760 (UK). **W** united.com

Package Holidays

Club Med
Tel 0845 508 1374 (UK).
W clubmed.co.uk

Corsican Places
Tel 0845 330 2059.
W corsica.co.uk

Simpson Travel
Tel 0203 603 5603 (UK).
W simpsontravel.com

Ferry Ports

Ajaccio
Tel 04 95 50 78 82.

Bastia
Tel 08 25 09 50 95.

Bonifacio
Tel 04 95 73 00 29.

Calvi
Tel 04 95 65 43 21.

L'Île Rousse
Tel 04 95 60 44 11.

Porto-Vecchio
Tel 04 95 70 06 03.

Propriano
Tel 04 95 76 04 36.

Ferries

Compagnie Méridionale de Navigation
Ajaccio. **Tel** 08 10 20 13 20. **W** lameridionale.fr

Corsica Ferries
Livorno, Savona, Toulon, Nice, Bastia.
Tel 04 95 32 95 95.
W corsica-ferries.fr

Moby Lines
Tel +49 (0)61 11 40 20.
Genoa, Livorno, Piombino.
Bastia. **Tel** 04 95 34 84 94.
Bonifacio. **Tel** 04 95 73 00 29. **W** mobylines.fr

Societé Nationale Maritime Corse Mediterranée (SNCM)
Marseille, Toulon, Livorno, Nice. Ajaccio.
Tel 3260 (France).
Tel 0825 88 80 88 (UK).
L'Île Rousse.
Tel 04 95 65 01 38.
W sncm.fr

Railway Stations

Ajaccio
Tel 04 95 23 11 03.

Bastia
Tel 04 95 33 71 03.

Calvi
Tel 04 95 65 00 01.

Corte
Tel 04 95 46 00 97.

L'Île Rousse
Tel 04 95 60 00 50.

Ponte Leccia
Tel 04 95 47 61 29.

Vizzavona
Tel 04 95 47 21 02.

Bus Companies

Autocars Santini
Tel 04 95 37 02 98.

Eurocorse
Ajaccio. **Tel** 04 95 21 06 30.

Société des Autobus Bastiais
Tel 04 95 31 06 65.
W bastiabus.com

Société des Autocars Cortenais
Corte. **Tel** 04 95 46 22 89.
W autocars-cortenais.fr

Car Rental

Ada
Ajaccio. **Tel** 04 95 23 56 57.
Bastia. **Tel** 04 95 54 55 44.
W ada.fr

Avis
Ajaccio. **Tel** 04 95 23 56 90.
Bastia. **Tel** 04 95 54 55 46.
Calvi. **Tel** 04 95 65 88 38.
Figari. **Tel** 04 95 71 00 01.
W avis.com

Budget Rent a Car
Ajaccio. **Tel** 04 95 23 56 63.
Bastia. **Tel** 04 95 54 54 09.
Calvi. **Tel** 04 95 65 88 38.
W budget.fr

Europcar
Ajaccio. **Tel** 04 95 23 57 01.
Bastia. **Tel** 04 95 30 09 50.
Bonifacio. **Tel** 04 95 73 10 99. Calvi. **Tel** 04 95 65 10 19. Corte. **Tel** 04 95 46 06 02. **W** europcar.co.uk

Hertz
Ajaccio. **Tel** 04 95 23 57 04.
Bastia. **Tel** 04 95 30 05 00.
W hertz.com

Motorcycle Hire

Corse Motos Service
Rte de Bastia, Immeuble Silla. **Tel** 04 95 70 12 88.

Rout'Evasion
10 Ave Noël Franchini, Ajaccio. **Tel** 04 95 22 72 87.

Boat Hire

Cap Evasion
Macinaggio.
Tel 06 81 70 38 48.

Corsica Voile
Port de Plaisance, Macinaggio. **Tel** 04 95 35 48 20. **W** corsica-voile. com

Dominique Plaisance
St-Florent. **Tel** 04 95 37 07 08. **W** dominique plaisance.com

L'Helice Aubert
13 Route Cala Rossa, Porto-Vecchio. **Tel** 04 95 70 23 97.

Leader Boat
Quai Paoli, Porto-Vecchio.
Tel 04 95 70 29 32.
W leaderboat.fr

Locamarine
Quai St-Erasme, Propriano.
Tel 06 48 14 28 20.
W locamarine.com

Marine Location
BP 55, Porto-Vecchio.
Tel 04 95 70 58 92.
W marine-location.fr

Multi-Services Plaisance
Santa Giulia, Porto-Vecchio.
Tel 04 95 70 29 13 or 06 10 83 59 25.

Nautimarine
Route de Calvi, Île Rousse.
Tel 04 95 60 00 73 or 06 22 70 92 26.

Societé des Loisirs Nautiques de Porticcio
Plage de la Viva, Porticcio.
Tel 06 74 98 06 21.

Toga Loca Nautique
Port de Toga, Bastia.
Tel 04 95 34 14 14.
W togalocation.com

Tra Mare e Monti
Port de Plaisance, Calvi.
Tel 04 95 65 21 26.
W tramare-monti.com

Union Nautique Insulaire
Port de l'Amirautée, Ajaccio. **Tel** 04 95 20 66 31.

General Index

Acknowledgments

Fabio Ratti Editoria would like to thank the following staff at Dorling Kindersley:

Publishing Manager
Anna Streiffert.

Senior Art Editor
Marisa Renzullo.

Publisher
Douglas Amrine.

Senior DTP Designer
Jason Little.

Cartographers
Casper Morris, Dave Pugh.

Dorling Kindersley would also like to thank all those whose contribution and assistance have made the preparation of this book possible.

Main Contributors
Fabrizio Ardito, a journalist and photographer born in Rome in 1957. Among his publications are several books on hiking. In the Dorling Kindersley Eyewitness Travel Guides series he has contributed to *Sardinia*, *Sicily* and *Jerusalem & the Holy Land*, as well as the following (so far published in Italian only, by Guide Visuali Mondadori): *The Dolomites, Northeast Italy, Central Italy, South Italy*. He has written texts and articles for various Italian publishers, periodicals and newpapers on the environment, geography and travelling in general. These include *Nuova Ecologia, Espresso,* Gambero Rosso-De Agostini, Touring Club, Giorgio Mondadori and *Unità*. He has also worked for the Italian State Television (RAI), producing various films and documentaries on nature, sports and the subterranean areas of cities.

Cristina Gambaro is a journalist who has contributed articles to the leading Italian periodicals. For Gambero Rosso-De Agostini she wrote *Guide to Italian Hotels*; for Clupguide she wrote *Sardinia* and *Pakistan*; for Airplane, *Scotland* and *Ireland*; for White Star, *The Castles of Scotland*. She was also a main contributor to the following Dorling Kindersley Eyewitness Travel Guides: *Sardinia, Sicily* and *Jerusalem &*

the Holy Land, as well as *Northeast Italy, Central Italy, South Italy* and *The Dolomites* (published in Italian by Guide Visuali Mondadori).

Additional contributions
Kathryn Tomasetti, Roger Williams.

Revisions Team
Cayetana Muriel Aguado, Thierry Combret, Géraldine Gonard, Marina Dragoni. For Dorling Kindersley: Kate Berens, Marta Bescos Sanchez, Julie Bond, Emer FitzGerald, Lisa Fox-Mullen, Michelle Arness Frederic, Anna Freiberger, Camilla Gersh, Laura Jones, Rupanki Kaushik, Sumita Khatwani, Maite Lantaron, Delphine Lawrance, Jude Ledger, Cathrine Lehmann, Norm Longley, Hayley Maher, Sonal Modha, Casper Morris, Claire Naylor, Helen Partington, Susie Peachey, Lucy Richards, Ellen Root, Farah Sheikh, Catherine Skipper, Karen Villabona, Dora Whitaker, Sophie Wright, Conrad Van Dyk, Vinita Venugopal, Ajay Verma.

Editors, UK Edition
Sylvia and David Tombesi-Walton at Sands Publishing Solutions, Lauren Robertson.

Additional Picture Research
Rachel Barber.

Additional DTP
Vinod Harish, Vincent Kurien, Azeem Siddiqui.

Additional Cartography
Uma Bhattacharya, Mohammad Hassan, Jasneet Kaur.

Factcheckers
Michelle Frederic, Irina Zarb.

Consultant
David Abram.

Proof-Reader
Jane Simmonds.

Indexers
Helen Peters.

Additional Photography
Max Alexander, Ian O'Leary, Tony Souter.

Special Thanks

We would like to thank the following persons for their contribution to this guide: Messieurs Xavier Olivieri and Jean-Philippe di Grazia, Agence de Tourisme de la Corse, Ajaccio; Madame Marie-Eugénie Poli-Mordiconi, Musée de la Corse, Corte; Monsieur Pascal Rinaldi, Parc Naturel Régional de Corse, Ajaccio; Madame Viviane Gentile, Domaine Gentile, St-Florent; Monsieur Jean-Noël Luigi, Clos Nicrosi, Rogliano; Ms Marina della Rosa, expert sailor; the chef Carlo Romito and his assistants Giorgio Brignone and Marco Fanti, of the Palazzo Granaio restaurant in Settimo Milanese, specializing in cuisine of the upper Tyrrhenian Sea; Mrs Delphine Jaillot, Sopexa Italia, Milan; Ms Charlotte Grant, Christie's, London; Dr Biondi, Scientific Committee, Palazzo Ducale, Genoa; Dr Campodonico, curator, Museo Navale di Pegli, Genoa; Dr Alessandro Avanzino, Palazzo San Giorgio, Genoa; the Associazione Amici di Palazzo Ducale, Genoa; the Museo di Sant'Agostino, Genoa; Gabriele Reina and Roberto Bosi, Franco Maria Ricci Publishers, Milan; all the Stations Touristiques in Corsica; the Musée Fesch, Ajaccio; the French Tourist Board, Milan.

Photography Permissions

The Publisher would like to thank the local bodies, associations and firms for the authorization to take photographs, in particular Archivio Electa, Milano; Musée de la Corse, Corte; Musée d'Antropologie de la Corse, Corte; Sopexa Italia, Milan.

The Publisher would also like to thank the cathedrals, churches, museums, galleries, restaurants, hotels, shops and all those who furnished material – too numerous to be mentioned here individually – for their kind assistance and valuable contribution.

Key:

a-above; b-below/bottom; c-centre; f-far; l-left; r-right; t-top.

Picture Credits

123rf.com: Marek Cech 66br. **Le 20123:** 175br. **4Corners Images: SIME** / Fantuz Olimpio 13br; **SIME** / Giovanni Simeone 85cl.

Agence de Tourisme de la Corse, Ajaccio: 21b, 35 (all photos), 38 (all photos), 39cra, 44cb, 44cb, 45br, 49bc, 53bc, 91tl, 103tc, 127br, 152tc, 166br, 167br 182br, 184cla, 192cl, 197cl.

Alamy Images: Jon Arnold Images / Doug Pearson 168cl; Peter Bowater 58; Juliet Ferguson 164tl; Robert Harding Picture Library Ltd: 204cra; LOOK Die Bildagentur der Fotografen GmbH 186cb; Justin Kase 169tl; a la Poste 202c.

Christian Andreani, Ajaccio: 103br.

Archivio Mondadori, Milan: 22clb, 22crb, 22bl, 23clb, 23tr, 23bl, 23bc, 23crb, 44cla, 44bl, 46–7c, 46br, 47tl, 47cr, 51ca, 52tc, 53tl, 73ca, 100cla, 106c, 126cl, 143cr, 146cl, 171tr, 199bl.

Archivio Scala, Florence: 40.

Ardea London Ltd: Stefan Meyers 30cla.

Enrico Banfi, Milan: 109tl.

La Cantina di l'Orriu: 178tl.

La Cantine du Golfe: 177b.

Contrasto, Milan: 53cb, 117cl, 117br, 170cl, 170c, 191tc, 192tr.

Corbis: Atlantide Phototravel 12bl; Walter Bibikow/JAI 1c; Stuart Black/Robert Harding World Imagery 54-5; Christophe Boisvieux 15br; Gary Braasch 169c; Boisvieux Christophe/Hemis 194-5; Marc Dozier/Hemis 2-3; Bertrand Gardel/ Hemis 13tc; Hervé Hughes/Hemls 14tl; Rene Mattes/Hemis 11tc; Photogolfer 98-9; Radius Images 86; Ellen Rooney/Robert Harding World Imagery 15crb.

Le Cosi: 172bl.

Louis Doazan, Corsica: 103cl.

Dreamstime.com: Allard1 191br; David Espin 19bc, 68-9; Fottoo 10bc; Holge Karius 14bc; Freddy Lecock 18; Dominik Michálek 144-5.

Flickr, TiDenis: 203cla.

Xiaoyang Galas: *Sea, Sunshine and Village* 8–9.

Getty Images: Michelle Bussellle 122–23.

Glacier du Port: 167tl, 178bc.

Gronchi Fotoarte, Pisa: 47tr.

Image bank, Milan: 37cra, 120tr, 140tr, 186tr, 190b, 191cl.

Gianmaria Marras, Milan: 185br, 205tl.

Grand Hotel Miramar: 159tc.

Groupe Boissons de Corse: 170bl.

Hotel Dominique Colonna: 165bl.

Hotel Les Mouettes: 158cr, 163tr.

Hotel Palazzu Pigna: 161cr, 163bc.

Hotel Le Pinarello: 159bl, 165tr.

Restaurant Le Pirate: 173tr.

Musée de la Corse, Corte: 34 (all photos), 39bl, 46cl, 48t, 48c, 49tc, 49crb, 49bl, 50–51c, 50tr, 50clb, 50bc, 51tl, 141bl; PH Lambert 141ca.

Office Municipal de Tourisme d'Ota Porto: 196br.

Overseas, Milan: 117cra, 117clb, 117crb.

Parc Naturel Régional de Corse, Ajaccio: 26cla, 27tl, 28clb, 28br, 29tc, 29ca, 30clb, 31tc, 31cra.

La Rascasse: 174bc.

RMN, Paris: 94tr, 94cl, 94bl, 94bc, 95tl, 95cra.

Anna Serrano, Barcelona: 22bcr.

Sofitel Hotel, Ajaccio: 185tl.

Sopexa, Italy: 171crb.

STA Travel Group: 197c.

Studio Aquilini, Milan: 104clb, 104bcl, 105cra, 118tr, 118bc, 188cr, 189b. **Superstock:** Walter Bibikow/age fotostock 10cla; Alvaro Leiva/age fotostock 156-7; Photononstop 12cr, 122-3; Pritz/F1 Online 134; Tips Images 110. **Syndicat d'Initiative de Piana**: 104tr.

La Villa Hotel: 162br.

Front Endpaper - **Alamy Images:** Peter Bowater Ltl; **Corbis:** Radius Images Lbl; **Superstock:** Pritz/FR ONLINE Rtc; Tips Images Rbr. **Jacket images:** Front and spine: **4corners:** Riccardo Spila/SIME; **Dreamstime.com:** Dominik Michaek bl.

All other images © Dorling Kindersley.

Special Editions of DK Travel Guides

DK Travel Guides can be purchased in bulk quantities at discounted prices for use in promotions or as premiums. We are also able to offer special editions and personalized jackets, corporate imprints, and excerpts from all of our books, tailored specifically to meet your own needs.

To find out more, please contact:
in the United States **specialsales@dk.com**
in the UK **travelguides@uk.dk.com**
in Canada DK Special Sales at
specialmarkets@dk.com
in Australia **penguincorporatesales@
penguinrandomhouse.com.au**

Corsican Words and Phrases

Although French is spoken everywhere, a few Corsican phrases can come in handy. Corsican is closer to Italian, in fact to Medieval Tuscan, both in its vocabulary and its pronounciation, but also shows a few other Mediterranean influences. Geographical terms appear in many sight names, and on the bilingual signs.

Basics

A'ringraziavvi: Thank you
Fate u piacè: Please
Ié: Yes
Nò: No
Và bé: OK
Induve: Where
Quandu: When
Chì: What, who, which
A'vedeci: Goodbye
A dopu: See you
Buona notte: Goodnight
Buona sera: Good evening
Buonghjornu: Hello
Cumu sì?: How are you?
Me dispiace: Sorry
(Nò) Capiscu: I (don't) understand
Parla inglese?: Do you speak English?

Geographical Terms

a marlna: beach
anse/cala: cove
boca/foce/col: mountain pass
calanca: gorge, ravine
casa: house
casatorre: stronghold
castellu/casteddu: fortified settlement
fiume: river
fiumicellu: stream
lau/lavu: lake
licettu: oak forest
muntagna: mountain
orriu: shelter under a large stone or boulder, sometimes bricked in
pianu: plateau
piscia: waterfall
ponte: bridge
stagnu: pool or pond
torre: tower
u paese: village
vignale/vignetu: vineyard

Directions

dritta: right
sempredrittu: straight on
sinistra: left
Induv'é…?: Where is…?

Shopping

aperta/apertu: open
Avetene…?: Do you have…?
basta: enough
buonu mercatu: cheap
chiusu: closed
grande/maio: big
Hè troppu caru: It is too much
menu: less
nulla/nunda/nudda: nothing
piccola/chjucu: small
pui: more
Quantu costa/Quanto hè?: How much does it cost/is it?
Vogliu…: I want…

Time, Days and Months

Chi ora hè?: What is the time?
oghje: today
ieri: yesterday
dumane: tomorrow
ghjurnu: day
simana: week
meze: month

Monday:	**luni**
Tuesday:	**marti**
Wednesday:	**mercuri**
Thursday:	**ghjovi**
Friday:	**venneri**
Saturday:	**sabatu**
Sunday:	**dumenica**
January:	**Ghjennaghju**
February:	**Febbraghju**
March:	**Marzu**
April:	**Aprile**
May:	**Maghjiu**
June:	**Ghjiugnu**
July:	**Ghjugliu**
August:	**Aostu**
September:	**Sittembre**
October:	**Ottobre**
November:	**Novembre**
December:	**Dicembre**

Seasons

auturnu: autumn
estate: summer
imbernu/ingnernu: winter
veranu: spring

French Phrase Book

In Emergency

Help!	Au secours!	oh se**koor**
Stop!	Arrêtez!	aret-**ay**
Call a doctor!	Appelez un médecin!	apuh-**lay** uñ med**sañ**
Call an ambulance!	Appelez une ambulance!	apuh-**lay** oon oñboo-**loñs**
Call the police!	Appelez la police!	apuh-**lay** lah poh-**lees**
Call the fire brigade!	Appelez les pompiers!	apuh-lay leh poñ-**peeyay**
Where is the nearest telephone?	Où est le téléphone le plus proche?	oo ay luh tehleh**fon** luh ploo prosh
Where is the nearest hospital?	Où est l'hôpital le plus proche?	oo ay l'opee**tal** luh ploo prosh

Communication Essentials

Yes	Oui	wee
No	Non	noñ
Please	S'il vous plaît	seel voo **play**
Thank you	Merci	mer-**see**
Excuse me	Excusez-moi	exkoo-**zay** mwah
Hello	Bonjour	boñzhoor
Goodbye	Au revoir	oh ruh-**vwar**
Good evening	Bonsoir	boñ-**swar**
Morning	Le matin	ma**tañ**
Afternoon	L'après-midi	l'apreh-**meedee**
Evening	Le soir	swar
Yesterday	Hier	eeyehr
Today	Aujourd'hui	oh-zhoor-**dwee**
Tomorrow	Demain	duh**mañ**
Here	Ici	ee-**see**
There	Là	lah
What?	Quel, quelle?	kel, kel
When?	Quand?	koñ
Why?	Pourquoi?	poor-**kwah**
Where?	Où?	oo

Useful Phrases

How are you?	Comment allez-vous?	kom-moñ tal**ay voo**
Very well, thank you.	Très bien, merci.	treh byañ, mer-**see**
Pleased to meet you.	Enchanté de faire votre connaissance.	oñshoñ-**tay** duh fehr votr kon-ay-**sans**
See you soon.	A bientôt.	abyañ-**toh**
That's fine.	Voilà qui est parfait.	vwalah kee ay parf**ay**
Where is/are...?	Où est/sont...?	oo ay/soñ
How far is it to...?	Combien de kilomètres d'ici à...?	kom-**byañ** duh is keelo-**metr** d'ee-**see** ah
Which way to...?	Quelle est la direction pour...?	kel ay lah deer-ek-**syoñ** poor
Do you speak English?	Parlez-vous anglais?	par-**lay** voo oñg-**lay**
I don't understand.	Je ne comprends pas.	zhuh nuh kom-**proñ** pah
Could you speak slowly, please?	Pouvez-vous parler moins vite, s'il vous plaît?	poo-vay voo par-**lay** mwañ veet seel voo play
I'm sorry.	Excusez-moi.	exkoo-**zay** mwah

Useful Words

big	grand	groñ
small	petit	puh-**tee**
hot	chaud	show
cold	froid	frwah
good	bon	boñ
bad	mauvais	moh-**veh**
enough	assez	assay
well	bien	byañ
open	ouvert	oo-**ver**
closed	fermé	fer-**meh**

left	gauche	gohsh
right	droite	drwaht
straight on	tout droit	too drwah
near	près	preh
far	loin	lwañ
up	en haut	oñ oh
down	en bas	oñ **bah**
early	de bonne heure	duh bon urr
late	en retard	oñ ruh-**tar**
entrance	l'entrée	l'on-**tray**
exit	la sortie	sor-**tee**
toilet	les toilettes, les WC	twah-let, vay-**see**
unoccupied	libre	leebr
no charge	gratuit	grah-**twee**

Making a Telephone Call

I'd like to place a long-distance call.	Je voudrais faire un interurbain.	zhuh voo-dreh fehr uñ añter-oorbañ
I'd like to make a reverse-charge call.	Je voudrais faire une communication PCV.	zhuh voo**dreh** fehr oon kom-oonikah-**syoñ** peh-seh-veh
I'll try again later.	Je rappelerai plus tard.	zhuh rapel**eray** ploo tar
Can I leave a message?	Est-ce que je peux laisser un message?	es-**keh** zhuh puh leh-**say** uñ mehsazh
Hold on.	Ne quittez pas, s'il vous plaît.	nuh kee-**tay** pah seel voo play.
Could you speak up a little please?	Pouvez-vous parler un peu plus fort?	poo-**vay** voo par-**lay** uñ puh ploo for
local call	la communi-cation locale	komoonikah-**syoñ** low-**kal**

Shopping

How much does this cost?	C'est combien s'il vous plaît?	say kom-**byañ** seel voo play
Do you take credit cards?	Est-ce que vous acceptez les cartes de crédit?	es-**kuh** voo zaksept-**ay** leh kart duh kreh-**dee**
Do you take travellers' cheques?	Est-ce que vous acceptez les chèques de voyage?	es-**kuh** voo zaksept-**ay** leh shek duh vwa**yazh**
I would like ...	Je voudrais...	zhuh voo-**dray**
Do you have?	Est-ce que vous avez?	es-**kuh** voo zavay
I'm just looking.	Je regarde seulement.	zhuh ruh**gar** suhl**moñ**
What time do you open?	A quelle heure vous êtes ouvert?	ah kel urr voo zet oo-**ver**
What time do you close?	A quelle heure vous êtes fermé?	ah kel urr voo zet fer-**may**
This one	Celui-ci	suhl-wee-**see**
That one	Celui-là	suhl-wee-**lah**
expensive	cher	shehr
cheap	pas cher, bon marché	pah shehr, boñ mar-**shay**
size, clothes	la taille	tye
size, shoes	la pointure	pwañ-**tur**
white	blanc	bloñ
black	noir	nwahr
brown	brun	bruñ
red	rouge	roozh
yellow	jaune	zhohwn
green	vert	vehr
blue	bleu	bluh

Types of Shop

antique shop	le magasin d'antiquités	maga-**zañ** d'oñteekee-**tay**
bakery	la boulangerie	booloñ-**zhuree**
bank	la banque	boñk
book shop	la librairie	lee-**brehree**
butcher	la boucherie	boo-**shehree**
cake shop	la pâtisserie	patee-**sree**

cheese shop	**la fromagerie**	*fromazh-**ree***
chemist	**la pharmacie**	*farmah-**see***
dairy	**la crémerie**	*krem-**ree***
department store	**le grand magasin**	*groñ maga-**zañ***
delicatessen	**la charcuterie**	*sharkoot-**ree***
fishmonger	**la poissonnerie**	*pwasson-**ree***
gift shop	**le magasin de cadeaux**	*maga-**zañ** duh kadoh*
greengrocer	**le marchand de légumes**	*mar-**shoñ** duh lay-**goom***
grocery	**l'alimentation**	*alee-moñta-**syoñ***
hairdresser	**le coiffeur**	*kwafuhr*
market	**le marché**	*marsh-**ay***
newsagent	**le magasin de journaux**	*maga-**zañ** duh zhoor-**no***
post office	**la poste, le bureau de poste, les PTT**	*pohst, booroh duh pohst, peh-teh-teh*
shoe shop	**le magasin de chaussures**	*maga-**zañ** duh show-**soor***
supermarket	**le super-marché**	*soo pehr-marshay*
tobacconist	**le tabac**	*tabah*
travel agent	**l'agence de voyages**	*l'azhoñs duh vwayazh*

Menu Decoder

l'agneau	*l'anyoh*	lamb
l'ail	*l'eye*	garlic
la banane	*ba**nan***	banana
le beurre	*burr*	butter
la bière	*bee-**yehr***	beer
le bifteck, le steack	*beef-**tek,** stek*	steak
le boeuf	*buhf*	beef
bouilli	*boo yee*	boiled
le café	*kah-**fay***	coffee
le canard	*kanar*	duck
le citron pressé	*see-**troñ** press-eh*	fresh lemon juice
les crevettes	*kruh-**vet***	prawns
les crustacés	*kroos-ta-say*	shellfish
cuit au four	*kweet oh foor*	baked
le dessert	*deh-**ser***	dessert
l'eau minérale	*l'oh **meeney**-ral*	mineral water
les escargots	*leh zes-kar-**goh***	snails
les frites	*freet*	chips
le fromage	*from-**azh***	cheese
les fruits frais	*frwee freh fresh*	fruit
les fruits de mer	*frwee duh mer*	seafood
le gâteau	*gah-**toh***	cake
la glace	*glas*	ice, ice cream
grillé	*gree-**yay***	grilled
le homard	*omahr*	lobster
l'huile	*l'weel*	oil
le jambon	*zhoñ-**boñ***	ham
le lait	*leh*	milk
les légumes	*lay-**goom***	vegetables
la moutarde	*moo-**tard***	mustard
l'oeuf	*l'uf*	egg
les oignons	*leh zonyoñ*	onions
les olives	*leh zoleev*	olives
l'orange pressée	*l'oroñzh press-eh*	fresh orange juice
le pain	*pan*	bread
le petit pain	*puh-**tee** pañ*	roll
poché	*posh-**ay***	poached
le poisson	*pwah-**ssoñ***	fish
le poivre	*pwavr*	pepper
la pomme	*pom*	apple
les pommes de terre	*pom-duh tehr*	potatoes
le porc	*por*	pork
le potage	*poh-**tazh***	soup
le poulet	*poo-**lay***	chicken
le riz	*ree*	rice
rôti	*row-tee*	roast
la sauce	*sohs*	sauce
la saucisse	*sohsees*	sausage, fresh

sec	*sek*	dry
le sel	*sel*	salt
le sucre	*sookr*	sugar
le thé	*tay*	tea
le toast	*toast*	toast
la viande	*vee-**yand***	meat
le vin blanc	*vañ bloñ*	white wine
le vin rouge	*vañ roozh*	red wine
le vinaigre	*veenaygr*	vinegar

Eating Out

Have you got a table?	**Avez-vous une table libre?**	*avay-**voo** oon tahbl leebr*
I want to reserve a table.	**Je voudrais réserver une table.**	*zhuh voo-**dray** rayzehr-**vay** oon tahbl*
The bill, please.	**L'addition, s'il vous plaît.**	*l'adee-**syoñ** seel voo **play***
I am a vegetarian.	**Je suis végétarien.**	*zhuh swee vezhay-**tehryañ***
Waitress/ waiter	**Madame, Mademoiselle/ Monsieur**	*mah-**dam,** mah-dem wah zel/muh-**syuh***
menu	**le menu, la carte**	*men-**oo,** kart*
fixed-price menu	**le menu à prix fixe**	*men-**oo** ah pree feeks*
cover charge	**le couvert**	*koo-**vehr***
wine list	**la carte des vins**	*kart-deh vañ*
glass	**le verre**	*vehr*
bottle	**la bouteille**	*boo-**tay***
knife	**le couteau**	*koo-**toh***
fork	**la fourchette**	*for-**shet***
spoon	**la cuillère**	*kwee-**yehr***
breakfast	**le petit déjeuner**	*puh-**tee** deh-zhuh-nay*
lunch	**le déjeuner**	*deh-**zhuh**-nay*
dinner	**le dîner**	*dee nay*
main course	**le plat principal**	*plah prañsee-**pal***
starter, first course	**l'entrée, le hors d'oeuvre**	*l'oñ-**tray,** or-duhvr*
dish of the day	**le plat du jour**	*plah doo zhoor*
wine bar	**le bar à vin**	*bar ah vañ*
café	**le café**	*ka-**fay***
rare	**saignant**	*say-noñ*
medium	**à point**	*ah **pwañ***
well done	**bien cuit**	*byañ **kwee***

Staying in a Hotel

Do you have a vacant room?	**Est-ce que vous avez une chambre?**	*es-kuh voo-**zavay** oon shambr*
double room	**la chambre pour deux**	*shambr ah duh*
with double bed	**personnes, avec un grand lit**	*pehr-**son,** avek un groñ lee*
twin room	**la chambre à deux lits**	*shambr ah duh lee*
single room	**la chambre pour une personne**	*shambr ah oon pehr-**son***
room with a bath, shower	**la chambre avec salle de bains, une douche**	*shambr avek sal duh bañ, oon doosh*
porter	**le garçon**	*gar-**son***
key	**la clef**	*klay*
I have a reservation.	**J'ai fait une réservation.**	*zhay fay oon rayzehrva-**syoñ***

Sightseeing

abbey	**l'abbaye**	*l'abay-**ee***
art gallery	**la galerie d'art**	*galer-**ree** dart*
cathedral	**la cathédrale**	*katay-**dral***
church	**l'église**	*l'ayg**leez***
garden	**le jardin**	*zhar-**dañ***
library	**la bibliothèque**	*beebleeo-**tek***
museum	**le musée**	*moo-**zay***
railway station	**la gare (SNCF)**	*gahr (es-en-say-ef)*
bus station	**la gare routière**	*gahr roo-tee-yehr*

tourist	les renseigne-	*roñsayn-*
information	ments	**moñ**
office	touristiques,	*too-rees-***teek**,
	le syndicat	*sandee-ka*
	d'initiative	*d'eenee-sya***teev**
town hall	l'hôtel de ville	*l'oh***tel** *duh veel*
private mansion	l'hôtel	*l'oh***tel**
	particulier	*partikoo-***lyay**
closed for	fermeture	*fehrmeh-***tur**
public holiday	jour férié	*zhoor fehree-***ay**

Numbers

00	zéro	*zeh-***roh**
01	un, une	*uñ, oon*
02	deux	*duh*
03	trois	*trwah*
04	quatre	*katr*
05	cinq	*sañk*
06	six	*sees*
07	sept	*set*
08	huit	*weet*
09	neuf	*nerf*
10	dix	*dees*
11	onze	*oñz*
12	douze	*dooz*
13	treize	*trehz*
14	quatorze	*ka***torz**
15	quinze	*kañz*

16	seize	*sehz*
17	dix-sept	*dees-***set**
18	dix-huit	*dees-***weet**
19	dix-neuf	*dees-***nerf**
20	vingt	*vañ*
30	trente	*tront*
40	quarante	*karoñt*
50	cinquante	*sañkoñt*
60	soixante	*swasoñt*
70	soixante-dix	*swasoñt-***dees**
80	quatre-vingts	*katr-***vañ**
90	quatre-vingts-	*katr-vañ-*
	dix	**dees**
100	cent	*soñ*
1,000	mille	*meel*

Time

one minute	une minute	*oon mee-***noot**
one hour	une heure	*oon urr*
half an hour	une demi-heure	*oon* **duh-mee** *urr*
Monday	Lundi	*luñ-***dee**
Tuesday	Mardi	*mar-***dee**
Wednesday	Mercredi	*mehrkruh-***dee**
Thursday	Jeudi	*zhuh-***dee**
Friday	Vendredi	*voñdruh-***dee**
Saturday	Samedi	*sam-***dee**
Sunday	Dimanche	*dee-***moñsh**

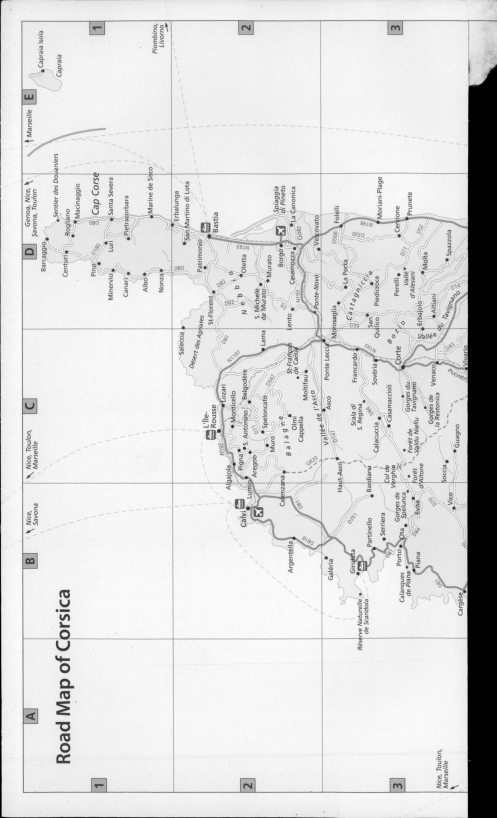

Road Map of Corsica